D0192643

THE SAS GUIDE TO TRACKING

New and Revised

THE
SAS GUIDE
TO TRACKING

NEW AND REVISED

Bob Carss
with
Stewart Birch
Foreword by John "Lofty" Wiseman
Illustrations by Roy Thomasson

THE LYONS PRESS
Guilford, Connecticut
An imprint of The Globe Pequot Press

To buy books in quantity for corporate use
or incentives, call **(800) 962–0973**
or e-mail **premiums@GlobePequot.com.**

Copyright © 1999, 2009 Bob Carss

First published in the UK by Constable & Robinson Ltd., 1999

First Lyons Press revised edition, 2009

Illustrations by Roy Thomasson

ALL RIGHTS RESERVED. No part of this book may be reproduced or
transmitted in any form by any means, electronic or mechanical, including
photocopying and recording, or by any information storage and retrieval
system, except as may be expressly permitted in writing from the pub-
lisher. Requests for permission should be addressed to The Globe Pequot
Press, Attn: Rights and Permissions Department, P.O. Box 480, Guilford,
CT 06437.

The Lyons Press is an imprint of The Globe Pequot Press

Library of Congress Cataloging-in-Publication Data is available on file.

ISBN 978-1-59921-437-5

Printed in the United States of America

10 9 8 7 6

To my son, Ben Carss

"It happened one day, about noon, going towards my boat, I was exceedingly surprised with the print of a man's naked foot on the shore, which was very plain to be seen in the sand . . ."

Daniel Defoe, *Robinson Crusoe*

CONTENTS

LIST OF ILLUSTRATIONS

FOREWORD TO THE
NEW AND REVISED EDITION

Bob "Bobby" Carss has used his wealth of experience to give insight into the secrets of the tracker.

Learning to read sign enables everyone to choose a safe route through life, staying safe and avoiding dangers.

Bobby tracks the trackers—a great book.

John "Lofty" Wiseman
Hereford, April 2008

PREFACE TO THE
NEW AND REVISED EDITION

My original purpose in setting down some of the lessons learned over years of tracking was to try to share with my young son and other young people the sense of adventure and discovery that I'd had with my father when growing up in Scotland. Although our territory would be the Wye Valley and Brecon Beacons rather than Roxburghshire, I knew that the lessons of tracking would be the same and that applying them could open a whole world of nature as well as establish habits of observation that would make my son's entire life richer. One of my father's greatest gifts to me was time spent together outdoors, guiding me with both words and example to be aware of the wonders around us that remain hidden to the uninitiated.

To my surprise, the book struck a chord not only with young people and experienced trackers in Great Britain, but also with a much wider audience throughout the world. Thus, letters and emails have come to me from environmentalists, bird-watchers, Scouts, police, and others in Canada and the United States, Australia, New Zealand, South Africa, and countries throughout Europe. Readers have made comments, shared their experiences, sought advice on specific scenarios—and asked why the book was so hard to find when they wanted another copy! The first edition had sold out swiftly, and those who had copies kept them to consult on day trips and longer expeditions as well as to use in setting up tracking courses. Thus, this new and revised edition meets a real need. Wherever one lives, the environment offers many opportunities for tracking, but practitioners are harder to find; this book can help you get started whether there is a helpful guide nearby or not.

Readers also asked for more real-life tracker stories and offered some stories of their own. Of course, the point of a tracking manual is to keep it brief so that it will be easy to carry and so that critical points are not overlooked. Thus, the new stories in this edition will, as before, be in the form of short examples. Should you wish to read longer accounts about how tracking has been employed, a few are suggested at the back of this edition—both true adventure stories and a few fictional ones in which tracking plays a part.

And readers of all ages reported that although they remembered lessons as they read and carried out the exercises chapter by chapter, they found it hard to bear everything in mind while on the trail. This is understandable: Tracking demands close observation, precise memory, and awareness of many other things simultaneously. The ultimate answer is study, practice, review, practice again—and lots of self-discipline! Even experienced trackers get rusty if away from tracking too long. But short checklists can be helpful in jogging the memory, especially in the early days and especially for such important drills as assembling equipment and moving through close jungle environments. Therefore, a new tracking aide-mémoire has been added in Chapter 26. This aide-mémoire can be used as a study guide as well as a refresher on key points before heading into the field.

Welcome to the world of tracking. Happy tracking trails!

Bob Carss

ACKNOWLEDGMENTS

My first debt of gratitude is to 22 Special Air Service Regiment and the New Zealand Special Air Service and all their highly talented jungle instructors who taught me tracking and, most importantly, introduced me to the Iban trackers of Brunei from whom I was able to learn a great deal by observing their methods.

Also I would like to thank Roy Thomasson, not only for his illustrations, which breathe life into the subject matter, but also for his support throughout this enterprise, especially in the early stages when his encouragement sustained me. Thanks are also due to Stewart Birch for his help in editing and writing, and Anne Harbour for her unstinting professional help in ensuring this edition became a reality.

Finally, I want to thank those members who are no longer with us for their contributions that helped me write this book.

INTRODUCTION

This book is about tracking—a serious subject in which I am passionately involved. It is not about the Special Air Service. I was fortunate enough to have served in the SAS for eighteen years and while there enhanced and developed my interest in tracking—that is the connection. Don't expect to find any state secrets in this book. The only secrets that I wish to pass on are those from nature, gained by the study and practice of the art of tracking. I hope this study will enrich your life as much as it has mine.

I was born in the urban environment of Newcastle. My mother and father moved when I was very young so I was brought up in Kelso, a small market town on the English/Scottish border. This was to be the start of my interest in country life and nature. I learned a lot fishing and walking with my father, listening to and watching local people, and spending many days wandering the countryside as a young boy.

By the age of fifteen I knew a great deal about the countryside and the wildlife it supported, absorbing some valuable lessons that were to become useful throughout my military career. Leaving Kelso at age fifteen, I joined the Army as a boy soldier. I enlisted as Junior Private Carss in the 1st Battalion of the King's Own Scottish Borderers (KOSBs) at Pennycuik barracks near Edinburgh. I felt immensely proud to join this infantry regiment. At seventeen and a half, after my "apprenticeship," I was posted to my battalion in Germany. I later served with them in a number of overseas postings. I enjoyed life in the KOSBs, but by 1971 I felt the need for a greater challenge so I applied for and passed selection for the SAS, which is based in Hereford—the city which has been my home ever since.

My service in the SAS took me all over the world, always in varied and interesting work. All volunteers for the SAS have to undergo jungle training, which forms an important part of the selection and continuation training. My initial jungle training lasted ten weeks, conducted by the very experienced Regimental Sergeant Major (RSM) "Geordie" Tindale and his very experienced and enthusiastic team of NCOs, who shared a passionate interest in jungle soldiering. The first phase of jungle training consisted of seven weeks 24/7, up at first light learning SOPs (Standard Operational Procedures); the second phase consisted of a two-week tracking course; and the third phase was spent looking for illegal loggers.

Learning to track with very knowledgeable and very experienced men—men who had survived years on operations throughout the world—brought to life all the things I had learned as a child roaming the countryside. It was hard work, but it suited me down to the ground and this early period in the SAS was a deeply satisfying time for me. The SAS, like any sound organization, tries to match jobs with people's interests and abilities, so I was often sent to work in jungle environments.

After twelve years' service, I came out of the SAS for a short period—and then decided to go back in. This second time I was 31 years old, not 21. I was fortunate to have two mates of mine rejoining at the same time: Stewart Birch, who helped me with this book, and Charlie C. We had all been in the same squadron and had served in the Oman War together. We completed, and passed, all of the the SAS selection again, including the jungle training, and we rejoined the same squadron we had left. The Sergeant Major was Roy Thomasson, who has also helped me to complete this book.

Fortunately, I was just in time for the Falklands War. After I came back from the Falklands, I had a serious talk with myself and decided that having lost twelve years' seniority, I was not going to become a general. Thus, the best way for me to put something back into the system was to concentrate on what I know best: hands-on field soldiering. With a few more trips to the jungle and a New Zealand tracking instructor course behind me, I started to teach tracking and survival proper.

Then I was asked if I wanted the job of chief instructor at the Jungle Warfare School. I took it and spent over two years there teaching tracking, long-range patrol courses run on the same lines as the SAS jungle training, jungle warfare courses, and jungle maiden courses. Not long after I returned to Hereford I was posted to the SAS Training Wing for two years, teaching mainly combat survival courses—that is, trapping, shelters, fires, food, and water—and going to the jungle to help set up jungle warfare training camps.

After two years on Training Wing, I was posted to a training area to assist a good friend of mine, RSM "Jock" Owen. Apart from other jobs to be done, I decided to build a Tri-Service Survival Area from scratch and to run survival weekends. The students in my first group were children with learning difficulties. The students in my second group were members of the TA (Territorial Army, comparable with the National Guard in the United States and with other such units around the world); the SAS still use this survival area today.

During my career with the SAS, I was fortunate enough to spend over 30 months actually in the jungle. Obviously I have omitted a lot of information about my career with the SAS in order to concentrate mainly on subjects that have enabled me to write this book. Counting my service as a Boy Soldier, I spent nearly 25 years in the British Army, 18 of them with the SAS. I was given the opportunity to do what I do best, hands-on field soldiering. In this book, I pass some of that experience on to you.

Back in civilian life I have continued to take an active interest in the outdoor, country life. There is a great deal that I would like to share with others. I look forward to when I can go out into the countryside with my son, Ben, to whom this book is dedicated, and share with him my enthusiasm for the natural world.

This book is designed to appeal to all ages from all backgrounds, and the use of male pronouns should be read as meaning both genders. It draws heavily upon my personal experience and my military career—especially my practical knowledge of the country-side. Although certain chapters are of more immediate significance to specialist groups, I recommend that all readers sample all chapters:—there is much to be learned from a cross-fertilization of ideas in tracking, as in many other interdisciplinary subjects. The outdoor pursuits teacher will learn from the jungle experiences of a soldier, just as much as an NCO instructor will profit from the lateral thinking of the psychologist.

The book starts by putting tracking into a modern perspective by briefly looking at its development and then showing the present applications, describing the attributes the tracker is trying to foster, and defining tracking terms. From this baseline the book progresses through a study of sign to development of the powers of observation, movement (stalking), and on to the track pursuit drill. Once the principles of the drill are established, we move to specific examples and chapters dedicated to advanced techniques.

A short summary in outline form appears at the end of each chapter. These summaries have been collated into the aide-mémoire that makes up Chapter 26. The serious student and the instructor will find these a useful tool, both for review in preparing for the next stage of tracking and as a critical prompt to memory in the field.

Finally, at the back of the book you will find two pages for you to record your own notes. Although you may wish to use a notebook, I thought it necessary to make the point that you never stop learning about tracking—you will learn new lessons from each experience.

This book will guide you stage by stage through the various practices that lead up to tracking itself.

If you are prepared to put the skills into practice as you read through the book, you will start to assimilate the knowledge immediately. By the end of the book you will be well on the road to starting your career as a tracker.

To be a successful tracker, as in any other occupation, you will have to adhere to the age-old adage that nothing is achieved except by hard, conscientious work.

Read the book!
Follow the spoor!
Good luck!

PART ONE

THE BRIEFING

1

TRACKING TODAY—SOME MODERN APPLICATIONS

People's first comment, or at least their first thoughts, when they hear an account of an incident where tracking has been employed is something along the lines of, "How unusual!" It is as if the skills associated with trackers and tracking had died out long ago, and the disciplines had no relevance to modern life. My aim is to dispel this misconception and to open up the benefits of tracking to a much wider audience. At the moment there are, it seems, only two groups who are aware of the usefulness of the tracker's knowledge in modern society.

First, there are the specialist military units who have kept the skills alive—despite great resistance from some quarters of the military establishment. And second, there are the rural police forces who have brought in trackers, usually ex-military, on a case by case basis but who rarely have a formal training program for their own trackers.

In my opinion this is a sad under-utilization of a wealth of knowledge that our ancestors have built up over millennia. I believe that tracking can play a wide and valuable role in modern society.

A historical perspective
The tracking skill initially developed because of man's desire for meat. Naturally weaker than most of his prey and having only primitive weapons, man was forced to use other skills. He had to

observe the areas frequented by and the habitats of the animals and birds he intended catching for food.

This basic feature is reflected even today in that some of the best game trackers in the world come from the more remote areas where they live a very unsophisticated existence close to nature. Often their way of life, customs and social habits are dominated by the "game chase" and the "after catch" celebrations. A classic example of this hunting-centered lifestyle was the Great Plains Indians of North America. They migrated with the game herds that not only provided them with food, but also clothing, ornaments, tools, shelter, and fuel. It is not surprising that their dances and their spiritual life were fashioned around the buffalo and the other animals that supported them. This is just one example of how fundamental hunting and therefore tracking are to mankind.

Even after man had domesticated animals and cultivated the land, tracking did not become redundant. It was a skill in his arsenal when warring against other tribes. He soon found that even with inferior numbers and weapons, by employing stealth, cunning, surprise, and superior knowledge of bush craft he was able to overcome and defeat his victims. Reprisals and revenge naturally followed, and so tracking and scouting skills were firmly established in warfare.

The vast majority of the civilian population and even military leaders and police chiefs are unaware of the potential use of trained trackers, but, with some imagination, it is not difficult to envisage tracking's many uses.

Law enforcement agencies
Tracking with most law enforcement agencies is orientated primarily towards scent tracking, employing highly trained tracker dogs. Their work ranges from the pursuit of law-breaking fugitives to the detection of explosives and narcotics. The U.S. border patrol is but one enforcement agency that currently employs these tracking techniques in its never-ending task of stopping illegal entry into the United States.

Scent tracking is established as a useful tool but the same enthusiasm has not yet extended to visual tracking, where expertise could equally well be used. To limit the use of tracking to scent tracking is to impose a severe limitation. The visual tracker can be especially useful in rural areas. Speaking from experience of having trained an anti-poaching unit (APU) in Botswana, I know how useful, and lethal, visual trackers can be—as do the unfortunate Zimbabwean poachers who tried to outrun and outshoot our APU.

In my opinion there are two areas in which visual trackers should be involved with police work. First, there should be a pool of federally certified trackers who are on call to local law enforcement—rather like interpreters are on call. And second, they have a briefing role: to explain to senior officers the applications of visual tracking and to make all officers aware of the importance of preserving the sign (see Chapter 2) for the tracker.

The military

Recent military tracking provides many examples of the application of this ancient skill. It is man tracking man, either to gain information or to kill him. The low-intensity, counter-insurgency wars of the post-colonial era provide many examples of the employment of trackers. It is such a rich and varied field that I have devoted a whole chapter to it (see Chapter 18). But even here, once the conflicts have been resolved, the tracking units are usually disbanded and the men reassigned, thus dispersing and eventually losing the pool of skills. The New Zealand SAS is one unit that has had the foresight to keep tracking skills as an essential component of the military curriculum.

The benefits of preserving the knowledge and skills of a tracker within a military establishment are twofold. First, the training that a tracker undergoes can be seen as honing the skills that any infantry soldier needs—observation, movement and concealment. And second, the skills are ready for immediate utilization by the higher commands in such remote area emergency situations as search and rescue of downed pilots, as in Iraq or Bosnia, when the TACBE (the emergency location beacon carried by aircrew) may have been lost, damaged, stolen, or removed if the aircrew have been captured—or it simply ran out of power.

Cave and mountain rescue

Rescue organizations are often called upon to locate missing persons. Unfortunately, they possess limited or no knowledge of the arts of tracking. Consequently a great deal of sign (see Chapter 2) is normally obliterated by the first person on the scene, making it almost impossible for any immediate pursuit by trained trackers. Vital time is wasted and the results can be tragic.

Conservationists

For the nature enthusiast, whether a professional paid conservation officer or the unpaid amateur working for the Royal Society for the Protection of Birds (RSPB), there is a great benefit to be had from a proper grounding in tracking. With a fuller understanding of what is happening in a particular environment they gain a greater satisfaction from their pursuits, and professionals are better placed to protect species and encourage the development of the wildlife.

Gamekeepers

As any professional gamekeeper knows, he is now protecting a very valuable asset for his employer. Land and livestock are under threat from ruthless, well-organized gangs, both local and, perhaps more importantly, from out of area. These criminals do not enter a region on a whim. They plan their raids with precision because they know the profits to be gained are huge. The knowledge that a trained tracker could elicit from studying the areas either where raids have taken place or, even better, where the reconnaissance and preparation for a raid have taken place would be an invaluable weapon in the anti-poaching units' armory. This is not just of relevance to the African government trying to protect its stock of rhino but also to the Yorkshire or Scottish gamekeeper trying to preserve stocks of pheasants and salmon.

A gamekeeper's use of tracking skills is not confined to anti-poaching activities; they can also be used to protect their charges from other wildlife predators. To catch, trap, shoot, or control the wildlife in their area of operation they must first be able to locate and identify the areas frequented by these animals.

Farmers and livestock owners

The activities of rustlers may conjure up romantic images of the Wild West but to the Welsh sheep farmer or the private zoo owner who has a rare species stolen, rustling is simply a matter of common theft. Often, though, the environment in which these crimes take place is ideally suited to the effective deployment of a tracker—if the owners are aware and do not foul the sign.

Country recreationalists

Any person who is interested in the countryside is seeing only a fraction of the life around him if he hasn't got the tracker's awareness of the observation of detail. This knowledge can enhance a country-based hobby beyond belief. It is the difference between an illiterate and a literate person standing in front of a signpost. Orienteers, field walkers, fishermen, hunters, botanists, and anyone with a love of or an interest in nature will find that their enjoyment and knowledge increase tremendously.

Educators

For the adult who has responsibilities for the personal development of the young and for the educator in general there is profound value in the study of tracking. It may seem paradoxical that a topic so readily associated with warlike activities should be proposed as being of use to the teacher in a liberal democracy, but I'm sure the following observations will banish any preconceived ideas.

Observation, memory, analysis, and deduction are all fundamental mental operations that need to be cultivated in the young mind—and they also happen to be the basis of the tracker's mental process. What better way to develop these processes than in an educationally fun environment for groups of all ages? I see this being extremely efficacious with children who have not responded well in a more formal teaching setting, or as an adjunct to an outdoor pursuits environment. As well as developing rational skills, emotional traits inculcated by tracker training are also of great worth: patience, determination, concentration, and an appreciation and respect for the countryside and its wildlife (see Chapter 5 for a full exposition of the qualities of a tracker and Chapter 17 for the material specifically for the teacher and instructor). The educational value of tracking should not be underestimated and there is a good argument for introducing tracking into any school syllabus for outdoor pursuits. One can see the development of a tracker as progress through several stages. First of all he must cultivate his powers of observation and attention to detail. Then he must develop and practice his memory and deduction. Along with these skills, habits of perseverance and patience are being encouraged.

I am sure that many in the armed forces, the police, and the cave and mountain rescue services will find invaluable, and possibly lifesaving, lessons in this book. For other groups such as conservationists, ornithologists, and country sportsmen and women this book will enhance their understanding and enjoyment of their pastimes.

And finally, for the young person, I hope this book fosters an interest in the countryside, conservation, and nature, just as the following incident did for me when I was lucky enough to have it explained by the gamekeeper. We were out walking one winter's morning when he pointed out where a rabbit had been crouching in the snow—there was a round patch about five by nine inches. Then he showed me how the rabbit must have been startled as it accelerated suddenly—the hind feet were ahead of the fore feet within a few paces. Then the rabbit's path became erratic. It was trying to escape but there were no other tracks. Then he showed me a few spots of blood. The rabbit had been attacked but by a hunter that left no track. To a six-year-old this was a mystery—obvious when the gamekeeper told me about hawks and owls. We then found a great deal more blood. And then the remains of the rabbit. The gamekeeper showed me the prints of the bird of prey in the snow by the rabbit's carcass. He was just about to outline in the snow the difference between a hawk's print and an owl's when the rabbit's attacker came swooping in to finish its meal and prove the gamekeeper right. The sort of incident you never forget!

2

SOME DEFINITIONS AND EXPLANATIONS

Before going any farther I would like to mention some of the terms used in tracking that you will find useful throughout this book. They are organized in like groups, so that the earlier entries will help to explain the later ones.

Tracking

Tracking can be defined as the art of being able to locate, identify, and pursue sign and, from intelligent interpretations and deductions, gain reasonably accurate information about the quarry concerned. The same skills apply whether it is a human being, an animal, a bird, or a vehicle. When applied to animals, in particular, it has been known by different names in different continents: trailing in North America, spooring in Africa, and pugging in India. Put simply, tracking is the following and interpretation of sign.

Sign

A sign is any physical indication left on or in the environment by the passage of any animal or inanimate object. The following are some examples of visual signs:

- Sap from a bruised root or trunk of a tree
- Disturbance to animal, bird, or insect life
- Change in color and unnatural formation of vegetation due to disturbance

- Lack of water and dew on vegetation
- Footprints in bare or muddy ground
- Mud, soil or sand on vegetation
- Animal droppings, fur, feathers, and bones
- Bruises, breaks, and cuts in vegetation

A sign is so important in tracking that a separate chapter, Chapter 3, is devoted to a more detailed breakdown and explanation of it.

Ground sign
These are ground-level marks or disturbances. (See also Chapter 3.)

Top sign
This is defined as any sign above the ankle. (See also Chapter 3.)

Conclusive sign
This is sign directly linked to the quarry, such as a boot print in soft ground. (See also Chapter 3.)

Substantiating sign
This is sign probably made by the quarry but it cannot be tied to it conclusively. (See also Chapter 3.)

Key sign
Key sign is the most prominent. The track may have 20 to 30 different types of sign and the tracker will have to be familiar with all these. But, in fact, he will be concentrating on a combination of two to three signs at any one time—these are the key signs. Because of the nature of the ground and changes in vegetation, key signs will change and one will become more important at any one time. The key sign will vary depending on the landscape, be it primary and secondary forest, scrub, swamp and grassland, or desert and snow-covered areas. Obviously, some signs are common to all areas, such as a footprint or a tire track. Key sign, like all sign, is affected by climatic and seasonal changes. It alters with the time of day and before, during, and after snow or rain, all of which will greatly influence the amount of sign left in any area.

Sign pattern

A sign pattern indicates the habits or the peculiarities of a quarry. This information may be of a particular individual or it may be building up a profile of the group or species. An example of this would be deer coming out of the forests at dusk to graze on the farmer's crops.

Time bracket

All sign in the initial stages is placed into a time bracket, that is, the time lapse between the earliest possible time that the sign could have been made and the time it was located.

Straight edge

This is the line found on leaves or blades of grass caused by the application of pressure. Most leaves, dry or green, are curled and if trodden on will break or bend in a straight line. Usually dry leaves will break and green or wet leaves will bend. From the straight edges on the leaves (see Fig. 1) we can tell the approximate size of the footprint, which, in turn, will help us to determine the size of the quarry. This can be demonstrated by treading on a small

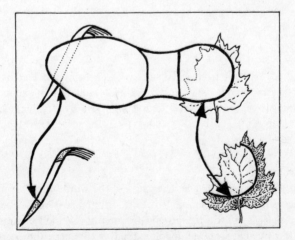

Fig. 1. Examples of straight edges on vegetation

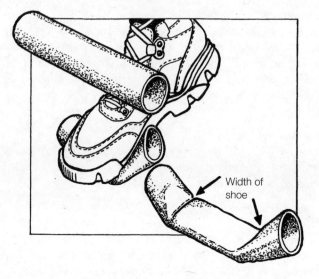

Fig. 2. Straight edges and their relationship
to the size of the footwear

cardboard cylinder, such as a toilet paper roll (see Fig. 2), which creates two straight edges. The width of your shoe would be shown by the distance between the "straight edges."

Spoor
The word "spoor" from Afrikaans derives from the Dutch word for footprint. Spoor is reserved for that sign left by an animal (including man), as opposed to the sign left by a vehicle or inanimate object.

The track
This is the line of sign. The derivation of the word "track" is uncertain but it is generally thought that the original sense described the line or mark made on the ground by anything hauled or dragged. Now the meaning of the word extends to include the mark, or series of marks, or any physical indication left by the passage of

anything—a wheel, the wake of a ship, a series of footprints, animal spoor, scent, any residual heat, and even microscopically recognized material in genetic tracking.

Visual tracking

This is the art of being able to track a human being, animal, or vehicle, by the marks it has left. It should be remembered that it is difficult for anything to move in an environment without leaving some sign noticeable to the trained eye. A visual tracker relies primarily on sight and is therefore unable to track by night except in very unusual circumstances such as brilliant moonlight, bright ambient light, with the use of a torch, or by using night viewing devices such as goggles or scopes.

Scent tracking

Scent tracking is normally performed by dogs. However, a well-trained visual tracker can follow a quarry, either human or animal, by its scent—the scent needs to be strong and fresh. In addition, the visual tracker may be alerted to potential dangers by detecting smells such as:

- Cooking odors
- Smoke
- Latrines
- Newly dug earth

Tracking picture

This is the overall picture gained by the tracker over any given length of track. It is like a story to a good tracker. To obtain the complete tracking picture you would have to follow the track until you could state with accuracy the complete details of the quarry being followed. The track picture builds up continuously with each new piece of information gained. An experienced tracker will be able to deduce part of the track picture after following for only a short distance.

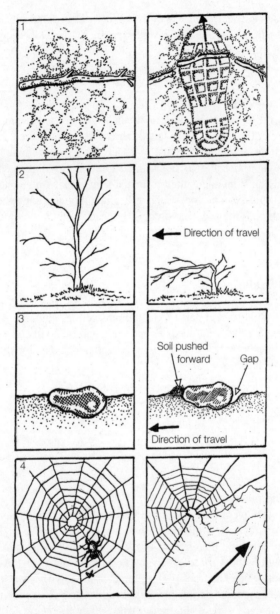

Fig. 3. Examples of pointers

Tracking medium

This is the generic term used for the material in which the sign was left by the quarry. For example, mud and sand are tracking media that obviously retain sign, whereas rock and water do hold sign but it is far more difficult to detect.

Exit and entry points

These are points or passageways through which a quarry may pass from one environment to another, for example, from a pine wood to a cornfield, from a grass field to a road, from a plowed field back into a wood.

Pointers

These are the signs that serve to indicate the direction of movement. They can either be ground or top sign (see Fig. 3 for examples). Low foliage, grass, and ferns when trampled on or brushed forward will remain in the direction of the movement until disturbed again. When a person or animal brushes past a small tree a number of leaves may become entangled. These may be seen from a distance after practice. If the base of the tree was tapped the leaves would fall back into their natural position. The leaves or branches will be tangled towards the direction of movement—these are the pointers. If the ground and top sign pointers contradict each other, it is possible that the quarry was walking backwards; that is, the prints on the ground would be facing one way but the evidence from the disturbed foliage would indicate a different direction of travel. On the other hand if the top sign pointers contradict themselves, in the case of a human quarry, then it could be that the sign has been rearranged. For example, a man using this deception tactic would deliberately bend vegetation in the opposite direction to his line of travel.

Foul track

This is defined as a track that has entered an area where numerous other tracks exist, for example, at a watering hole or a feeding area. Figure 4 shows some specific examples of individually fouled prints.

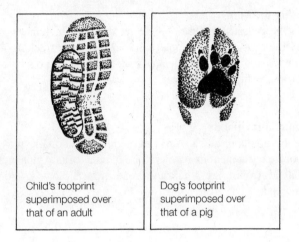

Child's footprint superimposed over that of an adult

Dog's footprint superimposed over that of a pig

Fig. 4. Fouled tracks

Deception

If a quarry knows it is being followed it will invariably try to lose the tracker by deception. Unless extremely efficient in deception methods this will more often than not "sign post" a change of direction (see Indicator Pace).

Indicator pace

This is the footprint immediately before or after an intended change of direction (see Fig. 5). The initial indications of this can be seen at the prints marked as 1 and 2, 1 being the indicator pace as it is now pointing, or indicating, a possible change of direction. The print marked as 3 gives the first full indication of the new direction of travel. At a walking pace a 90-degree change of direction will normally be indicated by two shorter paces as the turn is executed, in this case between 1 and 2.

Casting

This is the method of locating or relocating sign that has been lost, or where a tracker is endeavoring to locate a start point at an incident area (see Chapter 16).

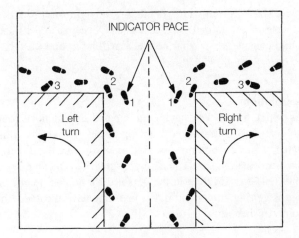

Fig. 5. Indicator pace

Tuning in

This is the initial reading of the sign that enables the tracker to think and act as the quarry. This will help the tracker anticipate future actions the quarry may take. The time taken for the tracker to tune into a new environment depends on his tracking ability. To give an illustration, imagine that you have been following a quarry through a wood for three hours and your main "key signs" were pointers, when all of a sudden the quarry's sign exits the wood and goes across a grass field. You will have to reassess the situation; the ground has changed and the "key sign" will now probably have changed to footprints. It may take you up to half an hour before you feel comfortable in pursuing the quarry's sign—it is in this sort of area that tracking crosses over from being a science to being an art.

Pace tracking

This is "pace for pace" tracking carried out during the "tuning in" period or when the track becomes difficult to pursue. It will be mainly ground sign that you will be following when pace tracking, and you have to start from a known quarry's sign, whether it is conclusive or substantiating sign. Then make a comprehensive study of that particular sign to gain as much information as you can:

direction, size of print, width, depth, left or right foot, fore or hind in the case of an animal, sex, and age. Once you have taken all these into consideration, your next task will be to find the next sign and so on.

Track isolation
This is where the tracker, having anticipated the intended route, is able to abandon the track and leapfrog ahead. To do this with any guarantee of success you must be able to extrapolate the direction of travel by information from some other source. This technique can be used not only to gain time in the pursuit of a human quarry but, if the sign is getting colder and older, you may have the added bonus of finding fresher sign.

Traits
These are the characteristic features or qualities distinguishing a particular quarry, for example:

- a limp
- a missing limb
- a pair of unevenly worn shoes
- a horse with a thrown or damaged shoe

Physique
This relates to the general appearance of the quarry.

Diet
This relates to the food and drink that the quarry regularly consumes.

Habitat
This is where the quarry lives. It can be described as:

- Rural
- Suburban
- City
- Remote—away from any population center

SUMMARY

DEFINITIONS

Tracking
Tracking can be defined as the art of being able to locate, identify, and pursue sign, and from intelligent interpretations and deductions gain reasonably accurate information about the quarry concerned.

Sign
This is any physical indication left on or in the environment by the passage of any animal or inanimate object.

Ground sign
These are ground level marks or disturbances.

Top sign
This is defined as any sign above the ankle.

Conclusive sign
This is sign directly linked to the quarry.

Substantiating sign
This is sign probably made by the quarry.

Key sign
This is the most prominent sign.

Sign pattern
This is the sign that serves to indicate the habits of or the peculiarities of a quarry.

Time bracket
All sign in the initial stages is placed into a time bracket, that is, the time lapse between the earliest possible time that the sign could have been made and the time it was located.

Straight edge
This is the line found on leaves or blades of grass caused by the application of pressure.

Spoor
This Afrikaans word derives from the Dutch word for footprint and is reserved for that sign left by an animal (including man), as opposed to the sign left by a vehicle or inanimate object.

The track
This is the line of sign.

Visual tracking
This is the art of being able to track a human being, animal, or vehicle by the marks it has left.

Scent tracking
Scent tracking is normally performed by dogs.

Tracking picture
This is the overall picture gained by the tracker over any given length of track.

Tracking medium
This is the generic term used for the material in which the sign was left by the quarry.

Exit and entry points
These are points or passageways through which a quarry may pass from one environment to another.

Pointers
These are the signs that serve to indicate the direction of movement.

Foul track
This is defined as a track that has entered an area where numerous other tracks exist.

Deception
When a quarry attempts to lose the tracker by leaving mis-leading sign.

Indicator pace
This is the footprint immediately before or after an intended change of direction.

Casting
This is the method of locating or relocating sign that has been lost.

Tuning in
This is the initial reading of the sign that enables the tracker to think and act as the quarry.

Pace tracking
This is "pace for pace" tracking carried out during the "tuning in" period or when the track becomes difficult to pursue.

Track isolation
This is where the tracker, having anticipated the intended route, is able to abandon the track and leapfrog ahead.

Traits
These are the characteristic features or qualities distinguish-ing a particular quarry.

Physique
This relates to the general appearance of the quarry.

Diet
This relates to the food and drink that the quarry regularly consumes.

Habitat
This is where the quarry lives. It can be rural, suburban, city, or remote territory.

3

SIGN IN TRACKING

The term "sign" as used in visual tracking can be defined as any evidence of change from the natural state that is inflicted upon any one geographical environment by the passage of the quarry, whether it be man, animal, or machinery. All sign is rigidly divided into two categories:

- Top sign—this is above the ankle
- Ground sign—anything below the ankle

Top sign
This is found in vegetation above the ankle; the zone extends to the height and width of the quarry. As the quarry passes through the undergrowth it brushes past and causes unnatural disturbances to the growing vegetation. In the case of birds this zone can extend to the height limit of the vegetation, while the downdraft of aircraft, especially helicopters, can create an enormous amount of top sign.

Some examples of top sign:

- Changes in the color of vegetation
- Unnatural position of vegetation
- Broken fences, gates, and turnstiles
- Disturbance to animals' and birds' nests
- Cutting of vegetation
- Disarranged cobwebs
- Chewed bark and roots

- Hand holds on trees
- Animal and bird roosting sites, quite often marked by droppings
- Bruised moss on trees
- Dew swept from vegetation
- Disturbance to the animal kingdom
- Broken twigs, branches, and leaves
- Man-made objects hanging on trees
- Scratches on trees
- Animal droppings, fur, feathers, and skeletons
- Shadow and shine irregularities on vegetation
- Birds and animals being put to flight
- Animal runs making tunnels through the vegetation or marks up trees

Ground sign
This is the sign left mainly by the quarry's feet. This occurs where vegetation from the ground surface has been disturbed by the quarry passing through and over the area.

Some examples of ground sign are:

- Foot and scuff marks
- Animal droppings, latrines, scrapes, and scent-marking areas
- Animal fur, feathers, skin, and skeletons
- Animal homes—rabbit burrows, fox dens, and badger tunnels
- Animal wallowing/rolling sites
- Bird nests
- Bird nests floating on water
- Bird dusting sites
- Footprints—shoes, hoof, claw, and pad
- Bruised or bleeding roots
- Disturbance to the insect life on the ground
- Disturbance or color change to the ground vegetation
- Mud, sand, and soil deposited by the quarry (see "Transfer" below)
- Disturbed leaves, stones, sticks, worm casts, mole hills, and pock-marks
- Debris dropped beside the tracks—cigarette ends, candy wrappers, and soft drink cans
- Debris blowing along the top of snow or sand that leaves marks

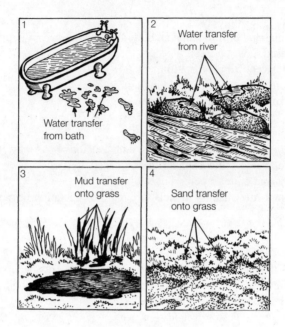

Fig. 6. Transfer of sign

- Disturbed water
- Dew swept from vegetation
- Flattening and color changes in the rest areas of the quarry
- Feather tip markings where a bird has taken off or landed—best seen in snow or mud
- Bruised, squashed, bent, and broken roots, berries, droppings, leaves, or twigs

Characteristics of sign
Sign may be identified by one or a combination of the following characteristics:

Regularity
This is an effect caused by straight lines, arches, or other geometrical shapes being pressed into the ground leaving marks not normally found in nature, e.g. boot marks, vehicle tire marks.

Flattening
This is the general leveling or depression caused by pressure on an area compared to the immediate surroundings, e.g. the quarry's resting or sleeping area in grass, sand, or snow.

Transfer
This is the deposit carried forward over an area after the quarry has moved from one environment to another, e.g. sand, mud, soil, or water not in its original position (see Fig. 6 for some illustrations of the transfer of sign). A couple of everyday examples of transfer are the drops of water left on the bathroom floor when someone steps out of the bath, not the footprint, but the drops that fall from the feet, and the droplets that fall from your hands as you reach for the hand towel from the washbasin.

Color change
This is the difference in color or texture of sign from the area that surrounds it, e.g. overturned droppings, stones, earth, twigs, or leaves will all give a color change to their immediate surrounding area when disturbed (see Fig. 7). Note that with continual use of the

Fig. 7. Color change in surrounding area:
1. rat; 2. squirrel; 3. mouse; 4. leaf

rat run (Fig. 7/1), the rat has worn a path—in this case, showing up lighter in color than the surrounding area. The area could be darker or lighter depending on the surrounding surfaces. The squirrel and the mouse (Figs. 7/2 and 7/3) provide examples similar to the rat's. Note that the leaf (Fig. 7/4) will be lighter in color on the underside compared with the weathered upperside.

Discardables

This is anything that is left behind by the quarry, e.g. fur, feathers,

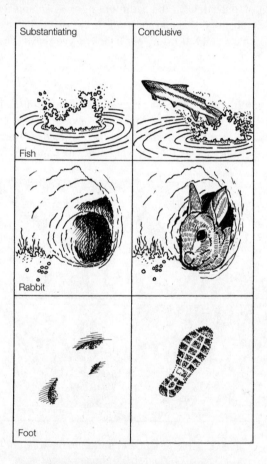

Fig. 8. Substantiating and conclusive sign

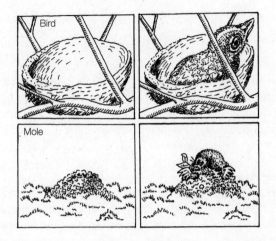

Fig. 8. continued

droppings, cigarette ends, candy wrappers, tin cans and the remains of food.

Disturbances
This is any other change to or rearrangement of the natural state of an area caused by the passage of the quarry, e.g. disturbance of the animal, bird, fish, and insect life, or to water.

Classification of sign
For tracking purposes we acknowledge four classes of sign:

• Substantiating
• Conclusive
• Temporary
• Permanent

Substantiating sign
These signs may or may not have been caused by the quarry. With experience and practice a tracker can, with confidence, classify these as conclusive. However, two or more may have to be identified to convince a learner that he is still pursuing the same quarry (see Fig.

8). Examples are broken twigs, bleeding and bruised roots, broken cobwebs, and disturbed water.

Conclusive sign
This class of sign indicates without any more evidence to a tracker the passage of the quarry through the area. This sign has definitely been made by the quarry you are tracking. Examples are a characteristic footprint, identifiable droppings, or a discarded piece of equipment.

Temporary sign
Some types of sign are termed temporary because they are particularly affected by weathering agents such as the wind, rain, snow, and the sun (see Chapter 4 for a full description). This is the unavoidable sign left during and after the quarry has passed through an environment, however careful he is. These signs will eventually settle down and return to normal after a lapse of time. Examples are broken cobwebs, movement of earth, leaves covering growing vegetation, and disturbances to the insect world.

Permanent sign
Sign is classified by a tracker as permanent when it is of a lasting nature—there is no specific time frame but rather a common sense approach is used to determine the correct classification. Permanent sign is very resistant to weathering, although even the hardest granite will eventually be eroded by rainwater, and man-made objects such as tin cans, newspapers, and clothing will eventually weather or rot away. Examples are badger tunnels, fox earths, rabbit burrows, bird and animal nests, broken or cut vegetation, dead animals, broken fences and gates, and discarded man-made objects.

How to study sign
Now that we have an understanding of the various categories and classifications of sign, let's move on to a practical illustration of how a tracker reads sign.

For this example let us look at the process of studying the sign left after a human has passed through a leaf-covered area. The first sign that is located is usually the ground sign. The tracker has to decide

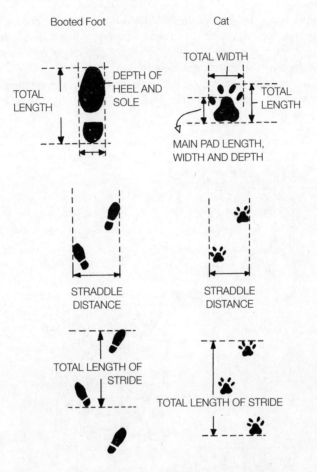

Fig. 9. Details of the first print that should be recorded

whether it is human or animal. Once this is established, the approximate height and size of the quarry can be determined by the extent of the top sign—remember, top sign is any sign above ankle height.

Initially the first sign must be studied carefully, that is, "the first footprint." This must be measured and recorded as a sketch. See Fig. 9 for the details that should be noted.

The approximate weight of the person may be found by comparing the depth of the sign left with that of your own imprint or the footprint of a known person with the same size foot. The experienced tracker will not jump to any conclusions at this stage about the weight of the person until he has seen other sign giving an indication whether the quarry was carrying a load or not.

The length of pace may indicate whether the person is tall, short, or carrying a pack. Top sign will normally verify this sort of information.

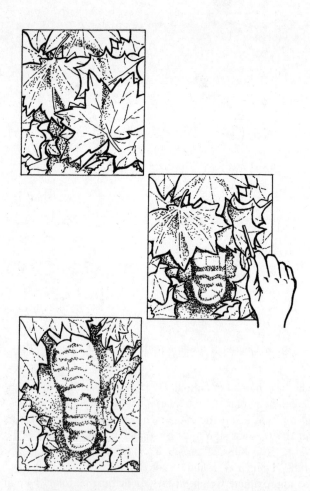

Fig. 10. Studying sign in a leaf-strewn area

Study the top layer of leaves, sorting out those that are bent or broken because they have been trodden on, remembering that some will be displaced. Mentally replace all or as many as possible of those displaced leaves and twigs. Pick up and examine each leaf in turn for what is called a straight edge. Remember where each leaf was taken from (see Fig. 10).

After removing and checking the top layer continue down to the next layer. If the conditions are wet this will be fairly pliable. Notice any distinctive bends that may indicate an edge of a boot.

Remove the next layer and study the earth itself. Look for squashed worm casts or indentations from twigs and nuts.

Establish the heel and toe and whether it is the left or right foot and, in the case of animals, whether it is the fore or hind.

Whatever the nature of the ground may be, always look up from the ground sign at frequent intervals. Where there are bushes and undergrowth, bits of hair and fur or shreds of clothing may be spotted. These will give a clue to the direction of the track and to the quarry's height and bulk.

A good understanding of sign and how to identify it is the vital skill that allows the tracker to build up the tracking picture. During the initial learning stages it is the most important part of visual tracking. With experience and practice, locating and identifying sign will become much easier and what was once a closed book will open and the track will come to life.

SUMMARY

CHARACTERISTICS OF SIGN

Regularity
This is an effect caused by straight lines, arches, or other geometrical shapes being pressed into the ground leaving marks not
normally found in nature.

Flattening
This is the general leveling or depression caused by pressure on
an area compared to the immediate surroundings.

Transfer
This is the deposit carried forward over an area after the quarry
has moved from one environment to another.

Color change
This is the difference in color or texture of sign from the area that
surrounds it.

Discardables
This is anything that is left behind by the quarry.

Disturbances
This is any other change to or rearrangement of the natural state
of an area caused by the passage of the quarry.

CLASSIFICATION OF SIGN

Substantiating sign
These signs may or may not have been caused by the quarry.

Conclusive sign
This sign has definitely been made by the quarry you are tracking.

Temporary sign
Some types of sign are termed temporary because they are particularly affected by weathering agents.

Permanent sign
Permanent sign is very resistant to weathering.

4

FACTORS AFFECTING SIGN

So much depends upon the state of the ground and the weather that it is very difficult to recognize the track under all circumstances. The difference between a track left by an animal or a man walking across a rocky outcrop and that left as he passes through an area with a clay-based soil is huge, but it is the track of the same quarry.

The best way to meet this difficulty, and to teach yourself how to recognize a track under varying conditions and on different kinds of soil, is to practice continually. Make a habit of imagining, as you walk along, what sort of tracks would be left by a man or an animal on the environment through which you are passing.

As we progress to the technical aspects of tracking you may find it useful to refer to the definitions in Chapter 2.

Sign is the crux of tracking. Sign, and consequently a visual tracker's ability to follow it, is influenced by four main factors:

- Spoor and sign left by other animals and vehicles
- Features of the terrain
- Climatic conditions
- Time

In general, all four factors are very closely related, a fact that has both advantages and disadvantages for the tracker. So it is important that you have an understanding of each of the four factors and how they interrelate.

Third-party spoor and sign
Spoor and sign belong to one of three groups:

- You the tracker and your team
- The quarry, which can be one or more animals, persons, or vehicles
- A third party

During a pursuit the quarry's sign is the most important thing to consider. However, a tracker must consider other spoor and sign in the area and how it is going to affect the track of the quarry.

You the tracker can and should govern the movement of your own group so as not to foul the track of the quarry, but you have no control over the activities of any third party that has previously left sign in the area and may already have fouled the track.

A tracker must consider the animal life in the area and know how to identify the difference between animal and human sign. It is fairly easy to identify the differences between animal and human spoor. For example the majority of animals with hooves leave a distinctive "chop" type mark as they move along a trail. This is caused by the shape of the hoof and the weight distribution. The hoof acts like a knife edge and the weight of the animal causes the hoof to cut into the ground. By contrast, humans tend to heel and toe their movements when walking, which is reflected in their spoor by an incised heel mark and a dragged part at the forward edge of the print where the toe scuffs the ground. Such identification is possible, even if the track advances across ground with a hard surface that does not allow a clear print (see Chapter 22 for a fuller exposition of animal prints).

There can be advantages and disadvantages to third-party sign. For example, prints superimposed on a quarry's prints may assist the tracker in gauging the age of the track if he knows when the third party passed by. But large groups of animals, such as flocks of sheep or herds of cows, may obliterate the sign of the quarry to such an extent that the tracker finds it impossible to continue any pursuit.

The terrain
The geographical features of the terrain may or may not assist the tracker. The following is a list of some of the major types of terrain that offer very distinctive attributes for the tracker:

- Grass and cultivated areas
- Rocky ground
- Sandy desert
- Primary forests
- Secondary forests and dense undergrowth
- Inland waterways and marshy areas
- The seashore
- Snow-covered regions
- Urban and built-up areas

Each type of terrain presents the tracker with a new challenge.

Grass and cultivated areas
Although it is difficult to obtain any clear impression of individual pieces of sign on grass, a track through grass will show up very clearly. The bruised and trampled grass can be seen some distance ahead and it is quite easy to decide in which direction the track leads. If, on looking at a field, you see a track that looks lighter than the surrounding grass, then you can be certain that whatever has made the track has been going away from you. See Fig. 11/1—in this case, a field of corn (or wheat). If, on the other hand, the track appears darker than the surrounding grass (Fig. 11/2), then you can be certain that whatever has made the track has been coming towards the place where you are standing. This visual aid is a result of the way in which light is reflected from the surface of the disturbed vegetation. The same feature can be seen when a lawn is mowed in alternate directions—there are strips of light and dark (see Fig. 11/3).

It is even easier to follow a track through grass that is wet with dew or light rain, or that is frosted. Most of us will have seen this kind of track on a football field or in a park in the early morning on the way to school or work. Once the sun rises higher and dries the dew off the grass, the track disappears to the naked eye. If following such a track, you would have to adapt pace tracking.

Frequently, places will be found where the grass has been nibbled if your quarry is a grass-eating animal, or where the ribs in the sole of a man's boot have torn off a blade or two.

If the grass is high, that is, above ankle height, tracks are relatively easy to follow because the grass is knocked down and will stay

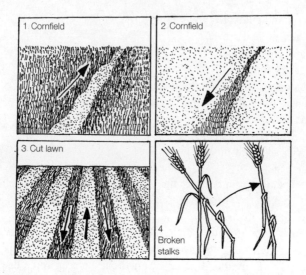

Fig. 11. Color changes in terrain indicating direction of travel

down for some time, depending on the weather. The shorter the grass, the more quickly it springs back into its original position.

The following points will assist when tracking in this type of country:

- Grass is normally trodden down and pointing in the direction in which the quarry is traveling—an example of pointers (see Fig. 11/4). The broken stalks of corn (or wheat) will eventually die. The wind and the rest of the long grass or stalks of corn will hold the stems up as if there is nothing affected. Only upon closer inspection will you see the broken stems.
- It presents a contrast in color to the normal undergrowth when pressed down—an example of color change
- If the grass has been wet with dew from the night before, the dew will be rubbed off by the passage of the quarry—an example of disturbance
- Mud or soil from footwear may appear on some of the grass—an example of transfer
- In dry grass, broken and crushed blades and stems and possibly footprints will be found

- If new vegetation is showing through, it indicates an old track
- In very short grass, that is, up to ankle height, hoof, pad, claw, and boots will damage the grass near the ground and invariably an impression will be found
- In general, color change as the quarry moves away from you is lighter and as it moves towards you is darker. An exception to this rule occurs if the grass is above your head. Then you may be following up to ten people moving away from you and find yourself going down a dark tunnel (contained shadow). The only way this will change is if more people use the track, making it wider and eventually letting in more light.

Rocky ground

At first it would seem an almost impossible task to track someone across rocky ground but there are a considerable number of aids. The professional tracker does not expect to find a perfectly formed boot print at every pace.

The following features will help you track over rocky ground:

- Impressions in any dust
- Displaced stones or twigs
- Different colored spots from which stones have been moved
- Scratches and marks on the rock surface made by the quarry; for example, humans wearing boots will leave rubber scuff marks, and animals will leave nail scratch marks
- Brittle rock is easily chipped and some rocks crumble when walked on, leaving a light patch
- Displaced rock chippings broken off by the quarry can be seen nearby
- The rocks may lend themselves to easy and obvious stepping places
- Lichen rubbed off or marked
- Moss growing on rocks can be dislodged by foot, hand, claw, pad, or hoof
- Vegetation growing in crevices may have been disturbed or bruised
- Differences in the color of soil from where a stone has been displaced—if the ground is very dry there will be a lighter shade and if the ground is damp, a darker patch will show

- Stones may be displaced and the side that lay on the ground will show darker if the ground is damp and lighter if the ground is very dry
- Soil under stones or rocks that have been trodden on will bear witness to the pressure of the foot upon the ground and will be a different shade
- On sandstone, shoe and hoof marks tend to show dark colors
- Stones on the side of hills tend to move slightly or roll away when walked on—this action takes place whether the quarry is walking up or down the slope
- Stones on a loose or soft surface are normally pressed in when walked upon, leaving either a ridge around the edge of the stone where it has forced the dirt out or a hole where the stone has been pushed below the surface of the ground
- Particles of stone sometimes catch in the sole of footwear and hoofs and are deposited farther on—these can show up vividly against a contrasting background; this is a good example of transfer
- Squashed insects may be seen that have not yet been removed by other predator insects, such as ants or beetles—this will give a tracker experienced in the particular environment a very good indication of the time lapse between the passage of the quarry and the sighting of the sign. If insects injured and immobilized by the quarry's tread are still alive, the quarry passed through recently.
- The quarry may be channeled by large rock formations that indicate to the tracker an obvious route
- Sign may be found in the area of soft ground near the base of large rocks and boulders

With the guidelines above the potential tracker will see that what could at first sight appear to be a "mission impossible" is entirely feasible.

Sandy desert
Soft, deep sand or dust does not give a clear impression, for the sand or dust falls in around the sign, blurring the edges and making it difficult to read with any accuracy.

The most significant aspect of tracking in sandy regions, especially in the desert dunes of areas such as the Sahara and the Empty

Quarter, is the part played by the wind. Even the smallest, faintest track left in these areas can remain in existence for days and weeks, but the imprint of the tires of a ten-ton truck can be completely obliterated in minutes by the strong desert winds that blow in certain seasons.

Anyone tasked to track in this sort of region must have a good understanding of the prevailing climatic conditions and the effect of the diurnal heat changes on the hardness of the sand surface. A track laid during the early morning, when the surface can be concrete hard, may barely be visible whereas a few hours later the same quarry will leave deep indentations in the surface of the sand.

I have found, through experience, desert tracking to be the hardest even though to the casual observer it might appear an easy tracking environment. And as this extract from *The Yom Kippur War* by Abraham Rabinovich shows, the tracker has to keep his powers of deduction engaged permanently.

> A week before Yom Kippur, Ashkenazi was in a half-track making a routine morning patrol eastward along the sandpit towards his rear base when he saw fresh footprints in the sand on both sides of the road. Whoever made them seemed to have circled the area, as if examining the lay of the land. The road was shut at night because it was vulnerable to commando landings from the sea. If anyone came down the road by day, Budapest was supposed to be informed beforehand, but there had been no such notification. The footprints, thought Ashkenazi, could have been left by Egyptian scouts landing from the sea, on one side of the road, or coming on foot through the lagoon, on the other side. He radioed headquarters and a vehicle with two Bedouin trackers arrived. They examined the footprints and concluded that they had been made by standard Israeli army boots.
> "If I were an Egyptian scout, I would use that kind of boot," said Ashkenazi.
> The trackers laughed. "Do you think they're that clever?"
> "Why not?" asked Ashkenazi.
> Twice more in the coming days he would find footprints along the route.

Primary forests

Tracking through primary forests is without doubt the most satisfying of tracking environments. Here trackers will find many ways by which they can track since the forest includes both undergrowth and mature trees, live and dead vegetation, streams with muddy and sandy banks, moss carpeting the forest floor and rocks, and an abundance of animal life.

The potential of tracking through this medium did not escape the attention of the military planners during the post-colonial counter-insurgency wars in the jungle areas of South-East Asia (see the military tracking anecdotes in Chapter 18).

During my attachment to the jungle warfare training establishment in Brunei, I made use of many of the following features of primary forests to assist me in my tracking exercises:

- Leaves on the forest floor when wet and disturbed will show much darker than those undisturbed
- Dry leaves when disturbed show a distinct dark brown on the underside in comparison with the biscuity color of the bleached upper surface
- Some types of vegetation, either leaves or twigs, become very brittle when dead. These crack and break under the pressure of a quarry walking over them.
- The underside of the green leaves of bushes, especially in the thick undergrowth on the edges of the forest, show up lighter in shade than the top of the leaf when it has been pushed aside or twisted by the passage of the quarry—this is a good example of both color change and pointers
- Broken twigs give the experienced tracker a good indication of the time since they were damaged. Freshly broken twigs are generally a creamier color at the break; this color gets darker with time. A tracker may break the twig again to get an indication, by comparison, of how long it was since the original break occurred. Only by experiment and experience will the tracker be able to determine the age of the break.
- Freshly broken green twigs usually retain the smell of sap for three to four hours
- Fallen and especially rotting trees will retain the impressions of any footprints
- Logs that have fallen across a path are usually scuffed by the quarry as he negotiates them and if he is careful to avoid this he will inevitably leave sign on either side of the log as he steps over it
- Roots crossing a path will show signs of having been walked on where they are bruised and bleeding

- Broken cobwebs across the path indicate the passage of animals or humans and if a tracker were moving along a jungle trail first thing in the morning and the cobwebs were broken at head height, it would be a very real indication of how close the tracking team were to the enemy
- Pine needles can be found in most European primary forests and a quarry passing over them will leave an expansive but shallow depression, similar to when a child stands on a soft duvet on a bed

When working in these surroundings the tracker student must be trained and encouraged to look *through* the forest and the vegetation and not *at* it. The jungle can easily become a mesmerizing green blanket that retains its secrets. The jungle tracker through careful observation, analysis, and deduction is able to transform the enshrouding blanket into a light, translucent veil that eventually fades away completely, leaving a clear, well-focused picture of the events.

Secondary forests and dense undergrowth
The 60-meter-high primary forest trees of the typical virgin jungle produce a canopy of vegetation that prevents the sunlight from penetrating to the jungle floor. The result is that in primary forests one finds the jungle giants spaced at fairly large intervals with very little growth in between. This type of jungle is often referred to as being clean—it is a pleasurable environment in which to work.

Secondary forests result when the primary forest has been cleared, either by migrating slash and burn aboriginal cultivators over hundreds of years, or by industrial logging companies over a few months. The vegetation is very thick due to the constant sunlight it receives.

The significance to the tracker is that any large animal passing through this type of undergrowth cannot fail to leave a lot of sign. When tracking in it the main points to watch for are:

- Broken branches, leaves, and roots
- Vegetation facing in the direction in which the quarry has gone— these are pointers
- Footprints on the ground
- Tunnels made by the passage of the quarry

- Broken cobwebs
- Pieces of fur and other animal coatings caught on the tangle of vegetation or on the thorns and spikes produced by some of the plants

Although this is a very arduous type of area to operate in, there is an abundance of sign, because it is impossible, even for the most devious enemy, not to leave evidence of his passage.

Inland waterways and marshy areas

This type of terrain includes rivers, streams, ponds, lakes, canals, marshes, and bogs. Contrary to general belief, tracking is possible where these circumstances exist. The wetter areas are very difficult to track in, except for shallow or still water where footprints may show up, or when following a very fresh track, where splashes on rocks and vegetation and muddy water will be telltale indications of the quarry's presence.

Signs to assist the tracker in these sorts of region are (see Fig. 12):

- Footprints on the bank where the quarry has entered and exited
- Skid, slip, and slide marks on banks—these will show as very distinctive color changes
- Footprints in shallow water—the tracker must examine the riverbed looking for color change, being very careful to avoid fouling the sign
- Stones on river beds are covered in a type of sediment. Therefore when the stone has been trodden on there is a definite color change.
- Mud churned up discoloring the water
- Rocks splashed with water in a quiet running stream—this is transfer
- Places on the bank where a person has sat down to take his shoes off, or to put them back on—this results in flattening of the area
- Foliage growing over a stream may be disturbed or broken
- Entry and exit points are usually obvious and channel the quarry; therefore time should be spent looking for these

As can be seen from this list, tracking is possible around inland waterways but I would like to give a word of warning, especially to the adult with responsibilities for training young people. All water-ways are potentially dangerous to the inexperienced and animals especially can lead the unwary into trouble. Remember it's quite easy for small animals, such as foxes, rabbits, badgers, and birds to walk on top of a bog without sinking and they can also easily swim across a canal, a pond, a river, or a lake.

The seashore
The seashore has many features in common with sandy deserts and also inland waterways—the unique salient feature for the tracker is the effect the tides may have on his task. Although the encroaching sea obscures sign, with a knowledge of the tides, the tracker can on occasion place sign within a specific time bracket.

Soft, damp sand will leave a very clear-cut impression easy to distinguish and follow. It will remain apparently fresh for a considerable time. But dry sand is badly affected by strong winds, as in sandy desert regions.

The main points to be considered are as follows:

- If the surface is inclined to be wet and hard, the footprint is very clear
- If the surface is soft, the footprints will be quite deep
- In the early morning and late afternoon the walls of the impression may cast a deep shadow because of the lack of relief and obstructions often characteristic of coastal areas

Snow-covered regions
After a fresh fall of snow anything that moves across it will leave a patently obvious track. See Fig. 13/1, where the quarry's footprints (in this case, human) are clear and easy to follow—probably the tracker's easiest tracking task.

The following are some of the distinctive features of tracking through snow:

- Secondary snowfalls—even if there is another fall of snow on top of the quarry's sign, under the right conditions you can still follow the track by the shadow under the surface layer (contained shadow) as long as the new snowfall does not get too deep (Fig. 13/2).

Example of a section of a slow-moving river in a pristine state, 20 meters by 10 meters. The river flows from left to right. (A) Large flat stones in the river bed. (B) The river bank. (C) The river.

Fig. 12a. A river before the quarry crosses

The same waterway as in (a) but this time after the quarry has crossed the river —in this case, a man. Points to note: (A) All the water downstream from the footprints is discolored and may take hours to clear depending on the speed and depth of the river. (B) Entry and exit points are darker in color. Slip and slide marks caused by the quarry entering and exiting the river.

Fig. 12b. The river immediately after the crossing

The same waterway as before but this time after 24 hours have elapsed. Points to note: (A) Look for debris downstream possibly caught up in the stones. (B) You may still see footprints on the river bed by their color change. With water flowing into the footprint it causes a distortion of the print on the downside i.e. down river. (C) You will see a definite color change on the stones on the river bed, as the lichen and moss have been rubbed off by the quarry's footprint. This may be lighter or darker than the surrounding stone.

Fig. 12c. The river after several hours

The same waterway as before. This time anything up to six months to a year old depending on how many quarry made the sign. Points to note: (A) Slip and slide marks will eventually disappear over time and weather and will return to normal. (B) Lichen and moss will also grow back onto the stones and everything will

Fig. 12d. The crossing point after days, weeks, and months

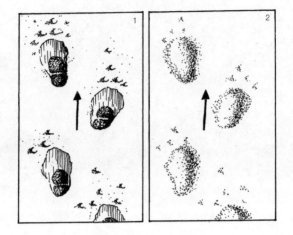

Fig. 13. Tracks in snow

- Hardness of the surface—this governs the prominence of the sign
- Differences in sign made by the same animal—this phenomenon occurs when, for instance, an animal leaves a recognizable, normal, clear track in snow an inch or two deep that has a hard surface, but in deep, soft snow the whole appearance of the track will alter. On hard snow a rabbit's track is easy to identify, but in soft snow it is very difficult to reconcile the large foot prints he makes with his size. Again, animals that do not leave a tail-mark on hard ground may leave a very distinctive and initially confusing tail-mark in soft, deep snow

I have not included ice-covered regions in this section because the skills required for tracking under such conditions are more akin to those recorded above in the section on rocky ground.

Urban and built-up areas
The skills required for tracking in built-up areas are not the sole preserve of the large town or inner-city because the tracker following a quarry through a predominantly rural area may suddenly find himself in a large farm complex, a disused airfield, or some such man-made feature.

The significant features of areas such as these are the hard artificial surfaces of which roads and railway lines are made and over which the quarry will move.

Fortunately, there is a great deal of commonality between built-up areas and other areas in which the tracker has to practice his skills—for instance there are many grassed areas and unsurfaced footpaths.

Invariably, though, tracking in built-up areas will involve foul tracks and will slow most trackers. However, although slowed to pace tracking the tracker may speed up his pursuit by carrying out a process of track isolation through the following:

• Look for exit and entry points
• Searching likely areas (see Chapter 16)
• Presence of particular sign pattern

And a tracker following a track into a built-up area should be aware of the following points about the quarry:

• He may have a rendezvous with someone
• He may be friendly with the local population
• He may live in the area

The climate

The student of tracking has to familiarize himself with the effects of the weather and climatic conditions on spoor and sign.

The three climatic factors that affect the track are:

• Direct sunlight
• Strong wind
• Heavy precipitation

All these factors will adversely affect the sign of a track. The degree to which this will happen varies and depends upon:

• The strength of the element
• Whether elements were working in combination or separately
• The duration the element impinged on the sign
• The type of terrain

Generally speaking, tracks sheltered from direct sunlight, strong wind, and heavy rain can still be recognized days, if not weeks, after they were made.

Direct sunlight
This causes sign to return to normal more quickly, although we have already seen how in certain circumstances the presence of sunlight can help the tracker to determine the quarry's direction of movement—a light path indicating movement away, a dark path indicating movement towards.

Strong winds
The wind encourages disturbed vegetation to return to its original position. This is particularly true of long grasses and tall cereal crops like corn, wheat, and barley. When a strong wind blows, any grass shoots displaced by the quarry tend to be tugged back up into their original position. In these circumstances a tracker will primarily be following ground sign and if you look at the lower part of the grass stem you will find that it will be broken and pointing in the direction in which the quarry traveled.

Strong winds may also conceal ground sign as debris is blown about.

For the observant, aware tracker the effects of the wind can be an advantage. It may have blown dust, dried grass, straws, leaves, or other debris over the marks. This feature, coupled with the observation as to when the weather was windy, will give you a clue as to the time the sign was made.

It is this type of detail that is always important. And it is this type of awareness of his surroundings that sets the good tracker apart, for he is continually monitoring significant changes and remembering what has happened.

Being aware of your surroundings and the interplay of factors is the reason why any tracker working a woodland area, whether it be jungle or temperate, is always alert to the dangers of deadfalls. Deadfalls are the result of old, dead, or rotten wood suddenly being displaced by the wind or rain. As they come crashing through the smaller, flimsier branches nearer the ground the unwary have little time to react.

Heavy precipitation
This will wash out some sign very quickly, particularly ground sign, and is probably the tracker's greatest enemy.

On the other hand, if there has been only a light shower, spots of rain may have pitted the sign, thus giving the tracker an additional clue as to the time it was made (see Chapters 14 and 15 for a full explanation of judging the age of sign and deductive skills).

Time

Time is the fourth of the factors that affect sign. To be able to assess the time bracket between when a spoor mark was made and when it is found is one of the crucial tracking skills. Only experience and practice will enable the tracker to judge accurately when sign was made.

Out of the four factors affecting sign, time probably poses the greatest challenge to the tracker. The following practical anecdote illustrates what I mean. The owner of a sheep station in Australia was riding with one of his stockmen. They were looking for a flock known to have passed through the area over a week before. The owner saw many tracks, assumed they were made by his flock, and suggested they should follow them. The aboriginal stockman contradicted him, reasoning, "No, these tracks were made only two days ago."

It would have been easy to be misled by the obvious tracks if the stockman hadn't taken into account all the facts and then applied them to his observations.

The following are some of the main indicators of timing:

- The track in question may cross other tracks for which the timing is known if, for instance, they are made by humans whom you have identified and whose movements you know or by animals whose habits are familiar to you
- Insects and worms that have worked across the marks can be useful to the locally experienced tracker
- The heat retained by the remains of fires, food, and feces
- Grass and other vegetation that has been bent will spring into normal place again in a few hours
- Broken vegetation will wither and die at set rates depending on the type of plant and the climatic conditions
- Observation and the ability to recall changes in the weather will also enable you to assess timings—for example a boot print with only a very small amount of water in it when it has been raining heavily for several hours would indicate the quarry is very close

- Water running back into a boot print on the edge of a puddle also helps to establish the passage of time
- The drying rate of soil disturbed and exposed to sunlight
- The obliteration rate of sign by strong winds
- Knowledge of the characteristics of various soils also helps the tracker to assess the time lapse. Most clay-based soils or earth will keep the impression longer and more distinctly than loamy or sandy soils.

To sum up, the tracker must be aware that the four factors that affect sign do not influence the track independently of one another. They work in unison on the sign and spoor to weather it and to alter its nature. Sometimes one of the factors becomes dominant, and at other times it is the interplay of the factors that produces the changes in the original sign.

SUMMARY

FACTORS AFFECTING SIGN
Four main factors affect sign:

• Spoor and sign left by other animals and vehicles
• Features of the terrain
• Climatic conditions
• Time

Third-party spoor and sign
Spoor and sign belong to one of three groups:

• You the tracker and your team
• The quarry, which can be one or more persons or vehicles
• A third party

The terrain
The major types of terrain that offer very distinctive attributes for the tracker:

• Grass and cultivated areas
• Rocky ground
• Sandy desert
• Primary forests
• Secondary forests and dense undergrowth
• Inland waterways and marshy areas
• The seashore
• Snow-covered regions
• Urban and built-up areas

The climate
The three climatic factors that affect the track are:

• Direct sunlight
• Strong wind
• Heavy precipitation

All these factors will adversely affect the sign of a track. The degree this effect will have is varied and depends upon:

- The strength of the element
- Whether they were working in combination or separately
- The duration the element impinged on the sign
- The type of terrain

Time
Time is the fourth of the factors that affect sign. To be able to assess the time bracket between when a spoor mark was made and when it is found is one of the crucial tracking skills.

Interdependence
The tracker must be aware that the four factors that affect sign do not influence the track independently. They work in unison on the sign and spoor to weather it and to change its nature. Sometimes one of the factors becomes dominant and at other times it is the interplay of the factors that produces the transformations.

5

THE ATTRIBUTES OF A TRACKER

A story I read as a boy has become a part of my personal philosophy. A party of academics and explorers were carrying out a scientific expedition in the interior of Australia in an area in those days appropriately known as the Great Thirstland. They came out of the area alive only because a little aboriginal girl was accompanying them.

The work of the expedition had been abandoned. Its members were dying of thirst and were desperately searching for water. The girl had noticed some ants creeping up the stem of a tree and making their way into a small hole in the bark. She realized that there would be a purpose behind their activity. She pushed a twig into the hole to explore. She discovered that water was contained in the tree trunk. She then stripped the bark from some green twigs so that they formed a succession of small tubes. She fitted them together to form a drinking straw and passed the end of this tube down through the hole into the tree enabling each one of the party to suck up his fill of water.

An illiterate fourteen-year-old, aboriginal girl saved the lives of the scientists. She had been able to perform her mercy mission due to powers of observation, deduction, and ingenuity. It hadn't been the sophisticated knowledge the members of the expedition had possessed that had saved them, but the natural knowledge of one who had been brought up to observe the essentials of life. These same skills are vividly displayed in the film *Rabbit-Proof Fence* set in 1930s Australia.

Trackers need to develop the sort of expertise that came so naturally to this young aboriginal girl. Good trackers are characterized by their outstanding ability to observe, remember, select, analyze and comprehend. The tracker when observing needs to look beyond mere recognition and go on to observe every detail. He must then remember all he's seen, smelled, heard, felt, and possibly tasted, usually without resorting to making notes. The salient points are then selected or collated for analysis. All this has to be done almost instinctively before he can arrive at correct deductions and an accurate comprehension of what has occurred.

The qualities of a good tracker

Anyone using tracking skills will soon realize that he is called on to make many decisions. He will be required to draw heavily on his training and experience. But above all else he will need acute observation, patience, and persistence.

He has to understand nature. He has to keep himself at a high standard of physical fitness. He has to have a good memory with which to retain and piece together the many small parcels of information—the sign left along a track.

The job of potential trackers is to think for themselves, to reason out statements for themselves, to discover the whys and wherefores of an activity for themselves. They may be helped to a certain extent by the advice and experience of others, especially if they are a member of a tracking team, but they should not become dependent on others. Trackers need to be self-sufficient, free-spirits. They do not blindly accept the obvious explanations.

To be a competent tracker you must develop the following qualities:

• Patience
• An inquisitive mind
• Honesty
• Perseverance
• Acute observation
• All five senses must be well attuned
• Above average endurance
• Above average standard of field craft

- Mental and physical determination
- A good knowledge of the local fauna and flora
- Curiosity

Contrary to common belief, people are not born with the natural instincts of a tracker. A tracker is not a special breed of person. Trackers come from all backgrounds and nationalities. Being country-reared, although an initial advantage, does not necessarily exclude the city dweller from becoming a competent tracker. Through dedication and hard work it is possible for anyone to become proficient in the art of tracking.

Generally speaking, a tracker is normally most efficient in his country of origin (see Fig. 14). Of course in a new country his effectiveness will depend entirely on his ability to adjust to a new environment. Once this is achieved a tracker is able to perform to his maximum efficiency. The sooner he gains first-hand knowledge of his area of operation, the better equipped he will be to follow through each tracking task successfully.

Self-knowledge
Good trackers are aware of their limitations, both in terms of fatigue and tracking ability. In short, they are honest with themselves and others.

First, they do not track on when tired because they know a tired tracker easily loses the track, becomes noisy and clumsy in his movements, and is less likely to see the quarry.

Second, they know their skill level and are confident without being overconfident. When a track becomes difficult and you are straining to follow the track, it is easy to see sign where none exists. Students of visual tracking are particularly prone to this tendency in their early days. Be aware; do not bluff yourself and others into thinking you are following the quarry when you are following an imaginary track.

I was told on my tracking course that I had to be prepared to follow a track for days and that it could be hard, frustrating work with many false trails, but that if I was destined to be a good tracker, eventually everything would click into place. There were others on the course who, by their own admission, couldn't track their way out

Fig. 14. The author with experienced desert tracker

of a paper bag, but their time wasn't wasted because over the eight-week course these soldiers began to realize that in a war situation a trained tracker can be deadly. They automatically started eliminating the sign that they left behind, realizing this could hinder a tracker.

Psychology of the quarry

Attempt to picture in your mind the party making the track. Try to get into his skin and into his mind. Your quarry may be leading the existence of a hunted animal. Don't underestimate his skill. He will be forcing himself to move very quietly and cautiously. He will be using all his skill and cunning to deceive you. Remember the possibility of a purposely misleading trail. Remember he may be in fear for his life and therefore a great threat to you.

As you build up the information about the quarry it is as though a transparent, ghostly image starts to take on a shape and then eventually you clothe and equip the person and finally enter into his mind. When a tracker is extremely adept at his skill he can anticipate the quarry's next move. This is not only of importance to the military or police tracker, but can be a life-saver for the mountain rescue team. As the tracker deduces the state of mind of the person being searched for, by analyzing the sign he is leaving, it is a small step from here for a tracker to foresee what decisions the victim will make at various junctures.

This knowledge of the quarry helps the military or police tracker develop his sixth sense and become aware of danger as he approaches the quarry. Needless to say, this cannot be achieved in a base camp surrounded by his fellow men and all the trappings of civilization—it is a result of being in the field and tuning in to the environment over prolonged periods.

The five senses

Good trackers have to learn one vital lesson early on in their development, no matter how the skills are applied: by hunter, conservationist, police, search and rescue, gamekeeper or military tracker. Trackers must let nothing escape their attention.

It takes a good deal of practice before a potential tracker can get into the habit of noting everything before him. Development of the memory and mental processes are key. Without constant training and practice the information provided by the sign becomes difficult if not impossible to decipher.

There seems to be no doubt that civilization has a tendency to dull all our five senses—sight, hearing, smell, taste, and touch. They become dull because we are not so dependent upon them, and because the opportunities for their use have been lessened. Towndwellers especially suffer in this respect. Vision is limited by walls and roofs, and sight is harmed by artificial light. Hearing is dulled by the continual grind and roar of modern traffic. Smell is clouded by the fumes of gasoline and oil that hang about the streets and by all the other pollutants associated with a modern city. Taste, which is so closely allied to smell, is very rarely fully engaged, except by a few skilled trades and professions. For the tracker all five senses are important. Sign is not confined to things that can be seen, but also includes things that can be heard, smelled, tasted, and touched.

Again, not only do the senses have to record an impression, automatically or subconsciously, but the tracker must train himself to remember it. An observation is useless unless it is crystallized into the memory. Observation cannot be divorced from memory if the tracker is going to benefit from the raw material his senses have given him.

SUMMARY

THE ATTRIBUTES OF A TRACKER
To be a competent tracker you must possess or develop the following qualities:

- Patience
- An inquisitive mind
- Honesty
- Perseverance
- Acute observation
- All five senses must be well attuned
- Above average endurance
- Above average standard of field craft
- Mental and physical determination
- A good knowledge of the local fauna and flora
- Curiosity

SELF-KNOWLEDGE
A good tracker is aware of his limitations both in terms of fatigue and tracking ability. In short, he is honest with himself and others.

PSYCHOLOGY OF THE QUARRY
Attempt to picture in your mind the party making the track. Try to get into his skin and into his mind.

THE FIVE SENSES
Sight, hearing, smell, taste, and touch have to be used to note everything and then remember it.

PART TWO

THE PURSUIT

6

OBSERVATION INDOORS

Observation is so closely linked to tracking as to be inseparable. Therefore, I think it only right that before I proceed to tracking drills proper, I spend some time explaining how to develop the powers of observation. This training can be undertaken in two stages. This chapter will deal with the first stage—the indoor stage. It is an added bonus for the teacher or youth group leader that you can progress with your tracker training course during the evenings or when the weather precludes outdoor activities.

A great deal of the indoor training revolves around the memory and observation training technique known as Kim's Game. This can mistakenly be considered merely as a party game but I can assure you that it is used as the basis of memory and observation skills training by some of the best surveillance units in the military.

Kim was the hero of the eponymous tale by Kipling. He was being trained for his secret service work on behalf of the British Raj—in the Great Game. His training was conducted using stones on a tray. Now slides and video clips are used but essentially the training is the same. The advantages of Kim's Game are that it is easy to conduct and it can be carried out indoors. It is directly relevant to tracking in that it develops and sharpens both observation and, just as important, memory.

Before I lay out the practical details for conducting Kim's Game as a training session, it would be beneficial to explain some of the basic principles of memory.

Memory training

If you are aware of some of the key processes that take place when you use your memory, you can take steps to improve its efficiency. It is worth spending some time studying the best ways to enhance your own memory. Although individuals differ, certain broad principles should be kept in mind.

Memory is the process of storing and retrieving information, or retention and recall.

Storage techniques:

- Association—the more facts that are associated with the object the better the chance of the object being remembered
- Groupings or clusters—organize in your mind similar items in a group
- Visualization—imagine some visually vivid image of the items you are trying to remember

Retrieval techniques:

- The Greek system of a familiar room—imagine a tour around a room you know intimately and associate the facts you are trying to remember with items in the room
- Knot in the tie or some item that is out of place—this immediately triggers the memory
- Mnemonics—produce your own mnemonic lists

Recall is state-dependent, that is, we recall better if the state we learned the facts in is the same as the one in which we are trying to recall them.

Memory is either short- or long-term. Phone numbers are designed to use the short-term memory function so they are usually broken into chunks about six digits long.

The physiological processes that come into play to transfer from short- to long-term memory are beyond the scope of this book but it is worth noting from a practical point of view that there are two sorts of memory. For instance, you may think that you have remembered some feature of the sign you observed three hours before but it may have registered only in the short-term memory and you may not be able to recall it later.

Another important part of the memory that we must be aware of is its opposite, forgetting.

This is defined as when information becomes inaccessible. It may be inaccessible because it is no longer in storage or it cannot be retrieved. Forgetting is a vital function; otherwise we would be overloaded with every sensory stimulus encountered.

Factors involved with forgetting:

- Time
- Interference—similar things interfere with each other, e.g. two vehicle registration numbers
- Distortions—due to what the person regards as most important. We try to reconstruct events into a previously recognizable pattern, as opposed to what actually happened, e.g. if a man passes a parcel to a librarian, we record it as being a book because that is what we are expecting.
- Memories can be entirely false
- Memories are not fixed but change over time and can also be affected by other memory inputs

We all have a memory, and it is a faculty that, with practice, can be improved. Exercises that allow us to make better use of our memories, consciously or subconsciously, are:

- Fantasy—a green limousine is remembered as a crocodile and the three passengers as three birds on its back
- Visualization—it is easier to recall concrete images, so try to see the vivid red of the mailbox that the man went to before he strode across the wide street to the sparkling lights of the restaurant
- Association—to remember a series of key words in the correct sequence, link them in your mind to articles in a room with which you are very familiar, ensuring that they are in the sequence you would see walking through the room
- Exaggeration—this is ideal for remembering the features of a person; if the person has long fingers this is remembered in an elongated fashion similar to how a cartoonist or caricaturist depicts his subjects

It is interesting that these are all positive acts; memorizing information is not passive. We are not sponges and although individuals have natural preferences for memorizing—some are more aurally aware than others, while some find the sense of smell an evocative trigger—all of these exercises can be actively employed to improve memory storage and recall. For a detailed description of these techniques I recommend you study *A Question of Memory* by D. Berglas and G. L. Playfair.

There are good reasons for a potential tracker to study and improve his memory. As you move along the track there will be many details of the sign. Some of these may appear irrelevant as you follow the three to five items of key sign, but when linked up to something further along the pursuit they may become a vital piece of the jigsaw indicating something very important about your quarry.

For instance you may be following the key sign of a booted man down a much used track where there is a great deal of other sign. But every mile or so a slight oval indentation about 3 or 4 inches in length appears alongside his boot print. If this was overlooked or not remembered, you may not realize the man was armed—that indentation being the butt of his rifle that he rested on the ground as he paused to read his map.

Exercise your memory. Engage your powers of retention and recall information positively during your daily life. Memory isn't a faculty that gets worn out!

Kim's game

The basic standard layout for Kim's Game is twenty small objects placed at random on a cloth. The items should be from a variety of uses and backgrounds. The students are allowed to study them for one minute and then the articles are covered. They are then asked to write down accurate and full descriptions of as many of the items as they can remember.

From the start an emphasis should be placed upon accurate and full descriptions to engender an attention to detail. For instance "a small metal object" is not sufficient for the description of a key. The type of description that should be aimed at is, "a Yale-type key, bronze colored, with a slight crack halfway down its length."

As a buildup fewer, larger objects can be used. The exposure time can be lengthened and the students can be asked to give verbal descriptions. Advice the instructor can give to the student after the first few attempts might be:

- Count the number of items
- Study the smaller things first
- Group the objects
- Don't hurry—keep calm

The instructor can vary the standard format of the game along many lines:

- Vary the types of items
- Alter the method of arrangement—use the floor, suspend them from the ceiling, scatter them around the room
- Use slides and video clips
- Play the game as a team
- Spring the game on a group of people without any kind of warning, or in the midst of another activity
- Interfere with the memory by introducing another task, or by planning a time lapse before writing the results down

Other variations on the theme are:

- A fleeting observation of one single article, for example, a look at an envelope reveals the postmark (foreign or domestic), the writing, marks on the envelope, the size, the shape (flat or bulging), the flap, the stamp, the color, and the quality of the paper
- Asking participants to remember the details of a room
- Before and after situations—"What is wrong?" or "What is missing?"
- The use of distance by holding up articles at the opposite end of the room
- Color can be utilized in two ways—first, to make an article insignificant by the fact that it is surrounded by other articles of more brilliant coloring, and second to aid the memory by grouping things of the same color

These changes of conditions are an important factor in the advanced application of Kim's Game. They prepare the student for the reality of an incident—you are not warned beforehand that something requiring observation is going to appear or to happen. If you have acquired the habit of observation, you will have recorded it; if not, you will be left startled and remember nothing.

The use of other senses
Most people's senses are dominated by visual stimuli but, as has been stressed previously, the tracker must be open to gain information from all five senses. It may be one of the seemingly less significant senses, such as taste or touch, that provides the conclusive evidence: Are the ashes in the fire hot or cold?

Hearing
The use of sight is not the only means by which the quarry's presence and activities can be detected. A trained tracker can gather valuable information by using his sense of hearing to locate the quarry. Trackers need to be trained to actively listen for sounds. They have to be able to differentiate between the natural and the unnatural. The following are some of the common sounds a tracker may hear:

- Metal against metal
- Vehicle movement
- Human movement
- Chopping
- Human noises
- Birds calling
- Foxes barking/howling
- Animals rutting/digging
- Birds flying
- Fish, birds, and animals splashing

Visual information is presented directly to the observer. Although many of the above sounds will be instantly recognizable to a trained tracker, the use of hearing requires deduction on the part of the hearer. Only with practice and imaginative training will accurate information be gathered through hearing.

The sense of hearing can again be sharpened by games conducted indoors. Noises Out is perhaps the best known and the most useful. All that is required in this game is for someone who is concealed behind a screen, or behind a door, to make a series of noises, either by dropping articles on the floor, or by moving articles about, or by using their mouth to make the sounds. The students are then asked to give their interpretation of what the sound represented, e.g. men whispering, a vehicle starting up, a man digging, cattle moving. The instructor can use tape recordings but it is probably still better concealing the source of the noise by a screen and interspersing non-recorded noises in the sequence.

Hunt the Watch is another game that can be used to stimulate the concentration on hearing. Everyone is blindfolded and they have to search for a ticking watch. This game teaches some of the rudiments of stalking, and brings home the importance of keeping quiet and of moving quietly.

This game helps develop a sense of direction by ear that can be practiced by various other means. For example, the group can sit in a wide circle with one of their number, blindfolded, in the center. He has to identify both the nature and direction of any sound made by the other members of the group.

Again, the elements of surprise should be brought into the training. During a lesson, plan for a sudden noise to be made outside the room. And then say, "Now note down all you can about that noise."

Important elements in describing noises are the tone and the rhythm. A potential tracker should be able to say whether one note was lower or higher than another.

Smell

It is a known fact that hot air rises during the day and cold air sweeps down the valleys and ridges at night. Therefore, smells drift uphill in the daytime and downhill at night. It is helpful for you to know the type of smells that occur and that are made by you or your quarry. Taking this point further, the sense of smell can be a double-edged weapon in a tracking scenario. This point will be reiterated in the chapters on stalking and on military tracking.

One method of training the sense of smell is to surreptitiously introduce a noticeable and characteristic smell into the room during another activity—you record the reactions and comments. This will at least make the students aware of the necessity of keeping all their senses alert. Items that can be introduced are:

- Burned paper
- An oily rag
- Fish-and-chip wrappers
- Cigarette smoke

Taste

Taste is related to and dependent on the sense of smell but the only relevance that it has to tracking is that if your taste buds are impaired by spicy foods it may also affect your sense of smell. It is all linked to having all your senses keyed up to a high pitch so that you are fully alert to your environment.

Touch

Touch is an interesting and overlooked sense with which a tracker can gain valuable information, especially with regard to texture and heat.

Cooking areas and sleeping areas can render a great deal of information about the age of the sign and how long the sites were occupied by the texture of soil—is it fresh or old? And if the occupation was more recent—how warm is the ground around the cooking and sleeping areas?

There is an interesting, unsavory story about a French Foreign Legion tracker in their war against Algerian rebels. When he came across human feces, he would test its age by poking his finger into it. Whether heat was retained inside and/or near the surface gave him some indication when the man defecated and therefore an indication of whether the enemy was close.

Detection exercises based on the use of touch not only lead to familiarity with shape and feel but also encourage trackers to use their deductive powers to gather information. For youngsters blind-fold obstacle races indoors are amusing and useful. Another exercise in touch is to let two blindfolded potential trackers loose in a room to find each other, and let the others watch in complete silence. Those looking on will also learn a lot about feeling their way in the dark—one of the most important aspects being that when one sense is restricted, others compensate and therefore in this exercise hearing and smell will come into play.

Another indoor exercise for the potential tracker is to find his way about in the dark, first of all in a known room and then in a strange room, or one in which the furniture has been rearranged. The fire services practice such drills with the very serious aim of being able to locate and rescue people in smoke-filled premises.

The identification of various objects by touch alone should be frequently practiced. The articles need not necessarily be small. It is possible to identify a person by passing the fingers lightly over the face. The blind can do this very readily, just as they learn to identify a person by the sound of his voice, or even the sound of his footsteps.

In time, after much practice, it will be found that it is possible to sense obstacles in the way before they are even touched.

I have attempted to demonstrate, especially to the adult responsible for training young people, that there is a great deal of scope for exercises related to tracking that can be carried out either in the winter evenings or during bad weather.

The subject of describing faces and individuals will be dealt with in Chapter 8 but, as will be seen, it also affords great scope and opportunities for indoor work.

A tracker must remember that his senses are his most valuable assets. It is important that all trackers continually exercise all their five senses—sight, hearing, smell, touch, and taste. They should avoid activities and habits that detune their faculties.

When the senses are at a high pitch, not only does the tracker recognize the sign of his quarry faster but his life is lived at a heightened state as he becomes more aware of his environment.

SUMMARY

Memory is the process of storing and retrieving information, or retention and recall.

Storage techniques
- Association
- Groupings or clusters
- Visualization

Retrieval techniques
- The Greek system of a familiar room
- Knot in the tie or some item that is out of place
- Mnemonics

Recall is state dependent.

Memory is either short- or long-term.

Forgetting is when information becomes inaccessible, either because it is no longer stored or it cannot be retrieved.

Factors involved in forgetting
- Time
- Interference
- Distortions
- Memories can be entirely false
- Memories are not fixed but change over time and can also be affected by other memory inputs

Enhancing the memory
- Fantasy
- Visualization
- Association
- Exaggeration

7

OBSERVATION OUTDOORS

Both the youth group leader and the military tracking instructor will find that as the training moves outdoors the students will become more interested. For the student the training and exercises become more closely associated with tracking proper.

With visual training skills outdoors there is one very important difference that has to be brought home to the potential tracker—visual training, now, is training to observe coupled with the knowledge of how to conceal yourself.

Outdoors observation has an added difficulty in that the range of vision varies. In some types of terrain, for instance, the sand seas of the large deserts, it is practically limitless, whereas in scrub or secondary jungle it is very restricted.

Those who are accustomed to living in open spaces have usually much keener eyesight than those who live in towns. And the specific environment affects the ability to observe over the full range. For instance, the desert-dwelling Bedouin has a remarkably clear long vision, whereas jungle aborigines have a keen eye for the detail of sign.

The town-dwelling Westerner can adapt but he must be aware of what he is trying to do and his limitations. However, he can make remarkable progress in a limited time. He will find that his learning curve is exponential. He will achieve a great deal at first, so long as he persists, but to emulate fully the Dyak or Iban trackers from South-East Asia would take him years of living in their environment.

There is an important lesson of observation to be learned from the following story. Common sense and a little reflection will often suggest to you the most likely places in which to look. While in Dhofar with the SAS in the early 1970s I became embroiled in a gentle challenge. One of the local hill tribesmen with whom we were operating tried, good naturedly, to get the upper hand of the foreign soldier by asking me how many goats were on the opposite mountainside. It was hardly possible to make out that there were any goats there at all, let alone count them. I could only make out a few whitish specks but not to be outdone, after admitting I couldn't count all the goats, I told him where the goat herders were, how many there were, and who they were.

I knew that the goat herders would be women and that there would be two of them—for company and as chaperones for each other. I couldn't actually see them but I guestimated that in the heat of the day they would be two black figures huddled under the largest, shadiest tree on the uphill side of the flock.

A look through the binoculars showed this to be correct.

Observe
Remember
Select and analyze
Comprehend and deduce

The use of sight is the primary means by which a tracker gathers and accumulates information, but seeing is more than just a question of looking. An understanding of why things are seen will assist a tracker in searching and detecting the quarry and its sign, and also help him to conceal himself. Six factors attract attention and determine why things are seen (see Fig. 15).

Shape
Personal equipment and the human body are familiar outlines to us all. They can be recognized instantly, particularly when they are in contrast to their surroundings. Distinctive shapes stand out and are more easily detected, for example, someone wearing a raincoat, a hat, rubber boots, or carrying an umbrella or a shotgun. Remember your shape and the quarry's shape can be easily disguised by standing motionless in front of the appropriate background.

Fig. 15. The six factors that attract attention

Shadow

Shadows are cast in sunlight, moonlight, and artificial light. An object casts a shadow, which may give away its presence. On the other hand, an object that is concealed in other shadows is harder to detect and does not cast a shadow of its own. The tracking student must be aware that as the sun, moon, or artificial light moves, so do the shadows. Objects that were concealed by shadow may now be revealed, as they themselves cast their own distinctive shadow, or as they come out of the obscuring shadow.

There is another category of shadow: contained shadow. Contained shadow is that which is within a space, for example, a hut, a room, a cave, or a tent. It is normally darker than other shadows and can therefore attract attention. You will have seen this type of shadow depicted in detective films where all that is seen of the murderer with his upraised arm and knife is his shadow inside the room or the tent (see Fig. 16).

Fig. 16. Contained shadow

A significant point about shadows relates specifically to sign. When a person walks over a carpet of leaves, they pile up in the direction of the movement. Depending on the light, a shadow will be visible, cast by the built-up leaves.

Silhouette

An object silhouetted against a contrasting background is conspicuous—smooth flat backgrounds such as water, snow, fields, or most extreme of all, the sky. An object may be silhouetted if it is against a contrasting background, for example, dark objects against a light background and vice versa.

Surface and shine

If the color and texture of the surface of an object contrast with its surroundings, it will be conspicuous. Shiny objects and white skin contrast violently with most backgrounds.

Spacing

Nature very rarely, if ever, spaces objects regularly. Therefore, the tracker should be alert to regularly spaced objects, even if they appear natural. Apart from the obvious explanation of trees and bushes planted by man, the items may be more sinister camouflaged objects.

Movement

Sudden movement attracts the eye. This is easily demonstrated by half-concealing a number of people and inviting others to spot them. They will do so with difficulty while those concealed remain still, but when they move they will spot them easily. Sudden movement is easily seen. Although the tiger is in its prey's line of sight, it is not seen until it launches its attack. You will realize the importance of stealthy movement when you come to practice stalking.

Observation techniques

Now understanding why objects are seen, we are able to study the next subject: the proper use of our eyes. This may seem a simple idea but if you have a technique on which to concentrate, you will not fall into the trap of looking and not seeing. In basic military training the instructor often spots the raw recruit whose head is turning back and forth as he patrols along on exercise. He seems to be alert but nothing that his gaze falls upon registers in his brain—he is looking without seeing. Consequently he will not; be able to remember anything from which to draw any conclusions; as a tracker he is worse than useless. There are two interrelated techniques—scanning and searching.

Scanning

This is a general and systematic examination of an area to detect any unusual or significant object or movement. To scan an area the following actions are recommended.

Divide the area into:

• Foreground
• Middle distance
• Distance

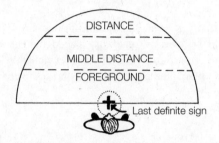

Fig. 17. How the tracker divides the area for scanning

Note: the size of the half-circle in Fig. 17 can be any size depending on the tracker's observational ability and the visibility.

Scan each area horizontally, starting with the foreground. To obtain maximum efficiency move the head in short overlapping movements. Moving the head as opposed to the eyes will minimize eye fatigue. The speed at which scanning is carried out will depend on the type of ground being observed, that is, whether it is open or close country. When the horizontal scanning is complete, scan along the line of the features that are angled away from the observation position.

As a tracker your eyes scan from about 5 to 10 meters out until sign is located. When you scan, your head and eyes must keep on moving slowly from side to side and in a figure eight pattern. This is especially important in close country such as secondary forest. This assists the tracker in looking through and not at the vegetation. Having picked up marks or signs, then move closer to inspect.

Searching
This is the next phase and may take place at any stage during the scanning. Any suspected movement or object spotted during the scanning requires an immediate more thorough visual study—a visual search of the area as opposed to a physical search.

If you are observing for movement, it is better to stare at a place for a while and only move the head and eyes occasionally. Anything that moves will then attract the eye.

Where to look
Sign is easier to find in some places than others. The following are places where sign will be most obvious:

- Near any source of water
- On muddy and sandy patches
- In high grass or thick undergrowth
- On steep hillsides
- On the edges of clearings
- Where obstacles have to be crossed

What to look for
As you are scanning and searching you should remember each of the factors that make an object visible:

- Shape
- Shadow
- Silhouette
- Surface/Shine
- Spacing
- Movement

On the move
Your eyes, ears, and nose are constantly monitoring the environment. Every few minutes, depending on how close you suspect the quarry to be, and certainly not less often than every ten minutes, you must stop and listen.

Eyes must be trained to disregard the general pattern of foliage immediately to the front and to look through rather than at it. Another invaluable tactic is to get down on the ground and look through the undergrowth for any sign or sighting of the quarry.

You have to survey both near and far and inspect objects both large and small. When any unusual sign or sound is noted, you must freeze quickly and silently. Do not move until you have investigated with a visual search.

Before and after studies
This is the application of very detailed observation to determine whether the quarry has entered an area or not. The basis of this technique is an in-depth study of what could be termed a micro-area to establish what its appearance is in its undisturbed state compared to the same area when the quarry has passed through it.

The format for this study is a description of the area in its pristine condition—the original state. This is then followed by a list of the alterations caused by the passage of the quarry. Finally, the tracker can take confirmatory actions to gain more evidence.

Some examples will illustrate the attention to detail necessary at this stage of the tracker's development. I include a generous list because this is excellent material for use by the tracking instructor.

Example 1 Leaf- and twig-covered area
Natural state:

- Dried twigs, flaking bark, and leaf surfaces will all be aged to the same degree

Disturbed state:

- No actual prints but depressions left
- Twigs squashed, bent, and broken
- Freshly broken twigs will be lighter in color and will have fine fibers left at the ends; where bark has been knocked off, the freshly exposed area will be darker or lighter and may have a layer of dried powder or granulated debris
- Overturned leaves will expose darker or lighter, sand-speckled undersides
- Squashed, crumbled, bent, or broken leaves will show the lighter colors of the fresh break, together with the exposed fine hairs of the tear

(In the case of both knocked-off bark and overturned leaves, you must compare pristine samples in the original state. This will confirm whether the underside of the leaf or bark is darker or lighter in that environment and whether there is a layer of dried power or granulated debris.)

Confirmatory actions:

- Check bent leaves for flexibility
- Lightly blow on tilted leaves to check their stability
- Study leaves for any transfer deposits—sand or mud

- Feel with the fingertips in any depression for the outline of a print
- Remove leaves from a depression and check for the impression of the print underneath
- Study worm casts under these leaves for evidence of disturbance

Example 2 Leaf- and twig-covered area with growing vegetation
Natural state:

- Same as Example 1
- No damage to the growing vegetation

Disturbed state:

- Same as Example 1
- Damage to the growing vegetation including bruising and scraping

Confirmatory actions:

- Same as Example 1
- Scrutinize any damage for sap evidence
- Make a comparative scrape or damage on an identical plant and note the differences in color, smell, and viscosity of the fresh sap
- Search for living leaves removed from their parent plant and study these for aging
- Use any scrapes to assess the direction of movement as well as age

Example 3 Leaf- and twig-covered area with exposed roots
Natural state:

- Same as Example 1
- Roots on earth mounds

Disturbed state:

- Same as Example 1
- Roots that have been rocked off their earth supports

- Sap flowing from damaged roots
- Imprint of the root adjacent to its original position

Confirmatory actions:

- Same as Example 1
- Force the root into the stepped-on position to give the direction of travel
- Compare the smell, texture, and color of the sap
- Check the roots for scuff marks

Example 4 Clumps of vegetation interspersed with rocks and stones
Natural state:

- This is usually open country exposed to the effects of the elements
- Large patches of clear, uniform earth

Disturbed state:

- Prints in the earth
- The earth crust around the sides of the stones and rocks will show signs of disruption

Confirmatory actions:

- Check for prints
- Study the vegetation for damage
- Compare disturbed stones with the surrounding stones
- Note any deposits of earth on stones and rocks. When cross-referenced with the time of the last rainfall, this will give a time bracket

Example 5 Forest floor with a deposit of twigs
Natural state:

- Same as Example 1
- Unbroken dead branches and twigs

Disturbed state:

- Same as Example 1
- Broken sticks

Confirmatory actions:

- Same as Example 1
- Examine the breaks. If the stick is in three parts (that is, there are two breaks), it is usually evidence, although not positive proof, that a man has trodden on the stick because of the way humans distribute their weight as they walk.
- The center part that is pushed in the direction of travel is a pointer

Example 6 A stand of saplings
Natural state:

- Trees are upright and parallel

Disturbed state:

- Some plants not in line with the rest

Confirmatory actions:

- Study the leaves on a broken stem to see whether they are still fresh—this gives an indication of the age of the sign
- Inspect the break on the trunk. If the ends are the same color, then the break is less than seven hours old; if it is an old break, the ends will have died and turned brown.

Example 7 Gradients
Natural state:

- Undisturbed

Disturbed state:

- Prints

Confirmatory actions:

- Are there slide marks? This indicates a tired person who is not confirming his step before transferring weight
- Check between the prints for walking stick marks as more information as to the state of the person
- Examine vegetation that may have been used as a climbing aid. This will give an insight into the morale, fitness, and training of the quarry (fit, well-trained troops would not be tempted into this practice because it can easily telegraph their location as the tops of the trees move)
- Direction of travel can be assessed by the relative depth of the parts of the print (even if the print is not distinctive enough to show a clear heel and toe). A person walking uphill produces a deeper print on the toe as opposed to the heel while a person walking down a gradient pushes debris in front of the print.

Some exercises for youth leaders

Just as there are indoor games that teachers and youth leaders can use to develop the powers of observation, memory, and deduction, there are also games and exercises suitable for outdoor use, such as laying trails of varying standards of difficulty and in a variety of scenarios. Also, during walks, whether in the town or the country, the group under training can be quizzed on items that they have passed. To ensure that the habit of observing becomes firmly entrenched, there should be an element of surprise and competition. (See also Chapter 17, dedicated to the training function.)

To emphasize to any group of students the seriousness of the topic, they can be subjected to a more advanced exercise based on the Royal Marine Sniper Test. In this modified practice twelve objects are placed in an arc in front of the observers up to 300 meters from the observers' position and invisible to the naked eye. The students are issued a copy of a panorama photograph of the arc. With the aid of binoculars the students are then told to observe the arc for 40 minutes, describe any foreign objects, and plot them onto the copy of the photograph. The standard can be adjusted for age and experience but the Marines fail any student with less than 8 out of the 12 and deduct fractional points for bad plotting or a poor description.

Reporting

There is another important factor connected with observation outdoors, and that is the necessity for recording in one's mind or on paper exactly what has been observed. A tracker is not much use to others unless he can communicate what he's observed. Your training in observation outdoors must of necessity include making reports, making rough sketch-maps and, as your level of expertise advances, making sketches.

SUMMARY

SCANNING AND SEARCHING
Divide the area into:

* Foreground
* Middle distance
* Distance

WHERE TO LOOK
The following are places where sign will be most obvious:

* Near any source of water
* On muddy and sandy patches
* In high grass or thick undergrowth
* On steep hillsides
* On the edges of clearings
* Where obstacles have to be crossed

WHAT TO LOOK FOR
As you are scanning and searching, you should remember each of the factors that make an object visible:

* Shape
* Shadow
* Silhouette
* Surface/Shine
* Spacing
* Movement

BEFORE AND AFTER STUDIES
The format:

* Natural state
* Disturbed state
* Confirmatory actions

Observe
Remember
Select and analyze
Comprehend and deduce

8

OBSERVATION OF THE
INDIVIDUAL

One distinct area of observation that is of great relevance to the tracker is the observation of people. This subject is of importance for three main reasons. First, it is an area in which the mental tracking skills of observation, memory, analysis, deduction, and comprehension can be practiced on a daily basis without any special preparation. Second, it concentrates the tracker's mind on the recognizable describable peculiarities of individuals. And third, for the teacher and those responsible for the development of young people, it has great practical application in the nurturing of the precise use of language, which is crucial to the ability to record and report.

Mental skills
When traveling and going about his daily business the potential tracker can exercise his skills by noticing every little thing about his fellow passengers and passers-by—their faces, their dress, the way they talk, and any other detail that would help him pass on a description of the individual to someone else.

Although we cannot always test the correctness of any deduction we make, it does add more interest both to the observation and the journey if we try to think of the personality and the occupation of the individual.

Judging character from appearances is difficult and can be very inaccurate but the mental skills it engages are some of those a tracker needs to polish to a high level of accomplishment. To reiterate, he observes, remembers, selects and analyzes, and then comprehends and deduces.

Apart from the rational application of the mind, the tracker's study of individuals exercises his imagination. It enables him to put himself in the place of another, to live his life, to enter his thoughts. This is of considerable importance in tracking.

Another interesting aspect of our ability to describe people is that individuals naturally differ in viewpoint and this affects the deductions they make. For example, a doctor was able to say that a man had been badly wounded some years previously in his left leg, because he noticed that, when the man was tired, his left shoulder dropped an inch or so lower than his right. The injured man had previously congratulated himself on the fact that no one who did not know could tell of his injury because he had no sign of a limp.

The description of individuals
Judging height and build is important in the observation of individuals, and special attention should be paid to these points. Anyone concerned with training beginners will notice that their descriptions pay more attention to the clothes a person is wearing than to the person himself, although it is easier for a person to change his clothes than his height and build. Similarly, a slight change in the facial appearance, such as the absence or addition of a moustache, will guard against a passing scrutiny, whereas a habit of gait or of carriage will give one away at once to a tracker, as these features will usually affect the sign.

To describe an individual with accuracy it is vital to have some scheme with which to break down the task into manageable portions. Also by using a format we ensure that we do not overlook any areas. The following format breaks down the description into logical sections. It is interesting for the instructor of a group to compare and contrast a group's descriptive efforts before and after being shown this layout.

Format for describing an individual
Sex
Age—in a 5-year bracket. Use their dress, the surroundings, the activity, as well as their physical appearance to assess their age
Height—in a 5-cm bracket. Use reference points (a door is 2 meters) or compare with a known person
Build—slim, medium, large
Posture—bent, straight, lopsided
Hair—color, parting, length, style, clean, dirty
Face—complexion, shape, features, facial hair, scars
Eyes—spacing, color, large, staring, glasses
Gait—speed, stride, limp, swagger, military
Dress—so as to avoid omissions work from the head to the feet
Carrying—describe any articles that the person is holding or carrying
Distinguishing features—if the person has any unusual characteristics note them
Other remarks . . .
Reminds me of . . . If it is possible, name a person to whom the individual has a likeness

One of the hardest parts of the person to describe but one of the best recognition features is the person's face. To overcome this problem it is very useful to use the breakdown of facial features in Fig. 18.

Language skills
I hope the following points will be especially helpful for people who have responsibilities for the personal development of the young. To be able to describe accurately and briefly demands the exercise and command of strong powers of expression. Therefore the practice of describing individuals can only help the communication skills of young people. To this end I again would draw your attention to how much detail can be given about a person's face by a good command of the language and a logical approach as is demonstrated by the drawings and descriptions in Fig. 18.

Finally, I would like to suggest some games for use in training the powers of observing people. Again, these will be of great assistance to the youth leader.

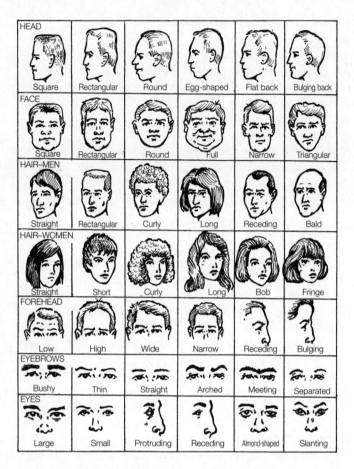

Fig. 18. Descriptions of facial features

Games for observation

Dressing statues

A person is arranged by one group in a pose and wearing specific items of dress. The second group then enters the room and is allowed two minutes to observe the figure. They depart and the figure resumes his normal dress and position. The group then re-enters

Fig. 18. continued

and has three to five minutes to rearrange the figure as it first saw him.

The unrehearsed incident
During an unrelated activity a predetermined incident is enacted. The incident should be dramatic and brief. The observers are then tested on what they can remember of the events. It will amaze them that the same events can be remembered in so many different ways.

Filming the original incident using a video can be very informative, exhibiting beyond any doubt what actually took place.

From "go" to "stop"
In this game the participants are to observe every action of a particular person from the word "go" to the word "stop." The person selected need only go through a few more or less ordinary actions such as taking off his coat and walking a few paces. As the skills of the group progress, the actions can become more complicated and the time extended.

Games to exercise the powers of deduction and imagination

Empty your pockets
A number of small articles, such as those carried in a man's pockets—a set of keys, a pen, a few coins, an old receipt, the return half of a railway ticket, a small notebook, and so on—are placed on a tray or table. A story is told of a man found wandering with loss of memory or a man found unconscious or dead. You are to try to identify him if possible, or give some useful guide as to his identification from the contents of his pockets. Naturally, the instructor needs to expend considerable thought in preparation so that the items from the pockets are compatible with the suggested answer.

Dressing up
The important part of a disguise is not so much dressing the part, which is comparatively easy, but acting the part. That is one of the reasons why play-acting is of undoubted use in persuading people to use their imagination and to try and get into the skin of the person they are following.

Clothing, beard, or hairstyle is only the first superficial layer. During the long hours spent in observation posts (OPs) in Northern Ireland, we usually recognized the target by gait long before we could confirm with a positive ID of the face.

SUMMARY

FORMAT FOR DESCRIBING AN INDIVIDUAL
Sex

Age—in a 5-year bracket. Use dress, surroundings, activity, as well as physical appearance to assess age

Height—in a 5cm bracket. Use reference points. A door is 2 meters. Compare with a known person to estimate

Build—slim, medium, large

Posture—bent, straight, lopsided

Hair—color, parting, length, style, clean, dirty

Face—complexion, shape, features, facial hair, scars

Eyes—spacing, color, large, staring, glasses

Gait—speed, stride, limp, swagger, military

Dress—so as to avoid omissions work from the head to the feet

Carrying—describe any articles that the person is holding or carrying

Distinguishing feature—if the person has any unusual charac-teristics note them

Other remarks . . .

Reminds me of . . . If it is possible, name a person to whom the individual has a likeness

9

THE PRINCIPLES OF STALKING

"Stalking" has ugly modern connotations, but in this book I use the word in its traditional sense, defined by the Oxford English Dictionary as "pursuing or approaching stealthily" (from late Old English; e.g. "bistealcian," "walk cautiously or stealthily"). Examples are a lion stalking a gazelle or a cat stalking a bird. The stalker's quarry in a hunt should never be aware of the tracker/stalker.

Having read the previous chapters on sign, the serious student of tracking will now realize what can be accomplished with well-practiced skills of observation. The next logical step along the trail of acquiring skills for tracking is to gain an appreciation of stalking. The following military tracking scenario will demonstrate how relevant stalking is to the life of the tracker.

I deliberately used the expression "to the life of the tracker" because to the military tracker that is what is at stake—his life. As the sign gets fresher and the trail hotter, so does the danger as the tracker closes with his quarry—the enemy. Man is more dangerous than the big game animals according to many SAS jungle soldiers, being more aggressive, better armed, and more cunning than any of the big five trophies the mollycoddled African safari hunter collects: lion, leopard, rhino, buffalo, and elephant.

Just as acute observation is essential for the tracker to be able to detect the sign as he nears his quarry, it is equally essential that he practice the skills of the stalker. This is as true for the conservationist, the ornithologist, the deer hunter, as it is for the soldier. I have decided to place stalking before other chapters on elements of tracking proper because it is another of the building blocks without which tracking proper is only half appreciated.

Also, for the outdoor pursuits instructor the stalking exercise described in Chapter 10 is far easier to administer and control than a tracking exercise. But the practice and the playing of stalking exercises will undoubtedly make the individual eager to go on to tracking.

I believe that it is necessary for every potential tracker to learn the main principles of stalking before he can practice tracking in its wider sense.

What is stalking?

Stalking is the art of approaching an object under cover or by stealth. It is more generally described as the ability to move rapidly, or fairly rapidly, from place to place, without being seen, heard, or otherwise detected, while at the same time seeing and observing.

Therefore, there are two aspects to stalking. The first is the concealment of the stalker. The second is the movement of the stalker. These two points are, of course, closely interrelated and interdependent.

Camouflage

The living natural world gives the astute student of tracking many important guidelines. Out in the countryside you rarely see birds and animals standing out against trees and bushes; they usually offer an indistinct outline, in or behind a bush. The camouflage of animals and birds is a subject in itself, a full study of which is beyond the scope of this book. What matters to us here is the principle of concealment.

The aim of the stalker should be to blend in with the background, remembering the reasons that things are seen: shape, shadow, shine, silhouette, spacing, and movement.

The first consideration for the tracker/stalker is the choice of clothing. The color of the material is very important. Colors should be of neutral tones, not too light or too dark. The color should not be uniform, as this helps to give shape to the person—an aspect that the stalker is trying to disguise. A ghillie suit (a camouflage suit to which has been added different colored strips of burlap and netting) is a prime example of how the shape of clothing can be altered to hide the shape of the person.

Often dark clothing with a top-up of local vegetation, combined with considered, well thought out movements, is better than military camouflage worn by someone who thinks that the jacket itself makes him invisible and proceeds in a lazy, slapdash way. A camouflage jacket is not enough on its own. In fact military camouflage is designed for specific theaters of operation—the jungle, desert, arctic—and if worn out of context, is more of a hindrance than a help.

Clothing and skin can be darkened by smearing mud on it but make sure that when dry it doesn't lighten too much. Another aid to personal camouflage is charcoal.

Nature gives some very good guidelines for the design and use of camouflage even to the extent that the underparts of birds and animals tend to be of a considerably lighter shade than their upper parts so that, whether viewed from above against the ground or from below against the sky, they still blend in. Aircraft camouflage tends to use this principle.

The color of the material is but one aspect. The outline shape the camouflage lends the stalker is of equal importance.

As the stalker moves through the countryside, especially the open countryside, he should continually monitor the changes in vegetation and adjust his camouflage as necessary by adding vegetation from the surrounding area. In forested and urban areas the addition of camouflage is used less. Here the use of shadow and the avoidance of shine and silhouette become much more important.

Concealment

The stalker will always be aware of his background. He will move position in order to place himself against a backdrop that conceals him. It is not necessary always to conceal yourself behind cover. The backdrop is just as important. Observing incorrectly from behind can lead to discovery of the stalker far more quickly than being in front of the appropriate backdrop (see Fig. 19).

Fig. 19. The art of concealment

The tracker should always be aware of being skylined. Apart from the obvious skyline, there are equally important intermediate skylines of which the tracker and stalker must be conscious.

If carrying anything shiny, such as binoculars, camera, compass, or if wearing a watch or a ring, ensure that it is covered from the sun; otherwise it will point to the wearer's position like a flashing mirror. It is a point that is often overlooked, but some clothing becomes shiny when wet.

Knowledge of the quarry
It is also a principle of stalking that you know as much as possible about your quarry. It is a mistake to underestimate this principle. The following is a list of questions about the quarry that the stalker should try to answer:

- How does it feed?
- Where does it feed?
- What precautions does it take to guard against surprise?
- How quick is it to take alarm?

- What sort of place does it frequent?
- What kind of cover does it go to?
- How does it get there?

When you have observed, analyzed, and understood, you are then ready to solve the problem of the final approach to the quarry.

It is vitally important for the military tracker and the big game tracker to have as deep a knowledge as possible of the quarry because of the threat it poses. Big game hunters will confirm the theory that it is possible to train up to a pitch where one becomes aware of impending danger. The development of this sense is necessary for the visual tracker. It is possible to be alert and efficient but relaxed, only becoming attuned and aware of danger when it is life-threatening. A tracker living every moment on his nerves while on a track will burn up too much nervous energy and will not last. Experience that almost gives a tracker a sixth sense cannot be gained from books, however detailed. This level of field craft can be gained only by practice and having the good fortune to accompany experienced trackers.

In the isolated areas of many countries, the native bird, insect, and animal life have their own ways of warning fellow creatures of danger from predators or intruders. Some examples will make this clear:

- The blackbird in the English hedgerow will soon realize the intentions of the small boy with his slingshot, and as it flies off, will give its loud warning cry alerting all the wildlife in the area
- The plover, often seen in Kenya near the basking crocodile, will hover over a stalking man, giving its warning cry
- The barking deer will shout to all in the area at the approach of a tiger or man in India
- Monkeys in the Far East not only shout to all around of man's presence, but I have known them to throw sticks down at you from the treetops
- A startled pheasant will cry its warning to the rest of the animal kingdom
- The domestic dog will bark its warning of the presence of a stranger
- Wild fish will dart away into deeper water when startled, warning others of a potential danger
- Often insects will warn of any intruder into the area by their silence

These are but a few of the cases where the wildlife may warn the tracker of possible dangers nearby or, alternately, warn the quarry of the tracker's presence.

First-hand knowledge of the habits and nature of the wildlife in any new area must be known and used to the tracker's advantage. Many a time during my trips to the jungle, if the breeze was blowing in our faces oncoming pigs would walk right past the patrol. I knew that the pigs were partially deaf and blind but that they had an acute sense of smell. So to avoid them alerting the rest of the jungle by rushing off once they smelled us, we would move quietly off to one side and they would pass unconcernedly on their way.

The wind

The wind is one of the stalker's greatest difficulties, and nothing but long practice will enable you to understand it completely. But it is very important to start to take this element into account, especially if your quarry has a well-developed sense of smell.

The tracker/stalker must also take into account the effect the wind has on the carriage of sound. Sometimes it has an adverse effect and sounds carry towards the quarry, whereas at other times the noise generated by the wind can cover the sound of your movements.

Again we can see how important it is for the tracker to get into the skin of his quarry—he must try to think like his quarry so that he can outfox him. He must know the strengths and weaknesses of the animal whose spoor he is following. I remember the Highland guide telling me as a boy that the red deer can not only see and hear you at a thousand yards, but that they can also smell you at that distance if you are foolish enough to be windward of them.

As you develop your tracking skills, you will start to realize that no one factor can be taken in isolation; this is just as true of the wind as any other feature in the tracker's world. The movement of air is affected by the topography of the area and the whole world of scent is affected by temperature and humidity because these factors affect the rate of evaporation.

The interaction of relief and airflow is very relevant to the stalker. On level ground the wind does not vary much without warning while a wind blowing uphill or along the side of a hill is usually steadier by far than one blowing downhill. The tracker has to bear in mind that strong smells will be carried for some distance by even the lightest wind before dispersing, and that any smell will tend to settle in low-lying areas and will linger in still air.

It is easy to find out the actual direction of the wind by wetting a finger and holding it up. The coolest is the direction from which the wind is blowing. Or you can throw up a pinch of dried vegetation to check the direction if it is a light breeze. If the wind is stronger the movement of the trees and bushes will indicate the direction. Another good indicator of the strength and direction of the wind is the movement of the clouds, but be aware that the higher clouds may be moving in a slightly different direction from those at a lower altitude.

Animals respond to warning received by their noses far more quickly than to warning by their sight or hearing. Unless you approach an animal with the wind, or even a breeze, blowing in from the animal to you, it is doubtful if you will get very close before it flees. In fact, your scent may so effectively advertize your presence that you may not even see an animal that has moved quickly away. If the wind direction is unfavorable when you first sight your quarry, it is best to make your way in a wide circle around the quarry until you are in a more favorable position from which to move forward.

As with all the features a tracker observes, he doesn't merely note the wind and record it but he continually monitors its changes. There is probably no feature of the environment that can change so quickly to the disadvantage of the tracker and stalker as the wind. One moment the deer herd is upwind to you. They gradually shift their location as they graze the hillside and before you realize you are obliquely upwind to them—disaster! In seconds their sentries have your scent and the alarm will go up.

Scent

As well as being conscious of how your quarry reacts, you must objectively study yourself. Don't forget that the human stinks to many animals. The world to a dog is one of scent leaving a trail even more permanent to the dog than visual sign is to the tracker. Your pet dog's mental map of your neighborhood would give a very different and enlightening view of the streets—as astonishing as when you first see a thermal imaging camera showing up the heat loss of an uninsulated house.

The tracker has to be aware of the scent that he may be giving out to alert his quarry whether human or animal. To eliminate any possible chance of the quarry detecting you by smell, it may be necessary to avoid any of the following for two or three days before going on a tracking task:

• Toothpaste
• After-shave lotion, scents, and deodorants
• Soap
• Hair gel
• Talcum powder
• Shaving soap
• Shampoo
• Medications such as liniments
• Spices and garlic

While you are on a tracking operation, it may be necessary to use only cold food.

Clothing can be given an acceptable smell by hanging it up on the clothes line to weather for a few days or hanging it up anywhere away from characteristic clinging smells. I would not recommend any other method, like burying your equipment or hanging your equipment over a fire, as this will only make you smell like a plowed field or a burned out fire and the quarry will be alerted.

The following are some of the scents that students may come across in their tracking exercises:

• Animal and human latrines
• Animal scent posts
• Animal homes—earths, tunnels, dens, and burrows
• Animal scent glands
• Dead animals
• Cooking fumes
• Smoke, burned wood
• Newly dug earth

In addition, the visual tracker, especially the military tracker, must use his sense of smell to warn him of any danger. The following would alert a soldier on a tracking mission:

- Cooking smells
- Human sanitation
- Domesticated animal smells
- Camp fires
- Slaughtered animals
- Freshly dug earth

Distinctive animal odors are dependent on the diet, and humans whose primary food is meat will smell differently from those whose diet is vegetarian. The diet of different races makes each one smell differently. Thus, the Chinese say that Europeans smell of milk.

Smoking
At this point I would like to touch on smoking. It is very difficult to give up smoking, but I do believe that if you are going to treat tracking seriously you should attempt to do so. Certainly, you should not smoke while on a tracking task and, if possible, a couple of days before going on a tracking task.

Smoking can:

- Affect your sense of smell
- Give away your position by the smell, the cloud of smoke, the glow of the tip, cigarette waste such as butts and ash, and a smoker's cough
- Reduce your concentration because of your concern about the next cigarette rather than the tracking task

Tracking and stalking can be seen as points on a continuum where one shades into the other, depending upon the closeness of the quarry or the enemy. Now that we have firmly established stalking within the tracking context, we will move on to the practical aspects of stalking.

SUMMARY

WHAT IS STALKING?
It is the art of approaching an object under cover, or by stealth. It is more generally described as the ability to move rapidly, or fairly rapidly, from place to place, without being seen, heard, or otherwise detected while at the same time seeing and observing.

PRACTICE OF CAMOUFLAGE AND CONCEALMENT
Remembering why things are seen.

KNOWLEDGE OF THE QUARRY
A principle of stalking is that you must understand and know as much as possible about your quarry. It is a mistake to underestimate your quarry. The following is a list of useful questions about the quarry the stalker should try to answer:

- How does it feed?
- Where does it feed?
- What precautions does it take to guard against surprise?
- How quick is it to take alarm?
- What sort of place does it frequent?
- What kind of cover does it go to?
- How does it get there?

THE WIND
Carries scent and sound. Sometimes it has an adverse effect and sounds carry towards the quarry, whereas at other times the noise generated by the wind can cover the sound of your movements.

SCENT
The tracker has to be aware of the scent that he may be giving out that will alert his quarry whether it be human or animal.

Eliminate any possible chance of the quarry detecting you by smell. It may be necessary to avoid any of the following for two or three days before going on a tracking task:

• Toothpaste
• After-shave lotion, scents, deodorants
• Soap
• Hair gel
• Talcum powder
• Shaving soap
• Shampoo
• Medications such as liniments
• Spices and garlic

In addition, the visual tracker, especially the military tracker, must use his sense of smell to warn him of any danger. The following would alert a soldier on a tracking mission:

• Cooking smells
• Human sanitation
• Domesticated animal smells
• Campfires
• Slaughtered animals
• Freshly dug earth
• Cigarette smoke, ash, or butts

10

STALKING TECHNIQUES

After successfully following the sign for several kilometers, or in some military situations, several days, it would be frustrating and dangerous to alert the quarry to your presence before you were ready. To that end this chapter will demonstrate the practical expertise the tracker has to gain so that he can covertly approach his quarry in the final stages of the pursuit.

Stalking is no longer natural to humans—it needs the study and practice of techniques. The actual practice is often difficult and uncomfortable as you crawl across rough ground and through tangled spiky vegetation.

The tracker/stalker's progress
The methods of movement available to the stalker approaching his quarry will be described in detail later in this chapter.

Cover can be very scant or non-existent but, by judicious route-planning, the stalker will make use of every crease and fold in the ground to approach his quarry. This approach will probably not be direct because it is following the best cover. With practice it is possible to move at a reasonable speed in comparative silence—steadily and carefully.

As the tracker/stalker moves, his gaze continually sweeps far and near, right and left, up and down, looking not only at bushes and trees but through and beyond them—he disregards the general pattern of foliage. The untrained stalker usually looks at a bush, failing to see what is behind or in it.

The tracker is conscious that completely new arcs of visibility are opening up in which the quarry may be waiting. To inspect the ground the tracker stops, goes down on one knee, waits for the cover man if he is a military tracker, and only then lowers his head to look at the ground. Whether the tracker is stationary or moving, only his eyes are ever directed towards the ground. He doesn't lower his head in order to look at the sign; this is especially important while he is moving forward.

He crouches down occasionally, as this often provides a better view through the vegetation, especially in what is termed close country such as you find in secondary jungle.

When working through woods and undergrowth, don't brush through the small bushes but slowly lift them aside with your hand and then ease them back into place—don't let them spring back. This technique not only cuts out a great deal of noise but it also eliminates unnecessary movement of the vegetation. Do not grab branches, saplings, or bushes for extra support, leverage, or balance when crossing an obstacle, getting up off the ground, or when climbing a hill because the slightest movement at the base is magnified at the top. This movement will give your position away. Flag-waving or telegraphing is the term given to this phenomenon, and the message is transmitted in all directions, not just forward. Avoid treading on dry leaves, sticks, or rotten wood. Don't allow yourself to become caught up in vines or overhanging creepers and, if you are, remove any spiky trailing fronds carefully and silently from your clothing.

If you think you have been spotted or you have been caught out in the open, remain perfectly still, freeze, until your quarry turns its head away. Then move slowly and quietly back into cover. Even when right out in the open there is no cause for alarm, provided your background harmonizes with your clothes, and you remain perfectly motionless. You will certainly arouse suspicion, and probably alarm, if you disappear suddenly. The only time when rapid movement back into cover is recommended is when it is a human who has surprised you; even then circumstances will dictate whether to freeze or flee, but if you move, any other animal will instantly be put to flight.

There is a specific technique to freezing, which again I will describe later.

Generally speaking, in stalking try to avoid working with the sun in your face, especially when the sun is low on the horizon in the morning or in the evening. There are several reasons for this. First, it is difficult to distinguish an object in the distance with the sun in your eyes. Second, it is easier for the quarry to spot you with the sun shining on your clothes. Unfortunately, owing to a natural paradox, it is easier to make out a track with the sun shining towards you casting a shadow on the track.

Listening halts

As the tracker approaches his quarry and the skills of stalking come into play, it is essential to take listening halts. You and your team should not make any noise that will travel beyond the distance you can see; otherwise the quarry or enemy may be aware of you before you see them.

Listening halts should be taken frequently. The tracker and his team should remain perfectly still and position themselves low down in shadow or shade, and against an appropriate background; otherwise the slightest movement on your part will attract attention.

To listen most effectively it is necessary to cock your head in the direction where you are listening, and to open your mouth slightly as this aids the working of the hearing function.

Stalking skills

If one word should be remembered by a stalker it is "stealthily." This word exactly describes the mode of progress that should be adopted. The actual method—walking, crawling, or slithering—varies according to the distance you are from your quarry and the kind of country you are moving through, but all the time you must use cunning and move stealthily.

I will now detail the different methods used by the tracker on his final approach—the stalk.

The cautious approach

This merely consists of walking calmly and quietly in the direction of the supposed quarry or in a direction you consider favorable to your purpose, having taken into account all aspects of the environment, including the terrain, obstacles, and the wind direction. You have not come to grips with the quarry yet, but there is no knowing when you may come to close quarters and so you have to be wary and take advantage of rising ground, of dips, of the cover afforded by trees and bushes, or the bed of a stream. Even this requires practice and an eye for ground, so that any casual observation does not lead you along a wrong line that will suddenly expose you to the view of everybody and everything within miles.

The upright crouch

When you are getting within range, your approach must be made still more cautiously. It is best to adopt what is usually known as the upright crouching position (Fig. 20). This requires practice in lifting the feet and in balance. The feet should point straight forward to offer the least resistance to any obstacles that may be encountered. If the toes turn out they act as hooks. The knees should be kept slightly bent and relaxed. The feet should be lifted well off the ground at every step, and not shuffled along.

Fig. 20. The upright crouch

Walk slowly and watch the placement of your feet. Tread on the outside of your foot first and roll your foot on and off the ground; be ready to withdraw the foot should it come into contact with anything likely to make noise. The ball of the foot should touch the ground first, followed by the heel. The weight of the body should be placed gradually on the sole of the foot to avoid snapping any twig that may be underneath it or kicking any stones. A firm balance should be obtained on each leg in turn before the other is advanced, so that at any moment, in any place, and in any position, you can remain poised like a statue, and as quiet. At the same time the arms should be kept still as you move and not be swung about violently.

Every movement should be stealthy, silent, and deliberate. In fact, you must put your brain into the soles of your feet and your eyes into your toes as you feel your way along. The best place to start to practice is a small wood or thicket strewn with dry leaves and sticks. To feel the ground better, try thin-soled shoes or just thick socks; depending on the surface and your feet, you can even try stalking barefoot to achieve even greater sensitivity.

The feline crawl

When the distance between you and your quarry is lessening and when cover is getting scarce it will be necessary to employ the feline crawl (Fig. 21). Any domestic cat can demonstrate this method to you. Watch a cat, study its methods and copy them—the cat family is probably the best at stalking. The hind paw comes automatically up to the position that the corresponding front paw has occupied.

Fig. 21. The feline crawl

You have to crawl along on hands and knees. The hands feel for suitable places on which to rest and the corresponding knee comes up to the same position. Care should be taken to lift the knee and foot from the ground and not to drag them, but equal care should be exercised so that the feet are not waved in the air. Also do not hump the body up in the middle like a camel; keep the back low. The head should be the highest part, and that, too, should be kept as low as possible, and certainly not bobbed up suddenly or jerked from side to side. As before, every movement that is made should be slow and deliberate.

The flat or belly crawl
Lastly, there is the flat crawl (Fig. 22). This procedure is used for the final stage of the stalk. It is slow and very tiring, especially for the abdominal muscles. It is necessary to go down full length on the ground, flat on the abdomen, with the head down. The body and legs should be kept stiff and the legs close together. The toes should be turned well out and the heels kept down so that practically the whole of the inner side of the foot rests upon the ground. If this is not done consciously, there is a tendency for the feet to come up and attract attention. You now have to work yourself forward, bit by bit, a few inches at a time, using the hands and the sides of the feet. This can be done by placing your forearm flat on the ground in front of your head and by bringing the other forearm up in front of it, and so on, the toes being used as levers on which to work. Instead of using the forearms it is possible to move forward by placing the hands on the ground close to, almost under, the body on a level with

Fig. 22. The flat crawl

the chest, and pulling yourself forward with them. Care should be taken to keep the elbows well down and close to the sides.

If it is safe to expose the head sufficiently to look round, then it is possible to do the flat crawl more on the side than on the stomach, and to bend the knees sideways and bring them up to help. Your movements will then be something of a cross between a feline crawl and a flat crawl.

With all methods of movement the stalker must be aware of the vegetation above and around him. If he is not careful with his movements, the grass and bushes will telegraph his progress towards the quarry.

Freezing

Frequently you find that when you are stalking, even when going dead slow, you suddenly burst out of cover and are liable to be spotted. In that case there is only one thing to do. You must freeze instantly and, when the opportunity offers, slowly and carefully work back to cover again, remembering that any sudden movement is liable to give you away.

In these circumstances, it is best to crawl backwards, keeping your body and legs stiff, and levering yourself back with your toes and hands working together. At the same time your face and hands should be kept close to the ground and steady. Even when back in cover, be very cautious about raising your head.

The art of freezing was touched upon earlier. It is not necessary to be behind something to remain unobserved. If there is a suitable background it is possible to assume a position right out in the open without any danger of being noticed, provided you keep your body, limbs, and especially your head still. This technique needs a good deal of practice so that whatever method of stalking you are using, you can instantly become still and then remain motionless for a considerable period. Although this technique is most effective with a non-human quarry, it has its place in the repertoire of skills to be used when stalking a human, although then the background, distance and light conditions are more critical.

Canadian hunters lay great emphasis on the best pose to adopt when freezing during a stalk. They not only remain motionless, but they adopt a pose which reflects the character of the surrounding

trees, bushes, and rocks. Thus, among perfectly straight trees they
would stand erect, whereas in an area with many uprooted trees they
would adopt a more irregular pose by bending and twisting their
body and arms. Obviously, they slowly and cautiously take up these
shapes, they don't snap into them.

Lying still

The practice of lying or sitting perfectly still, during the day or at
night, and letting the wildlife in an area become used to your presence enables you to learn a great deal about what is happening. The
novice will be amazed how the wildlife starts to return and totally
ignores you if you stay still for a long period. I've been fortunate
enough to see some remarkable sights as I've lain perfectly motionless for hours in observation or sentry positions—vibrantly colored
hummingbirds within arm's length beating their wings at a rate that
defies the eyes as they hover to draw out the nectar from jungle flowers; vixens bringing out their cubs to play by the safety of the den
entrance.

A sophisticated version of this habit takes place in the blind the
bird photographer constructs. The detailed subject of hides is
beyond the scope of this book. But it should be noted by the serious
student of tracking that a hide acts as a good observation post for any
individual who desires to study nature.

Tree hides can also be effective, provided the observer realizes he
is not hidden when he sits across a branch. You must conform to the
lines of the tree.

Route-planning

Apart from the techniques of moving silently and covertly, another
very pertinent subject is often overlooked entirely by the amateur,
and that is route-planning and selection (Fig. 23). When given a target to stalk, military snipers are also issued aerial photography and
stereoscopes so that they can plan the approach to the enemy with
meticulous precision. Chapter 20 is devoted to the associated skills
of map-reading.

The route will seldom be the most direct but the experienced
tracker will take all the following points into consideration before
embarking on the final stage of the pursuit.

Wind direction and strength
We know the wind carries not only smell but also sound. Therefore
you should stalk with the wind in your face.

Vegetation
As vegetation cover alters, the stalker has to select new material to
top-up his personal camouflage.

Movement
Each leg of the stalk will require a different method of movement. It
is useful to split the route into bounds; hence the expression to move
in bounds. See the numbers in Fig. 23. For instance, if you are
behind a hedge and not visible from the quarry a crouching posture
will be ideal, whereas if you are working your way through a wheatfield overlooked by the quarry, it will be necessary to adopt the
feline crawl.

Landmarks
During the stalk you will require reference points for orientation
purposes. These must be visible without exposing yourself, for
example towers, trees, high ground, and the sun, moon, and stars.

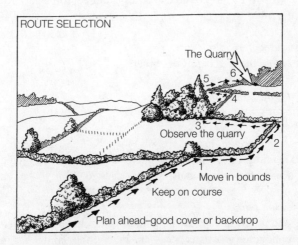

Fig. 23. Route selection for the stalker
(numbers denote stalker's bounds)

Cover
Check that the obvious features—such as ditches, walls, hedges, buildings, river beds—will actually cover you to your destination and that the cover is complete. Many hedges have gaps in them and ditches can terminate abruptly in impassably small drainage pipes.

Dead ground
This is a military term used to describe an area that, although over-looked by an observer, is a blind spot to him because of the folds in the ground. It is of great importance to the stalker; he can move through such areas with impunity because he is out of sight. To the inexperienced stalker it can be unnerving in dead ground in open country, as he feels completely exposed, but it is far safer than fol-lowing a broken hedge in full sight of the target. Of course, you may have to consider the wind and scent.

Obstacles
The route-planning has to take into account any obstacles before the stalker sets off. He should have a good idea in his mind as to how he will overcome each and every obstacle. A prime consideration in obstacle crossing is skylining—avoid it but if it is unavoidable do it briefly, keep as low as possible and, for example, roll away from the crest of a hill.

Roads and waterways
Plan to cross these at bends or corners.

Plowed land
Use the furrows as cover.

Long grass or cereal crops
Keep changing direction so that there isn't a uniform, predictable movement of the foliage causing color change.

Observation points
There should be pre-planned points at which you will halt and observe the quarry. This is necessary in case the animal has moved or the human quarry is planning any actions that could affect you. It

is imperative that you can see without being seen, so pick observation points that allow you to look through cover rather than over it.

Noise
The stalker has to take advantage of existing noises, such as streams, wind, rain, vehicles, the sea, or aircraft to cover any sounds that he may make. He should ensure that the contents of his pockets and any equipment that he is carrying do not make any sound that will carry. Before a stalk this can easily be checked by jumping up and down a few times. The stalker selects his clothing with the elimination of noise in mind because many fabrics, especially waterproof ones, rustle when in contact with vegetation. Watches that chime or beep should be left behind, along with pagers, mini cassette recorders, and mobile phones. Remember that sound travels in all directions. Visibility in close country can be very limited, so the visual tracker must ensure that sounds made will not travel beyond the distance he can see. Thus he will avoid alerting an unsuspecting quarry of his approach. Silence is essential at all times. All extraneous noise has to be excluded—this refers both to voice and movement. Because the tracker has to eliminate all sounds, military trackers have developed a series of hand signals for communicating within their group (see below).

Animals
As previously mentioned, any wildlife that you disturb will alert the quarry and the curiosity of domesticated animals will, apart from the more obvious barking of dogs, be noticed by the observant enemy.

Hillsides
If you are stalking on a mountain or hillside, try to put yourself into a position above the quarry but avoid skylining. Animals tend to look for danger coming from below. On mountains the stalker has to avoid displacing rocks.

Stalking animals
Grazing animals tend to raise their heads at frequent but irregular intervals, so do not be tempted to make a sudden dash or any quick movement, as you can be caught out and they will be put to flight.

Alternative routes

After choosing the main route, consider other paths in case you have to abort or modify the stalk for reasons such as a change in the wind direction, movement of the quarry, or third party interference.

Hand signals

The hand signals military trackers use are a refinement of infantry hand signals. Such is their importance that trackers always rehearse them immediately before a patrol. The group may have its own variations relevant to that particular theater of operations. The number of silent hand signals is kept to a minimum so as to avoid confusion—remember, these are being used to communicate vital, perhaps life-saving information, at a time when the patrol is within hearing distance of the enemy. See Fig. 24 for some of the more common hand signals used.

The tracking/stalking group

The tracker has to be aware that he must control the group that he is with. He either does this himself or the commander of the group is mindful of the tracker's work and manages this role. The party has to be controlled for the following reasons:

- Silence is paramount
- Preservation of the sign—the tracker's group must not inadvertently spoil the sign

Exercises and practices for the instructor

Stalking is usually associated with the wilds, with big game hunting, and with deer stalking. But it is not necessary to have something very large to stalk. You can get a great deal of good experience stalking a dog, a cat, or any of the smaller wild animals, such as rabbits.

Before students are asked to undertake a stalk they should be well practiced in adopting the different stalking positions and in moving across the ground by the different methods. Preparatory drills should include, at intervals, the instruction to freeze.

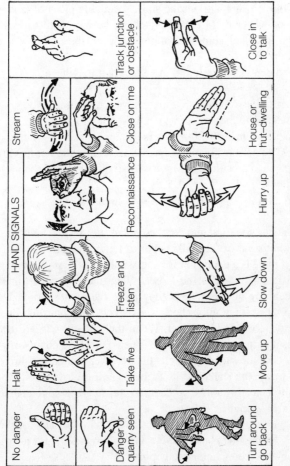

Fig. 24. Hand signals for the stalker/tracker

Now we are able to undertake a full-scale stalking practice. To emphasize the seriousness of stalking, the students can be told that this exercise is based upon a test military snipers have to take.

For the instructor all that is required for this exercise is an observer or two with binoculars, controllers who walk near the students who are carrying out the stalk, a suitable piece of land either private or where there are not likely to be any disturbances from other groups, and communications between the observer and the controllers.

The students are briefed to the effect that they have:

- A start point—about 1,000 meters from the observer
- Boundaries to the area in which they can move
- To get within 150–200 meters of the observer—rough limits should be outlined by the controller as to the extent of this bracket
- To be in a position to observe the quarry from their chosen position
- A time limit—approximately 45–60 minutes

The students then attempt to accomplish the task. The controllers stay within sight of the stalkers but as far from them as possible. It is best if there is a controller for each stalker as the stalkers may take very different routes to the target. When the observers think they have seen any of the stalkers they radio the controllers and direct them to where they think there is a stalker. The controller does not aid the observer or the stalker. When the student is in position, he declares it to the nearest controller. The controller then moves within 10 meters of the stalker and tells the observer that he has three minutes to locate the stalker. If he is unsuccessful the controller moves to within 5 meters and the procedure is repeated—and then finally to within arm's length.

The outdoor pursuits instructor can switch the roles for the students by letting them be observers and controllers in turn so as to see the problems from another standpoint.

The type of terrain chosen is a very important consideration. To avoid discouraging the student in the early stages, the mission should be achievable. As the group's level of expertise increases, the stalking problems can be made more difficult.

In the debriefs they will soon realize the golden rule of stalking: you take your risks early in a stalk, when the target is farther away. As a rule, the nearer you are to the quarry, the lower and slower you need to be.

The stalking practice above will impress upon the tracking student the patience, planning, and skill required to carry out a successful stalk.

To summarize:

- Routes must be planned
- Avoid impassable obstacles—marshes, open ground
- Move in bounds
- Keep a check on your course
- Observe without being seen
- Remember . . .

The golden rule of stalking
Take
Risks
Early

SUMMARY

STALKING
If one word should be remembered by a stalker, it is "stealthily."

METHODS OF MOVEMENT

The cautious approach
This consists of walking calmly and quietly.

The upright crouch
The ball of the foot should touch the ground first, followed by the heel.

The feline crawl
When the distance between you and your quarry is lessening and when cover is getting scarce, it will be necessary to employ the feline crawl. You crawl along on hands and knees. The hands feel for suitable places on which to rest and the corresponding knee comes up to the same position.

The flat or belly crawl
This procedure is used for the final stage of the stalk. It is necessary to go down full length on the ground, flat on the abdomen, with the head down. You work yourself forward, bit by bit, a few inches at a time, using the hands and the sides of the feet.

Freezing
Used if you are liable to be spotted. This technique is most effective with a non-human quarry. It does have a place in the repertoire of skills to be used when stalking a human, although then the background, distance, and light conditions are more critical.

ROUTE PLANNING AND THE STALK

Wind direction and strength
As we know, the wind carries not only smell but also sound; therefore, you should stalk with the wind in your face.

Vegetation
As the vegetation cover alters, the stalker has to select new material to top-up his personal camouflage.

Movement
Each leg of the stalk will probably require a different method of movement. For instance if you are behind a hedge and not visible from the quarry a crouching posture will be ideal, whereas if you are working your way through a wheatfield overlooked by the quarry it will be necessary to adopt the feline crawl. Divide the route into bounds.

Landmarks
During the stalk you will require reference points for orientation purposes.

Cover
Check that the obvious features—such as ditches, walls, hedges, buildings, and river beds—will actually cover you to your destination and that the cover is complete.

Dead ground
This is a military term used to describe an area that, although overlooked by an observer, is a blind spot to him because of the folds in the ground.

Obstacles
The route planning has to take into account any obstacles before the stalker sets off.

Roads and waterways
Try to plan to cross roads and waterways at bends or corners.

Plowed land
Use the furrows as cover.

Long grass or cereal crops
Keep changing direction so that there isn't a uniform, predictable movement of the foliage causing color change.

Observation points
There should be pre-planned points at which you will halt and observe the quarry.

Noise

The stalker has to take advantage of existing noises such as streams, the wind, rain, vehicles, the sea, or aircraft to cover any sounds that he may make.

Animals

Any wildlife that you disturb will alert the quarry. The curiosity of domesticated animals will, apart from the more obvious barking of dogs, be noticed by the observant enemy.

Hillsides

If you are stalking on a mountain or hillside, try to put yourself into a position above the quarry but avoid skylining.

Stalking animals

Grazing animals tend to raise their heads at frequent but irregular intervals, so do not be tempted to make a sudden dash or any quick movement as you can be caught out and they will be put to flight.

Alternative routes

After choosing the main route, consider other paths in case you have to abort or modify the stalk.

REHEARSE HAND SIGNALS

CONTROL THE TRACKING GROUP

The tracker has to be aware that he must control the group that he is with.

THE GOLDEN RULE OF STALKING

**Take
Risks
Early**

11

NIGHT MOVEMENT

Because of the huge differences in the methods that have to be used at night compared to those that we use by day, the subject of night movement deserves a chapter to itself.

The major difference is the switch in emphasis away from sight to hearing, touch, and smell. Even when the ambient noise level is the same at night as during the day, one's hearing seems to be more acute. It is as if the senses are compensating for one another.

The importance of the other senses compensating when the visibility is poor is well illustrated by the experience of a friend of mine. He wasn't tracking, but he was the lead scout in a patrol in an enemy stronghold during the Dhofar War in the early 1970s. The patrol was operating in very close country. The monsoon mist was like a heavy shroud over the scrub, especially during the first light period just before dawn. He was able to alert the rest of the patrol to the presence of the enemy because he detected the smell of camel meat being boiled over an open wood fire. The adoo (the enemy) were preparing their breakfast. Although they were still involved in a heavy fire fight, things could have been a great deal worse without that moment's forewarning.

The sense of smell is an aid not only to discover your quarry but also to fix your whereabouts if you are in known country. Smoke, whether of tobacco or of a fire, can be smelled at incredibly long distances at night.

Night vision

We can see in the dark.

The retina of the eye is made up of light-sensitive cells. These are either cone-shaped or rod-shaped. The rods provide us with our night vision. They only distinguish between black and white, and they have a reaction time before they are fully effective. If you walk from a lit room into the night, you find yourself temporarily blind while the changeover from cones to rods takes place. Full night vision takes about forty minutes to come into operation. However, the process is a gradual one. The rods adapt very quickly at first and then slow down gradually, so you have most of your night vision within the first five to ten minutes.

Observe the effects of night vision for yourself. Walk from a well-lit situation into the darkness outside. At first you will see nothing, but you will be aware of a red tint to the darkness. After only a few seconds, the outline of larger objects will be visible; the details on those objects will begin to show after a few more minutes. After ten minutes the detail on the faces of people around you will be easily recognizable, and you may also be able to recognize larger individual plants at ground level. To pick out distant detail at night, flick your eyes on and off the object or look slightly to one side of it. The one major problem with night vision is that it is instantly lost as soon as a light shines into your eyes. To get night vision back you must go through the forty-minute process once more. There are a few things we can do to avoid losing night vision. If you sense a light is about to shine in your eyes, simply close them. If you need to make use of that light, but still retain night vision, close just one eye. Night vision will be preserved in the eye kept closed, although you will be left with a strange lopsided feel to your vision for a few minutes.

When a flashlight or several flashlights are to be used, ensure the carriers are aware of night vision and the effect that light has on it. Get them to shine flashlights at the ground, not in the air or in people's faces. As much as possible, try to avoid using flashlights at night—they illuminate only a short distance in front of you, whereas night vision will reach the horizon and thus is far more suitable for observation or navigation purposes. A group of people walking at night, all with flashlights switched on, will be walking in a bubble of light. The immediate ground will be well lit, but the eyes will not be able to penetrate beyond the bubble.

One compromise is to use red or green filters on flashlights to help preserve your night vision.

To summarize, at night:

- We see less than in daylight
- We see shapes not detail
- We see skylines and silhouettes—and so does the quarry
- We may see movement
- If caught in the light of a vehicle, freeze, quickly close one eye to protect your night vision
- Use night vision aids if available

Direction finding

Loss of sight brings with it loss of direction—people eventually walk in a kind of spiral, and one often hears of people lost in the jungle or in mist coming back on their own track. To remedy this inevitable tendency it is necessary to take precautions when you start on your night stalk.

If it is a clear, starlit night you will experience no difficulty, as the stars will give you direction, provided you take your bearings when you start.

There may be a slightly stronger light in the west, or in the east, depending on the time of night, which will give you a rough indication of direction.

Even in the dark, try to make a note of the landmarks that you pass, taking care to glance back at them after you have passed so that you will recognize the differences in their appearance from the other side.

If there are no stars to guide you, your difficulties are increased. The wind may help, if it is constant, and if you note its direction at the start.

At night, when there is stillness in the air, a man's voice, the bark of a dog, or the rumble of a train will carry a long distance compared with these same sounds by day. This can be a guide to the direction if you have sufficient local knowledge.

Sounds carry through the ground, so if you place your ear to the ground, or against the end of a stick that is touching the ground, you can frequently hear footsteps a long way off. If it is difficult to identify the exact quarter from which a sound comes, it is a help to block one ear.

Noise

On the other hand, the noises that you make will be correspondingly intensified and so it behooves you to be very careful as you move. At first you will find that you are certain to make more noise as you night stalk. Do what you can to move only when there is covering noise, such as the wind in the trees or, in heavily populated country, the noise of a car passing down an adjacent road.

Balance

The methods of movement at night are basically the same as those used in the day (see Movement at night below), but you will find it more difficult to keep your balance. Because of this you will find the obstacles more difficult to negotiate. If you want to carry out a simple experiment to prove how losing the sense of sight disturbs the power of balance, stand on tiptoe and, still standing on tiptoe, shut your eyes. Almost immediately you will discover a tendency to over-balance, probably forward.

Skylining

It is best to keep as low as possible. The dangers of the skyline have been referred to before but are especially grave at night.

Shadows

During night stalking, shadows can be just as much a danger as an advantage. The stalker can use the shadow to conceal his presence, but on the other hand he has to be aware of letting his own shadow fall on a lit patch of ground (see Chapter 7 for a full explanation of the effects of shadow).

Movement at night

Daylight movements are not suitable at night; they have to be adapted. The actual method—the ghost walk, the cat walk, and the kitten crawl—varies according to the distance you are from your quarry and the type of country you are moving through, but all the time you must use cunning and move stealthily.

The ghost walk

To walk quietly in the dark demands greater use of touch. Feel the ground in front with the toe before placing the foot fully down. Hold the hands in front of you and slowly move them up and down the full length of the body to detect branches, wires, or the person in front of you if you are part of a team (Fig. 25). An alternative to using the hand is to use a thin stick in one hand and to move this up and down.

Fig. 25. The ghost walk

The cat walk

The technique for this is to crawl on your hands and knees, searching the ground ahead for noise-making vegetation. You move the knee forward to where your hand has searched (Fig. 26).

The kitten crawl

This is quiet but slow. It is also very tiring. The stalker has to lie on his front. He searches ahead for noise-making vegetation. Then he lifts his body on his forearms and toes. He presses forward and then lowers his body gently to the ground (Fig. 27).

Fig. 26. The cat walk

Fig. 27. The kitten crawl

In summary:

- At night remember that you hear and smell more than you see—turn your ears towards any sound
- Stop and listen, keep close to the ground
- Freeze if you hear a noise
- Keep quiet
- Don't have loose equipment—jump up and down before starting the task to check for loose or noisy items
- Remember that the dangers of skylining and creating a shadow are still present and even graver at night
- Move carefully. Use the ghost walk, the cat walk, or the kitten crawl
- Clear your route
- Don't step on dry vegetation
- Use any available cover

- Be aware that vehicle lights turn night into day
- Use your ears
- If the quarry is near check on his movements frequently by putting an ear close to the ground
- Breathing into the air on cold nights will create an obvious cloud above the stalker—breathe into your jacket or the grass or disperse your breath with a scarf

A note on safety for instructors

There are so many valuable lessons to be learned from a night stalk that it is an essential part of any stalking training and therefore any tracking training.

But any person involved with training, especially training young people, must take note of a safety point. It is foolish, almost criminal, to initiate night stalking training on an individual basis—this must be built up to.

We all have a fear of the dark. The trees and fences become magnified, sounds become intensified, the ground becomes more uneven, until gradually we feel a sinking sensation inside that warns us it is time to take a grip of ourselves. When we have become accustomed to these apparent changes we begin to appreciate the subtle beauty of the dark and become quick to read the noises of the night.

Walk out at night, in a group at first, and practice by listening for sounds and learning their meaning, by looking at the stars and the lighter horizon, by distinguishing shadows from objects at a distance, by using the sense of smell to find out what is happening round about, and by feeling and identifying different objects in the dark. Become accustomed to the unfamiliar by degrees. Then stalks should be arranged for pairs before individual night stalks are attempted.

SUMMARY

NIGHT VISION
- We see less than in daylight
- We develop night vision
- We see shapes not detail
- We see skylines and silhouettes—and so does the quarry
- We may see movement
- If caught in the light of a vehicle, freeze, quickly close one eye to protect your night vision
- Be aware that vehicle lights turn night into day
- Use night vision aids if available

DIRECTION FINDING
- Hearing and smell become more important—turn your ears towards any sound
- Stop and listen, keep close to the ground

NOISES
- Freeze if you hear a noise
- Keep quiet
- Don't have loose equipment (check before starting out)
- Be aware of skylining and shadows

MOVEMENT AT NIGHT
- Move carefully using the ghost walk, the cat walk, or the kitten crawl
- Clear your route
- Don't step on dry vegetation
- Use any available cover
- Breathing into the air on cold nights will create a cloud above the stalker—breathe into your jacket or the grass or disperse your breath with a scarf

12

THE TRACK PURSUIT DRILL

The serious student of tracking now has the theoretical knowledge and, if the earlier exercises have been mastered in the field, also the practical experience to approach meaningfully the linchpin of tracking—the track pursuit drill.

The track pursuit drill (TPD) is a distillation of lessons learned in the art of tracking. It has been devised and formulated by the military to provide a framework from which the tracker can work. It is particularly useful for the student because he has the guidance of a sequence. So, as its name suggests, the TPD is a sequence of activities, a drill, which the tracker employs while in pursuit of his quarry. Some of the steps in the sequence are thought processes and some are actions. If the drill is followed in its correct sequence it gives the tracker the best chance of following his quarry. There are seven steps that are, in effect, a cycle; when the end of the cycle is reached, the sequence is started again. This drill continues until the culmination of the track.

This chapter introduces the process of interpretation of sign and its interrelationship with the TPD. It gives an overview of the TPD's seven steps leading into a full explanation of each stage of the process.

Interpretation of sign
Once a person knows what to look for, following the sign can be likened to following a series of signposts. But for the sign to become obvious, the tracker must first interpret what he has observed.

The following assists the student in interpreting the sign:

- The sign must be studied very carefully
- Distinguish the sign from among the many others
- As soon as possible, the condition of the quarry being followed must be assessed—that is, whether it is lazy, tired, alert, confident, or any other indication as to its state
- Idiosyncracies and traits must be noted
- Any slight change, no matter how small, in its sign must be investigated thoroughly
- Anticipate the quarry's moves, the direction of travel, and any likely deceptions
- Build up a complete picture from all the available sign
- Continuously monitor the ground and country in relation to the direction of travel

An overview of the track pursuit drill
For the visual tracker to be able to follow and make contact with the quarry the TPD must be implemented. There are seven separate steps to this drill. Each step has been formulated for a specific purpose, and it is essential that every potential tracker learns and at all times follows this drill. I will now give you a brief outline of the drill and then analyze each stage separately.

Step 1: assessment of the general direction
The tracker looks ahead along the perceived track to the maximum visibility and back to where he is standing for the general direction of the track.

Step 2: eliminate all openings and finalize the general direction
If there are two or more openings, compare the ages and eliminate old tracks, assuming you know the track that you are following is the most recent one.

Step 3: look for the farthest sign and connect it back to your position
This is to ensure that there is not a split track or that no other form of deception has been practiced. This ensures that you, the visual tracker, are still following the same track.

Step 4: look through the vegetation for the quarry
This step is, in reality, an ongoing process and that is the reason it is placed midway through the sequence. It is very important and must be carried out at every opportunity. The visual tracker must always be aware of the possibility that the quarry is close.

Step 5: check the area to the left and right for deception tactics
By carrying out this drill you ensure that your quarry has not gone off your line of travel and that there isn't any access to the sides. There are many ways in which the quarry can confuse the tracker and these will be dealt with fully in Chapter 13. This step is to combat being led astray.

Step 6: plan and memorize your next footsteps
Here the tracker is working out the best route to the farthest visible sign made by the quarry. The tracker makes a mental note of all obstacles to be negotiated because once he starts to move forward, he will be looking ahead and not at the ground. He memorizes the footsteps and notes particularly any sound-making vegetation. It is important to remember that in steps 1 to 6 the tracker has remained for the most part stationary. This is because the eyes do most of the work. You are alert to all sounds, smells, movement, and vegetation in an unnatural state. Remember we are minimizing all unnecessary movement, which could give our position away.

Step 7: move forward with stealth
The most vulnerable time for the visual tracker is when he is moving. Any sudden movement might catch the quarry's eye. This will result in the quarry being put to flight or, in the case of a military tracker, in your being ambushed. The tracker must retain a mental picture of the track and the footsteps to be taken. With the head held up and the eyes carrying out the drills, the tracker moves forward, alert to all areas ahead and for any sign of the quarry. Trackers must develop good peripheral vision. When the tracker arrives at the farthest sign of the quarry, he again visually checks all the area to the front for the quarry's presence before restarting the cycle.

For ease of explanation the following description is based on an area with vegetation but, even though tracking in desert areas or anywhere without vegetation may be harder, the same basic principles of the TPD can still be applied. Let us now have a more detailed look at the seven steps of the TPD.

Step 1: assessment of the general direction
Start tracking from a definite point where the signs are those made by the intended quarry, for example, outside an earth, a tunnel, a den, a burrow, a nest, a campsite, or an incident area. If this is not possible, you have to rely on information about a sighting of the quarry itself from a reliable source. For the nature conservationist this may be a fellow club member; for the military tracker this may be the local security forces. Once in the immediate area of the sighting your first task is to stand back and observe the area as a whole for the quarry itself. Use binoculars for this in open country. On drawing a blank you must then close in on the location of the last sighting of the quarry and cast about the immediate area until you locate the quarry's track, sign, or spoor.

Once a start point has been confirmed (see Fig. 28), look carefully at all signs in the immediate area and estimate the age of the sign. This can be checked against the information received from your informant. If your sign is two to three days old and the sighting of the quarry took place four hours ago, you are on the wrong track. The physical evidence and your information should confirm each other. If not, you must repeat the casting drill (see Chapter 16) again until you locate and verify the correct sign left by your quarry.

At the start of the track try to estimate the number in the party or group, or the numbers and types of vehicles. By estimating the age of the sign and the number of quarry at the start of the track you will subsequently be in a better position to recognize the following:

- Where the quarry has rested
- Overnight stopping sites
- Watering points
- Feeding areas

It is highly probable that you will find fresh tracks over old tracks at many of the places mentioned above and that the quarry may have moved off again in a different direction. The track that you are following may well have foul tracks on top of it, giving you the problem of distinguishing old from new and verifying which is your track.

Now stand beside the last definite sign facing in the general direction the quarry was last traveling and look ahead 20 to 30 meters. Look for all the possible openings made in the undergrowth and trees to determine the general direction of the track. These openings are recognized and become apparent by eliminating areas the quarry could not possibly have moved through, such as natural obstacles, and areas where there has been no breaking of the undergrowth or disturbance to the vegetation—no physical sign. It is possible that two or three openings of the undergrowth to your front are large enough for the quarry to have passed through. Ensure that you have checked the complete area to your front and also that you are looking as far ahead as is possible and through the undergrowth for any possible signs or sightings of the quarry.

Put yourself in the quarry's place and ask yourself, "Which way would I go?" If the quarry is unaware of being followed, you can often locate the general direction of travel quite easily. Step 1 of the TPD has established the general direction of travel.

Step 2: eliminate all openings and finalize the general direction
Whenever an animal or human moves through any environment, he will always cause disturbance that in some way will alter the natural appearance along the "line of march" when compared with the surroundings. A tracker, through training and experience, begins to recognize these changes and by a process of elimination is able to narrow the options down to the most probable direction of the "line of march."

Still in the same position (Fig. 29), the tracker should take each opening in turn and carry out the following drill:

- Look forward to the maximum visibility for ground and top sign
- Remember the age of the track that you are following and do not be drawn forward by ground and top sign of a different age from your track
- Eliminate openings to the left and right that do not coincide with the age of your quarry's track
- Endeavor to end up with one opening, which you now perceive to be the general direction of the track left by the quarry. If it is not

possible to eliminate all but one opening and you end up with two options then you must:
- Remember the possibility of a split track, that is, when a group separates and takes different routes
- Remember, if there is a definite split, you should follow the quarry that has left the most sign
- Remember that you may have two or more general directions but on inspection all but one can be eliminated

Having completed Step 2 of the TPD you should have eliminated the openings and finalized the "general direction."

Step 3: look for the farthest sign and connect it back to your position

If it has been established that there are visual tracking signs of the right age to your front and that the quarry could have physically passed from where you are standing to the point where you have sighted the furthest sign, we are then ready for Step 3 of the TPD, which is to confirm that the track that we have followed so far is, in fact, the same track as that spotted out front. Without moving from your position (see Fig. 30) you then look at the farthest sign, back-track with your eyes, noting signs along the way to link up the far-thest sign with your present position. Here the tracker is going through a process to confirm that the track being followed is the clearest track. This backtracking with the eyes and connecting signs will often serve to eliminate false openings and false tracks.

A visual tracker must not get into the habit of connecting track from the nearest sign to the next sign ahead unless he is specifically carrying out pace tracking (see Chapters 2 and 17). The reason for this is twofold. First, it is quicker—if you have good top sign and conclusive ground sign 20 to 30 meters to your front, you can move straight on. The tracker has to be conscious of the fact that as the dis-tance increases between him and the quarry, the track gets older, colder, and more difficult to follow. Second, if an inexperienced tracker is concentrating on the ground sign and pace tracking (a pro-cedure that is sometimes unavoidable but very time consuming) he is likely to miss an actual sighting of the quarry ahead.

It is important to mention here that a tracker should always have conclusive or substantiating sign in front before proceeding to the

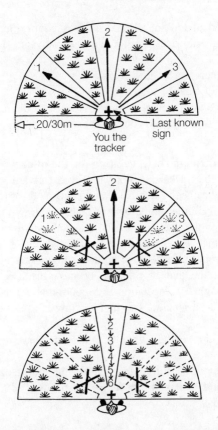

Figs. 28, 29, and 30. The track pursuit drill

next stage, especially in areas where little sign is left due to the nature of the terrain. During the early learning stage it is advisable that the visual tracker stand just behind the last definite sign and not on it while carrying out the TPD, to avoid obliterating the sign with his own feet. This is just in case of need to refer to the last definite sign again, as in the lost track drill (see Chapter 16).

To examine ground sign immediately in front of him, the tracker goes down slowly onto one knee. He doesn't attempt to examine it from a standing position because his forward peripheral vision is severely reduced and also he needs to get as close to the sign as possible to observe all the detail.

The method of looking ahead and then connecting the farthest sign back to the tracker's position has many advantages:

- Speed, as mentioned above
- Split tracks are easier to identify
- The track picture becomes more obvious with the tracker merely using individual signs to confirm the track picture

Step 4: look through the vegetation for the quarry

At this stage the tracker has not yet moved forward, but we know that the track has been established and confirmed for the next 20 to 30 meters. Depending on the type of quarry, you will be looking at ground level, in the trees, in the sky, or even underground.

In Step 4 the visual tracker must visually clear the area to the front. This should also be done before the commencement of Step 1—that is, at the end of Step 7—because the TPD is a cycle. Looking through the vegetation is a continuous process, but it is included here as a separate step halfway through the TPD because:

- During the intervening period the quarry may have moved into the area
- The importance of attuning oneself to being aware of the quarry's presence and the possible danger associated with it must be emphasized

If necessary, the tracker crouches or kneels to check at ground level through the vegetation. He checks through the tunnel-type runs made by the constant use of animals. The tracker should move from side to side so that areas behind obstacles can be seen.

We have now proved the track out to 20 or 30 meters. We have built up the track picture and feel confident that the quarry is not in the immediate area.

Remember: look through the vegetation, not at it!

Step 5: check the areas to the left and right for deception tactics

Deception tactics are mainly the concern of trackers working with the military or the law enforcement agencies. Both the enemy soldier and the criminal can be expected to use various forms of deception tactics to hinder or even ambush the tracker and his team. There are many ways of confusing a tracker or follow-up party. These tactics will be covered in detail in Chapter 13.

We are now in the position where the track has been established and confirmed, and we have checked out the immediate area and have not sighted the quarry. The police or military tracker has to be as sure as is possible that the fugitive or enemy are not present, that they are not in ambush positions, or that they have not laid booby traps. It is vitally important that the military tracker has a full understanding of the types of booby traps associated with the enemy that he is tracking.

Step 5 is not solely for trackers following a human quarry. Some of the large game animals have been known to ambush the unwary hunter by circling around behind him.

The visual tracker must now concentrate on detecting any deception tactics the quarry has used to lead the visual tracker astray. The tracker looks along the confirmed track, concentrating on the areas to the left and right of the track to check for signs of "drop-off" tracks. The slightest irregularity in the vegetation will be noted for confirmation later during Step 7. The tracker must have a thorough knowledge and understanding of all known deception tactics and must always be conscious of their possible use.

On occasion a visual tracker may deliberately follow up on a deception tactic to gain a greater understanding of the quarry. The cunning and cleverness, the degree of alertness and stealth with which a deception tactic has been carried out will certainly assist the visual tracker in understanding the way the quarry thinks and acts. Getting to know and understand the reasoning, thinking process, and habits of the quarry will assist the visual tracker in making an intelligent appraisal of the quarry's intentions. If ever the track is completely lost, the tracker will be in a better position to have an appreciation and make assumptions of where to look when carrying out the "Likely Areas Probe" (covered in detail in Chapter 16).

Step 6: plan and memorize your next footsteps
The track has been located and confirmed; there have been no sightings of the quarry; and the areas left and right of the track have been scrutinized for deception tactics.

Still in a stationary position (Fig. 31), in Step 6 the tracker has to work out the best route to the farthest sign, making a mental note of all obstacles to be negotiated. The principle behind this is that the tracker should only move forward while observing the area to his front—not the ground and where he is going to place his feet.

The tracker now looks at the ground. He notes and memorizes the placement of each foot for the move forward to the farthest sign or the next ten to twenty steps. The tracker will note roots and vines across the track that could possibly catch the feet. I have seen many trainee trackers take a tumble when moving forward because they have not studied the ground in sufficient detail.

Noise is another factor for consideration at this juncture. The tracker will not wish to place a foot on or through any vegetation that would create a noise. In areas of dense vegetation, noise will often travel farther than one can see, so particular care is required to avoid alerting the quarry to your presence.

Bearing in mind that nature will not move vegetation in isolation, the visual tracker should note all vegetation to the front that, if disturbed, could cause the movement of isolated branches, treetops, bushes, or any other interconnected vegetation. These can telegraph the tracker's presence ahead. When moving through areas of close vegetation, the inexperienced or tired person will often be heard first and then give their position away by movement of the undergrowth before they are actually sighted. At this stage the visual tracker has not taken one step forward. During Step 4 the tracker has merely moved from side to side and up and down. In Steps 1 to 6 for the most part the tracker has remained stationary with his head up and looking ahead so that he can immediately catch any movement and hear the slightest sound to his front.

Remember we are minimizing all unnecessary movement that could compromise the tracker's position.

Step 7: move forward with stealth
The tracker now moves forward with stealth to the limit of the confirmed track (see Fig. 32). He places each foot on the predetermined locations. It is important to note that, at this stage, new areas to the front will be opening up—areas not thoroughly checked. Once

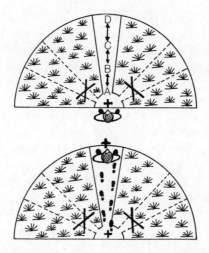

Figs. 31 and 32. The track pursuit drill

moving, the tracker becomes more vulnerable and obvious to any watching quarry.

The visual tracker when moving forward must never look at the ground. He has no need to after the study he made of it in Step 6. If the tracker does need to check the ground or confirm possible deception tactics he must stop, go down on one knee and inspect the ground. To endorse the significance of this point, the military tracker always has a "cover man" following at a suitable distance behind in order to protect the tracker.

While moving forward, the tracker ensures that his position is not telegraphed ahead by undue movement of vegetation. He must also ensure that no sounds are made that could travel beyond limits covered by his vision. During this step the tracker is trying to spot, locate, and discover the quarry without the quarry being alerted to his or his team's presence.

If no quarry is sighted, and this will happen most of the time when the visual tracker arrives at the farthest point and before beginning Step 1 again, the tracker will visually check all the area to the front for signs of the quarry. The drill is repeated over and over until the information about the quarry is obtained or contact is made.

An example of the TPD in action

The scene is set in a cold temperate area, in spring. The start point of the follow was a sighting in the early hours of the morning by a dairy farmer. He saw a small group of soldiers crossing the road by his farm. They seemed to be carrying one of their colleagues on a stretcher. We've been following the patrol of soldiers for 3 kilometers through mixed farmland. It has been easy to deduce that the group is eight men strong by a close study of their prints as they passed along a clay section of ground (see Chapter 15 for details). Also we have confirmed that they are carrying a heavy stretcher by the impression it makes in the ground when they change over bearers. The last section across a dew-soaked field was very clear before the sun evaporated the moisture. We have now entered deciduous woodland. The ground sign is a great deal less obvious. It is now a question of applying the TPD more slowly than before. We approach the entry point into the wood very cautiously, since this would be an ideal place to ambush any pursuers. But because they have a casualty and their border is near they are probably going as fast as they can for safety.

Step 1: assessment of the general direction
I look through the trees. They are widely spaced mature oaks with little undergrowth, but my first thought is to ensure the area is clear of the quarry—it is. The continuation of the direction across the field into the wood is blocked by a small rocky outcrop angling away to the left. The general direction could either be angling away along the outcrop or they have turned sharp right and paralleled the treeline.

Step 2: eliminate all openings and finalize the general direction
To the right the dead vegetation on the forest floor is undisturbed. Along the line of the rocks there is an indication of leaves being disturbed. To the left of this the ground is pristine.

Step 3: look for the farthest sign and connect it back to your position
Five meters along this line is a stream. On the far bank are numerous skid marks. This is the stretcher party negotiating the obstacle.

Step 4: look through the vegetation for the quarry
The rocky outcrop to my right is cause for concern but after a prolonged scrutiny nothing untoward is registered.

Step 5: check the area to the left and right for deception tactics
Nothing is evident.

Step 6: plan and memorize your footsteps
The first couple of paces are on mossy ground—no trouble there with noise. But just before the stream there's an area covered with old dry twigs. I identify a couple of places where I can place my feet without cracking the twigs.

Step 7: move forward with stealth
Continuing to look to the front, scanning and searching the vegetation for the quarry, I proceed to the next sign, which turns out to be conclusive as we can identify several of the individual boot prints in the mud on the stream bank.

This will give you an indication of the type of thoughts that are going through the tracker's mind as he continually runs through the TPD.

Overshooting a track
There is a specific drill laid down for the eventuality that the tracker loses the track. This will be dealt with fully in Chapter 16, but the student should note at this stage the indications that he has overshot the track. They are:

• Individual tracking signs, conclusive or substantiating, are absent
• The ground is fresh—each step will cause leaves and small twigs to crack and break, worm casts will crush, and the general underfoot feel will be different
• Cobwebs that would normally be broken by the quarry you are following are intact, especially in the morning
• Dew is still present on the vegetation and ground, whereas it should have been brushed aside by the quarry if the sun has not had a chance to evaporate the moisture

- Vegetation as a whole will be in a natural state, showing no signs of disturbance, color change, or pointers and you, the tracker, will find yourself making new openings in the undergrowth

The tracker's first problem now is not finding the track but exercising self-control. Sit down and silently deliberate about the chances of re-establishing the track. Take plenty of time to think. Then look carefully and patiently.

Never give up
The trail is there
Somewhere!

The future and some encouragement

The full Track Pursuit Drill may seem a laborious process but during the early periods potential trackers must follow each step of the TPD until the sequence becomes second nature. Eventually, as competence and confidence improve, the visual tracker will be able to combine steps, performing several parts of the procedure with one quick glance and the periods of time spent between successive steps will soon become imperceptibly short pauses.

Another seemingly insurmountable obstacle will be stealthy movement but this also will become as natural as taking a breath.

In conclusion, remember the seven steps:

1. Assessment of the general direction
2. Eliminate all openings and finalize the general direction
3. Look for the farthest sign and connect it back to your position
4. Look through the vegetation for the quarry
5. Check the area to the left and right for deception tactics
6. Plan and memorize your next footsteps
7. Move forward with stealth

SUMMARY

INTERPRETATION OF SIGN
The following assists the student in interpreting the sign:

- The sign must be studied very carefully
- Distinguish the sign from among the many others
- As soon as possible, the condition of the quarry being followed must be assessed, that is, whether it is lazy, tired, alert, confident, or any other indication as to its state
- Idiosyncracies and traits must be noted
- Any slight change, no matter how small in the sign, must be investigated thoroughly
- Anticipate the quarry's moves, direction of travel, and any likely deceptions
- Build up a complete picture from all the available sign
- Continuously monitor the ground and country in relation to the direction of travel

THE TRACK PURSUIT DRILL (TPD)
The TPD is a distillation of lessons learned in the art of tracking. It has been devised and formulated by the military to provide a framework from which the tracker can work. It is particularly useful for the student because he has the guidance of a sequence. There are seven steps that are in effect a cycle: when the end of the cycle is reached, the sequence is started again—this drill continues until the culmination of the track.

Step 1: assessment of the general direction
The tracker looks ahead along the perceived track to the maximum visibility and back to where he is standing for the general direction of the track.

Step 2: eliminate all openings and finalize the general direction
If there are two or more openings, compare the ages and

eliminate old tracks, assuming the track that you are following is the most recent one.

Step 3: look for the farthest sign and connect it back to your position
This is to ensure that there is not a split track and that no
other form of deception has been practiced. This ensures that
you, the visual tracker, are still following the same track.

Step 4: look through the vegetation for the quarry
This step is an ongoing process and that is the reason it is
placed midway through the sequence. It is very important
and must be carried out at every opportunity. The visual
tracker must always be aware of the possibility that the
quarry is close.

Step 5: check the area to the left and right for deception tactics
By carrying out this drill you ensure that your quarry has not
gone off your line of travel and that there isn't any access to
the sides. There are many ways in which the quarry can confuse the tracker and these will be dealt with in full in Chapter
13. This step is to combat being led astray.

Step 6: plan and memorize your next footsteps
Here the tracker is working out the best route to the farthest
visible sign made by the quarry. Remember we are minimizing all unnecessary movement, which could give our position
away.

Step 7: move forward with stealth
The most vulnerable time for the visual tracker is when he is
moving. Any sudden movement might catch the quarry's eye.
This will result in the quarry being put to flight, or in the case
of a military tracker, in being ambushed. When the tracker
arrives at the farthest sign of the quarry, he again visually
checks all the area to the front for the quarry's presence
before restarting the cycle.

SIGNS THAT A TRACK HAS BEEN OVERSHOT
- Individual tracking signs conclusive or substantiating are absent
- The ground is fresh
- Cobwebs that would normally be broken by the quarry are intact
- Dew is still present on the vegetation and ground
- Vegetation as a whole will be in a natural state showing no signs of disturbance

13

DECEPTION TACTICS

This chapter is primarily applicable to tracking a human quarry.

It is a physical fact that a human will always leave sign of his presence. The conspicuousness of the sign depends on the environmental factors discussed in Chapter 4, but the value of the sign is dependent upon the experience of the tracker.

Any military unit or any fugitives who consider that their pursuers will deploy trackers will be very wise to employ deception plans. The aim of any deception is to gain time and distance and in some military contexts to ambush the pursuers.

A look at basic deception tactics will make the tracker realize that there are many different ways in which a determined quarry can confuse, delay, and possibly lose a tracker and his team. Determination and imagination will often need to be called on by the tracker when tracking through deception tactics. But unless the group laying the deception plan is extremely efficient, they will more often than not signpost their deception by leaving a piece of sign that is obviously out of place to the experienced eye of the tracker.

The following is a list of the deception methods that can be employed:

- Walking backwards
- Conversion of sign
- Brushing the track
- Stone hopping
- Tiptoe walking
- Fade out

- Splitting up if the quarry is in a group
- Crossing or walking in a stream or river bed
- Looping back

A sophisticated enemy may deploy a whole series of deception methods to make the tracker team waste time and effort. But even this, although it slows the tracker, is in itself an indication as to the state of the enemy—they are alert, highly skilled, and therefore very dangerous. The military tracker would then be seriously considering the possibility of the track being booby trapped or of his team being ambushed.

I will now detail each of the major deception methods. With each tactic I will indicate the clues that tell a tracker a deception tactic is being employed against him. The student will notice that some of the methods are more appropriate to certain types of environment than others.

Walking backwards

This is the equivalent of Dick Turpin putting the horseshoes back to front on Black Bess—it would throw the unobservant tracker off the line of march by a complete 180 degrees. But to the tracker aware of this ploy it is as clear as day for several reasons (see Fig. 33):

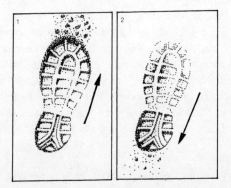

Fig. 33. Walking backwards versus forwards

- When a person walks backwards the length of his pace is shortened
- The toe and the ball of the foot will be more pronounced, the heel not so much
- Loose dirt, dust, sand, long grass, ferns, and foliage will still be dragged in the direction of movement (see Fig. 33/1, walking forwards, and 33/2 walking backwards)
- The feet are placed wider apart for balance

Conversion of sign
Unless a person is reasonably good, this practice only serves to signpost his direction. People sometimes try to mask their prints by making animal tracks over them, usually pig tracks, by the use of shaped sticks.

Brushing over the tracks
Again to an experienced tracker, this technique only signposts the track and thus the intentions. The quarry attempts to hide his sign by brushing over it or placing over it leaves, sticks, stones, and earth. The sign leads to the area that has been brushed; the tracker has then to ask himself, "Why did they brush the track at this point and where did they go?"

Stone hopping
This is attempted as a deception if there is an area of large stones that are firm and do not move when stepped on. The stones or rocks have to be very large otherwise there will be sign left, because after a stone has lain for some time, dirt and sand will build up around the base. Once stepped on, this wall will crumble and what appears to be a shadow will appear around the base—a coloration difference at the lower edge of the stone. This is an extremely difficult and arduous deception tactic to follow especially if it is used for some distance.

One strong indication is that there will be fine particles of dust, sand, or dirt left on the surface of the stone—transfer of sign.

Tiptoe walking
This is a very tiring procedure and is almost impossible over a long distance. It is relatively easy for a good tracker to detect because the toe is obviously very prominent and the pace is much shorter.

Fade out

This is where members of the group jump off the track. The tracker should notice the amount of sign being tracked and that it is starting to dwindle. By checking the sides of the track you should be able to find the "jump off" points. These can give a surprising amount of intelligence about a group as it becomes more relaxed, assuming that the deception has worked. A fade out may be the enemy's start to his daily lying-up drills or even his preparations for an ambush on your party. This sophisticated, coordinated technique should alert the tracker.

Splitting up

This is similar to the fade out. In fact, at first it is indistinguishable from the fade out but with the latter the tracker will start noticing that the group has started to reunite. Again the indication to the tracker is that the amount of sign decreases. The rule in this case is to follow the sign that is the most prominent or where the sign indicates the larger group went.

Crossing or walking in a stream bed

It is normally done where the water is rippling in the vain hope that it makes the sign much harder to locate, whereas in fact it makes it easier because the small stones on the stream bed are disturbed and their light undersides revealed. If the quarry cross in deep water, exit points will normally be prominent as water splashes will be transferred, muddy banks marked and overhanging branches used to pull themselves out.

Looping

Although not strictly speaking a tracking deception tactic, looping is worth mentioning here to give a full picture of what is mainly military tracking. If the track starts to change direction in a gradual but similar direction, thus describing a loop, it is a fair assumption that the enemy have looped their track so that any follow-up party will be passing in front of their observation position. Depending on the freshness of the track, this could be dangerous but if the sign is old, a tracker should be thinking about seizing the opportunity of coming across an old lying-up position to gain intelligence about the enemy.

In conclusion, it is extremely important for a tracker to have an understanding of deception tactics. A person involved with the training of trackers should build into the training the use of deception tactics during the middle stages of the course in a gradual and controlled fashion.

If trackers can identify deception tactics used by the quarry, they will be able to counter them and it will give trackers a greater understanding of the quarry.

Always remember deception tactics are mainly used by man. Man, when he is a quarry, is a very dangerous animal. He uses deception tactics against trackers for three main reasons:

To gain time
To lose the tracking team
To kill the tracker

SUMMARY

DECEPTION TACTICS

The following is a list of deception methods:

- Walking backwards
- Conversion of sign
- Brushing the track
- Stone hopping
- Tiptoe walking
- Fade out
- Splitting up if the quarry is in a group
- Crossing or walking in a stream or river bed
- Looping back

Reasons for using deception tactics

- To gain time
- To lose the tracking team
- To kill the tracker

14

JUDGING THE AGE OF SIGN

The student of tracking who has been applying the skills so far described in this book will now be realizing how important it is to be able to give an accurate estimate of the age of the sign. Chapter 13 highlights this fact in what may be a life or death situation.

This chapter and the next will enhance the practical skills of the tracker. We are now moving more into the area of the application of our reasoning powers.

Judging the age of a track is the most difficult aspect of visual tracking and can only be achieved with confidence and a good degree of accuracy after practice and experience in an environment.

The importance of the time bracket
The sign needs to be placed into a time bracket for the following reasons:

- To distinguish between old and fresh sign
- To determine the approximate time lapse since the quarry passed through the area—this will give you some indication of your position in relation to that of your quarry
- To establish the correct track picture—this is building up the story of the trail as a whole and it is imperative that the time bracket is assessed correctly in order that no confusion occurs in the tracker's mind
- To use foul tracks to your advantage and not to be misled by them
- To gather information for use by intelligence analysts

The four factors
As stated in Chapter 4 four factors affect the quarry's sign:

- Time
- Features of the terrain
- Climatic conditions
- Spoor and sign left by third parties

We are now going to focus on the time element and study how sign alters over time with the others factors remaining constant.

The terrain as a medium
It is worthwhile in many cases to view the physical terrain as a medium upon which the quarry writes or draws as he passes over or through it. What he writes is the sign. What we are now interested in is whether the medium has a nature that will retain the sign or not, and if so, for how long.

The concept of permanency of the sign was hinted at in Chapter 3 when two of the classifications of sign were given as permanent or temporary. For the purposes of judging the age of the sign, the physical surface is:

- Soft—where disturbance or damage is easily inflicted, for example: soft soil, mud, sand, snow, green leafy plants, ferns, crops, grasses, roots that bleed, most types of dead or dry foliage (leaves, pine needles), ant hills, worm casts, and animal droppings
- Hard—being matter or material that is resistant to damage or disturbance, for example: hard packed or sun-baked soil, frozen ground, rocky ground, roads, tracks, resilient mosses, tussock grass, many man-made objects (plastic, metal—usually classed as discardables in tracking terms)

Exposure to the climate—weathering
Having isolated the time part of the formula, we have now to concern ourselves with not only the climatic factors but how long they exert their influence on the sign. If the medium upon which the sign is written is exposed to the elements, it will obviously be affected more than sign sheltered from the weather.

An example will illustrate the point. An object such as a piece of cloth, a newspaper, a used fire, or animal droppings will age at a different rate depending upon whether it is in a plowed field or under the canopy of a thick forest.

The tracker has to assess the exposure of the sign and has then to remember the weather over the preceding period.

Methods for judging the age of sign
To be able to judge age accurately to within hours will only come with experience and continual application and practice. And however talented the tracker is, certain types of environment will only give him a broad time bracket in which to place the quarry's passage. But, applying the skills of Chapter 15, the most difficult terrain may reveal the quarry's secrets to within a few minutes, if all the evidence is used.

Having considered the type of physical surface (the medium) and how much or how little it has been exposed to the climatic elements, the tracker now has to use other techniques to attain a greater degree of accuracy. The following are the methods available to assist his judgment.

Comparison of color
An indication of the age of a track may be gained by the state of dryness of cracks and splits that appear in grasses that have been trodden on or disturbed. When fresh they are green, but after a few days they turn brown.

Breaking and comparing sticks and twigs
A tracker who is trying to use a break in a twig, for instance, to assess the time when the quarry passed by may break a similar piece of vegetation and compare the fresh break with that the quarry made (Fig. 34). A fresh break will be a lighter color and a study of the ends may show fibers protruding. These fibers disappear over a period of time and the color darkens.

Comparison of impression
By comparing your print beside that of the quarry's and contrasting the color change and the degree of definition, an assessment can be made of the age of the quarry's sign.

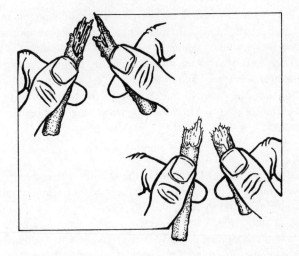

Fig. 34. Comparing a freshly broken twig with the sign

Time brackets created by precipitation
Rain, mist, or dew will pockmark tracks and they will appear to lack definition. Therefore these sorts of tracks will have been made before or during the rain. If they are not pockmarked they will have been made after the rain. Pockmarking can also be caused by mist or dew dripping from trees which, when considered by a tracker with knowledge of the local weather conditions, will give an estimate of the age. An example will explain: if a track was found at midday and there was a heavy downfall of rain at 0200 hours, and the track was clear, you can say it was made since the rain, placing it into a ten-hour time bracket.

Wind
In forests, leaves and pine needles are always falling from trees. The amount of foliage that falls on the sign will depend on the season and on the wind and precipitation over the period since the quarry passed—a further indication of the age of the tracks.

Superimposed game tracks
Most wild animals lie up during the day and move at night. Many species such as deer will move up and down the same track to and

from their resting place to their source of food and water. If human prints on a main game trail have animal tracks superimposed and these tracks show that the animal has moved in both directions, the tracker can estimate that the human prints are probably at least one night old. If the tracks show that the animal has moved only in one direction, then human tracks were probably made during the night—after the animal has moved down to water and before it has moved back.

Wildlife

By studying and noting the habits of the wildlife with regard to feeding, watering, and movement, the tracker can gain information to assist him in assessing the age of the quarry's sign. As mentioned, most wild animals feed and move during the hours of darkness, but most birds feed during the day. If they lay sign that affects or is affected by the quarry's sign, knowledge of the timings of their activities gives the tracker another time bracket with which to encapsulate the quarry.

Apart from disturbances to worm casts and insect life, as noted below, the existence of broken cobwebs should also be taken into consideration to try to place your quarry's movement within a period. Awareness of all your natural surroundings will be a great aid in judging the age of sign.

Prints in mud

The state of dryness of a track in mud or soft ground must be noted. If the track is very fresh, water will not have run back into the depression made by the quarry's footprint. Later the water runs back, and later still the mud pushed up around the print and kicked forward by the quarry's foot leaving the ground begins to dry (Fig. 35).

Exposed earth

Freshly exposed earth, whether dug or plowed, has a unique smell and a characteristic appearance. Weather and exposure will eventually take away the fresh smell and the new look. Closer examination of freshly disturbed earth will reveal two things. First, it smells different because the newly exposed earth uncovers a greater area of freshly disturbed, squashed, crushed roots and insects, but more

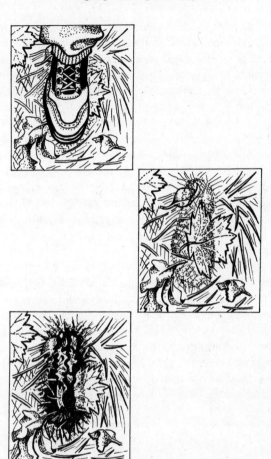

Fig. 35. How water refills a print

importantly it contains more moisture. When that moisture begins to evaporate, it gives off the distinctive odors. Second, it will be noted that freshly disturbed earth is in a completely unnatural position—clods and lumps of earth will be balanced one upon the other. This is the state of freshly disturbed earth whether it is plowed, dug or, of more interest to the tracker, disturbed by the passage of the quarry.

The visual tracker will see the similarities between the fresh skid, slide, and scuff marks of the quarry and the newly dug or plowed piece of earth. Shoes, hooves, and pads leave exposed earth. When this is fresh, it will have flat surfaces with straight edges outlining the pattern of the print. Both the color and the smell will be different; close examination will show many examples of small particles—grains of sand, soil, and mud balancing one upon the other. As the sign becomes exposed to the elements the wind, rain, sun, and snow will start to blow away the finely powdered earth and level the balancing grains. The heat of the sun will dry up and age the whole appearance and alter the smell radically. The fresh print has now changed its appearance; it has become dull in color, vague, and unclear.

If the ground is frozen or very sandy, it will react more like rock or pure sand respectively.

Dry leaves

With a fresh track over dry leaves the visual tracker will have to look for the following. The overall disturbances will cause a color and appearance different from the surrounding area. The effect will be greater shadow and so a darker color. Tilted leaves will be in an unbalanced state. Each leaf that has been stepped on will either bend, break or crumble, and the edges of broken and torn leaves will be lighter in color than those of weathered surfaces (see Fig. 36/1). On freshly walked-over leaves there will be more evidence of transfer (see

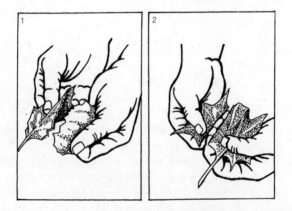

Fig. 36. Broken dry leaf

Chapter 2). Rain will pat each leaf down into its natural position and so eliminate shadow and color; sand on leaves and the smaller particles of leaves will be washed off. As the sign is exposed to weathering, the transferred material will tend to be removed. Unbalanced leaves will resettle themselves. The darker shadowing will disappear as the old pattern re-establishes itself. If sunshine follows rain, after twenty-four hours all signs of freshness will have gone from this sort of sign. The exposed, freshly broken ends will begin to darken and the fibrous ends will curl up and disappear. You, the tracker, can tear a similar leaf found in the immediate area and compare the fresh break with the one the quarry made (see Fig. 36/2).

Sticks
What has been said above about leaves applies equally to sticks and twigs, with the addition that often the undersides will be darker in color and may possibly have small particles of either sand or decaying vegetation adhering to them.

Growing vegetation
The state and position of trodden vegetation must be noted. Various grasses have different degrees of resilience. Prior knowledge of the response of flora to being crushed, pushed aside, broken, cut, and squashed will assist in determining the age of the sign.

Only by studying flora present in areas of operation over a period of time can the tracker become skillful with this method.

Think of a vase of freshly picked flowers with no water and put out in direct sunlight—they soon wither and die. In water and in shade they will stay fresh and alive-looking for a much longer time. Next think of the many different kinds of flowers, some of which when cut and given water and shade will last only two to three days, while others will be in bloom over two weeks later. The visual tracker should be aware of these differences in aging.

Pulpy leaves with a high water content will wither and die faster than vegetation with a low water content. The tip leaves of most branches, which are the new tender leaves, will be the first to show signs of aging. Plants with a low water content when subjected to heavy rain will rot and darken in color at a rapid rate.

The visual tracker must also be aware of a plant's reactions to cutting, breaking, or bruising.

So far I have described the effect on the removed section—the growing section must also be considered. First, sap will appear then congeal or dry up. Next when the cut end has dried it will start to turn brown. The speed of browning will differ with different species and exposure to weathering.

Growth will begin again from the next bud or shoot down. The process can take from two to nine months, depending on the species.

Man-made objects

If man is the quarry he will probably have many man-made items with him for his support. These can be broadly categorized into items for sustenance, medical, sleeping and shelter, navigation, weapons, and communications. When a visual tracker locates an old camp site or a recently vacated one, he will need to know the speed of aging of the different items listed to estimate when the camp was last used. You will need to know that, for instance, a metal can constructed to hold a liquid with acid content will be more durable and stay newer-looking longer than metal constructed to hold a liquid with an alkali base. The quality of the product, which can be determined to some extent by the country of manufacture, should also be noted, as this affects the speed of aging. The tracker should be able to assess the age of a variety of objects such as: paper products, including cigarette packs, writing paper, candy wrappers, newspaper, as well as textiles, plastics, and metal objects.

Fires

Fires can be an invaluable guide to a tracker if the particular fire site can be linked to the quarry. Not only does the retained heat at various levels give an indication of the fire's recent use—up to twenty-four hours ago—but the changes to the ash brought about by rainfall and to the food remains by decomposition can give clues to the age of the sign.

Worm casts

In the early hours of the morning worm casts are soft; after they have been exposed to the sun for some time they dry out. Therefore, armed with this knowledge and his memory of the exposure that the cast will have had to sunlight (local weather conditions), the tracker can estimate the time bracket. The quarry will have either trodden on the ground before the worm appeared and therefore the cast will be superimposed on his print, or the quarry will have trodden on a moist cast, which will produce a flat circular formation, or a dry one, in which case the cast will be powdery.

Ants and termites
Ants and termites on the move can give you a good indication of the time the quarry passed by, as long as you know by conclusive sign that it was your quarry that disturbed them. Depending on the amount of damage inflicted on them by the quarry, it can take them up to two hours to resume their natural formations.

Animal droppings
All animals produce either solid or semi-solid feces. Although there can be a variation within a species and even from the same animal depending upon its age, condition, and diet, usually droppings can be used to identify a species. But more usefully, the state of the droppings can be used as a time indicator. Either droppings can be used as sign if tracking the animal who produced the droppings, or the droppings can be the medium for the quarry's sign.

The fact that many animals are creatures of habit and have regular defecating places and use their urine and scent glands to mark their areas can also assist the tracker in placing either the animal's movements or some other quarry's movements within a time bracket if the tracker is familiar with his environment.

Smell
Smell, whether the sap from a freshly cut branch, wood smoke hanging in still air, or the smell of freshly dug animal homes, recent droppings, or newly marked scent posts will all indicate a fresh track. Where there is no smell, this will indicate that the sign is not fresh.

An advanced technique—age stands
If a professional tracker is intending to operate in an area over a protracted period, or if he is training other trackers to operate in an area (see Chapter 17), he will employ the following method to enhance

his skills in judging the age of sign and provide continuous up-to-date information on the effects weather has on this. He will construct what is called an age stand. It is necessary to construct two: one in the open, subjected to the elements, and a protected one as the control in the experiment.

All that is required is two identical patches of prepared ground each measuring 3 meters by 3 meters. What is placed in the age stands depends upon the environment being studied and for what the tracker is preparing. The following items could be included:

• Materials to make a small fire
• Cigarette butt
• Animal fur, wool
• Matches used and unused
• A slice of bread
• A handful of rice (cooked or raw)
• New coin
• Empty tin cans, both acid and alkali containers
• Candy still in its wrapper
• Small pile of animal droppings appropriate to the area
• Newspaper
• Magazine—glossy paper
• A candle
• A small amount of seed
• Thin green saplings
• Dry sticks
• Shavings from a freshly cut stick
• Pile of leaves
• Pile of pine needles
• Sapling cut in half
• Animal and human prints (which will be added after the stands have been constructed)

I have found the following procedure the best to adopt when constructing the age stands:

1. When you come to constructing the fires (remember everything is duplicated), make a small circle about 30 cm in diameter with stones about the size of your fist. Do not use man-made stones

as they can explode when heated. Then add your tinder, dry grass, small dry sticks, papers, and other kindling and fuel.

2. Light the fires at the same time, using more than one match. Blow the matches out when burned halfway down the stem. Leave the matches just outside the stone circle. Next to these used matches place several unused matches.
3. Light a cigarette, place it on the stand and leave it to burn down. This is included in the age stand in case the tracker comes across the remains of cigarettes left by the enemy.
4. Light the candle and let it burn for five to ten minutes.
5. Keeping the leaves on, bend the saplings and stick them in the ground—three saplings about 30 cm in length.
6. Snap in half a couple of dry sticks, making sure not to damage the small, fine, fibrous hairs, and place them on the stand.
7. Plant the seed as per the instructions on the packet
8. Footprints—dig a small patch in the stand to accommodate a footprint of a bare foot and a booted foot. Make an impression with the bare foot and the booted foot in the soft soil, withdrawing the foot carefully.
9. Spoor—as for 8 above, but use a plaster cast to make the imprint (see Chapter 24) or a compliant pet.

The age stand protected from the elements is to be laid out in the same way as the first stand but protected by overhead cover. It is up to the individual what materials are used in the construction of the sheltered stand, as long as it has a roof and plenty of ventilation. The ideal procedure is as follows:

1. Make sure that the back of the stand is pointing into the prevailing wind.
2. Drive two stakes into the ground 3 meters apart, making sure that you leave at least one meter of each stake above the ground.
3. Strap, nail, or tie a crosssection just over 3 meters long across and on top of the two stakes.
4. Before going any farther, assemble the items that are going into this age stand, lay them out in exactly the same way as you have done in the first age stand, and light the fire.
5. Once the fire is out, place the roofing material on top of the frame so that you end up with a slanting roof. Make sure that

the roof is secured with something heavy or tied, but not nailed down. It has to be easily removable so that the sign can be inspected.

The stage is now set. With continual inspection of the stand over the next few days, weeks, months, and even years, and by keeping a log of the changes, the tracker is able to build up a reference work for his area for judging the age of sign.

Being able to assess the age of sign is a vital tool of the professional tracker. It saves him hours of frustrating effort, as he avoids being misled by foul tracks. Applying the techniques above, he can take much of the guesswork out of assessing age and this, coupled with the skills depicted in the next chapter, will provide a tracker with an ability to extract the maximum information from the sign left by his quarry.

SUMMARY

THE IMPORTANCE OF THE TIME BRACKET
The sign needs to be placed into a time bracket for the following reasons:

- To distinguish between old and fresh sign
- To determine the approximate time lapse since the quarry passed through the area
- To establish the correct track picture
- To use foul tracks to your advantage and not to be misled by them
- To gather information for use by intelligent analysts

THE FOUR FACTORS AFFECTING SIGN
- Time
- Features of the terrain
- Climatic conditions
- Spoor and sign left by third parties

THE TERRAIN AS A MEDIUM
The terrain is the medium upon which the quarry writes as he passes. What he writes is the sign. Is the medium of a nature that will retain the sign or not, and if so, for how long?

WEATHERING
Consider if the sign has been exposed to the elements or sheltered.

METHODS FOR JUDGING THE AGE OF SIGN
- Comparison of color
- Breaking and comparing sticks and twigs
- Comparison of impression
- Time brackets created by precipitation
- Wind
- Superimposed game tracks
- Wildlife
- Prints in mud
- Exposed earth
- Dry leaves
- Sticks
- Growing vegetation
- Man-made objects
- Fires
- Worm casts
- Ants and termites
- Animal droppings
- Smell
- Age stands

15

DEDUCTIVE SKILLS

Deduction is the final phase of the mental process that the tracker employs. To recap, the full process is:

Observe
Remember
Select and analyze
Deduce and comprehend

The tracker observes and remembers. He selects and collates the relevant facts and analyzes the interplay of the observations he has remembered. From this analysis he arrives at deductions about what has happened. From these deductions he gains an overall understanding and comprehension of the track picture.

When the tracker arrives at the start of the pursuit, the quarry is like a ghost, without substance, but after a while the tracker not only fleshes him out, but clothes him and eventually determines his emotional state.

A couple of tales from antiquity will illuminate the thought processes that the tracker should try to cultivate. These stories are from Judea and show the application of reasoning to observed facts—not only must the tracker look but he must also see.

The first:

Two men were reduced to slavery on Mount Carmel. Their captor, following behind, overheard one of them telling the other, "The camel that went before us is blind in one eye, is laden with two skin bottles, one containing wine and the other oil, and is driven by two men, one an Israelite and the other a Gentile."

172

"You stiff-necked people," cried the captor, "how do you know all this?" They replied, "The grass is nibbled on one side of the road only. The drops of wine on one side are sunk into the ground; whereas the oil drops remain above it. One of the drivers has relieved nature at some distance from the road, the other (a Gentile indecency) on the road."

The second:

The story is told of a man who bought a servant to accompany him on his journey home. Having paid the money, he discovered to his dismay that the servant was blind in one eye. "Be comforted," said the dealer, "though he is blind in one eye he can see much better than persons who have two."

The man departed with his servant. When they had gone a little way, the one-eyed slave said, "Master, there is a traveler ahead of us. If we go fast enough we shall overtake him."

"I see no traveller," said the master.

"No," said the slave, "but I know that he is just four miles distant."

"You are mad," said the master. "How can you know what passes at so great a distance, when you can scarcely see what lies before you?"

"I am not mad," said the slave, "moreover, the traveller is accompanied by an ass, who, like myself, is blind in one eye. She is big with young and is laden with two skin bottles, one of which contains vinegar and the other wine." The master, who thought the slave was either insane or making fun of him, was wild with rage.

They traveled on, however, and after a time overtook the traveler. When the master found that everything was as the slave had predicted, he asked him to explain how he could know all this without seeing.

The slave replied, "Although I have not seen what I described, yet I knew the traveler was four miles ahead of us, for the almost imperceptible impressions of the ass's hoofs in the road indicated that she was at least that distance or the impression would have been more distinct, and could not be farther or they would not have been visible. The grass, having been eaten away at one side of the path and not the other, plainly showed that the ass must have been blind in the one eye. Again, the impression the animal left on the sand when she rested showed clearly that she was with young. Further, the impression of some liquids that leaked onto the sand appeared spongy while others were full of small bubbles caused by fermentation. These clearly indicated the nature of the liquids."

To put what may have seemed a mystical and baffling process into perspective, I propose to give some solid, practical cases that will convince the student that the thought processes of tracking are a part and parcel of the totality.

Deductions from a single print
A single print can give a range of information about the quarry:

- The size of a footprint gives an indication as to height
- The depth of the impression, all other things being equal, is in direct relation to the weight of the man and his equipment
- The angle of the print with respect to the line of march is indicative of the posture of the person—an athletically built person tends to walk with his feet parallel
- Any scuff marks around the edges would suggest an idiosyncratic gait
- The footwear itself will lead to other deductions based upon its manufacture, style, and state of repair—such as the country of origin, and socioeconomic group

Deductions from a series of prints
A series of prints from the same quarry lets the tracker judge:

- The speed
- The gait
- The load being carried—the heavier the load the shorter the pace

See Chapter 21 for more details.

Estimating numbers in a group
A group of more than ten humans will automatically leave such a well-defined track that following it will present no real difficulties at all. The estimation of the numbers in a large group can only be made with any degree of accuracy when either a resting place or an overnight camp or bivouac area has been located and the individual resting places counted.

When estimating the size of smaller groups, follow the track to soft ground, then take what would be an extra large step (see Fig. 37). Now make two lines across the track, one line level with the back of the heel of your rear leg and one level with the toes of your leading foot. Remember the unit of comparison ordinarily adopted is that of a normal walking pace. Now count every variation of footwear or part of the visible impressions left by footwear within the space between our two lines (our extra large step). Having counted the prints divide by 2 and if the result is an odd number, say 7, then the estimate is 3 or 4 people. If the estimate is an even number, say 8, then the answer is 4 people. You might be able to confirm this number by counting the different types of footwear within our extra large step. If tracking children under the age of ten, halve the extra large step and carry out the same drill as for adults.

There is a possibility of inaccuracy if the first person to move through the soft ground weighed, say, 80 pounds and had small feet, while the average weight of the people in the group was, say, 160 pounds. The first person's prints could be completely obliterated. This problem can be overcome by repeating the process whenever soft ground is encountered.

By counting from the extra large step (Fig. 37) we get 12 impressions of footwear, partial or whole. Using our formula this gives us an estimate of 6 people. However, from Fig. 38 we can see that only 5 people made the track. A closer look at our extra large step will reveal that it is out of proportion to the average length of each step made by the group—it is nearly the distance of two steps. The Adjusted Method gauges the average distance of each step. Then we take an extra large step based on our assessment of the average. In this case the adjusted extra large step is smaller than our original one and is more in proportion to those of the group we are tracking. Our new calculations arrive at the figure of 10 footprints (whole or partial) which, when divided by 2, gives the correct answer.

As always, when producing estimates, try to confirm as and when the opportunity arises.

Analysis of groups

In Fig. 39, a total of 12 prints will be observed within the extra large step. Four canine prints equals one dog. Four juvenile prints, divided

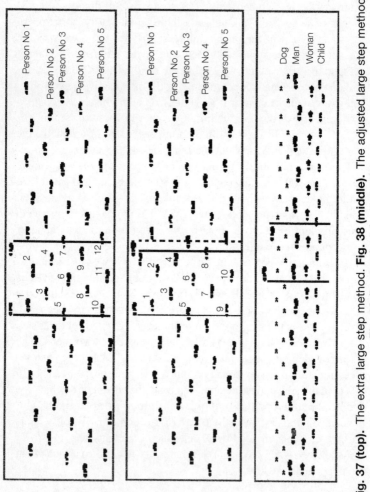

Fig. 37 (top). The extra large step method. **Fig. 38 (middle).** The adjusted large step method. **Fig. 39 (bottom).** A family outing.

by 4 (because we have taken an extra large step based on an adult pace) equals one child. Four adult prints, divided by 2, equals 2 adults. On further examination of the human prints we can deduce the sex of the adults. The print pattern has indicated one dog walking beside an adult male, probably on a lead. On the other side of the adult male is an adult female with a child—because of the evenness of the child's pace, probably holding hands with the adult female. The picture is that of a family going for a walk.

By careful analysis of the prints in a group, one can work out the order in which they were walking. First of all pair off the sets of prints into left and right. Then concentrate on the prints of the quarry and see how many of the others make foul sign over its prints at any stage. For example, if there were eight in the group, walking in single file, and the set that you had isolated was fouled by three of the others, he must have been marching at number five in the group.

The analysis of peripherals
Apart from the quarry's footfalls his passage through the tracking medium is indicated by sign left by his equipment and clothing, for example:

• Scuff marks on trees from load-carrying equipment
• Impressions left by items of equipment such as weapons
• Marks from a walking stick
• Discarded items of equipment and rubbish
• His urine and feces
• Fires and cooking places
• Sleeping places
• Prayer stations

Fig. 40 depicts an overnight stop by a patrol. Fig. 41 shows the same area after the man has departed and reveals:

(a) Weapon butt print and scuff marks
(b) Cigarette ends
(c) Marks from hammock cords on both trees
(d) Rubbish pit, halal ration wrappers
(e) Prayer mat marks, facing Mecca

Figs. 40 and 41. An overnight stop by a patrol

(f) Scorch marks from a Tommy Cooker
(g) Scuff marks and heel marks where the person sat under the tree
(h) Marks where load-carrying equipment was placed
(i) Area used as toilet, urine marks on tree
(j) Marks from kipsheet/poncho cords

All the above should be actively searched for by the tracker as they will provide vital evidence to indicate the following:

- Nationality
- Health
- Diet
- Morale
- Customs
- Traditions
- Religion
- Military/Civilian

The importance and the amount of information that can be deduced from a track can be seen by the importance the military place on a tracker's report. They expect to be able to assess the following from a tracker's observations:

- Direction of movement
- Age of the track
- Number in the group
- The speed
- Loads
- Tactics
- Weapons
- Sex

The military process
When the military apply the deductive process to the work of their trackers, they use the following system:

- Facts—something that is physically present
- Interpretation ⎫
- Deduction   ⎬ the tracker's reasoning
- Assumption   ⎭
- Reaction—this is to the conclusions from above
- Confirmation of the reasoning and the reaction
- Reporting of the sightings
- Recording—this is the final stage of the process when the written report is submitted

Inter-deduction

Interpretation and deduction, "inter-deduction" in tracking terminology, is the essence of the tracker's mental processes. The tracker starts by making a list of all known facts. He then asks himself:

• How did it occur?
• Why is it like it is?
• When did it happen?
• Who caused the sign?

He then lists all the deductions from this questioning.

The tracker then brings into play his insight and imagination and makes assumptions, but he is careful to distinguish this purely mental process from the facts provided by the sign. With these assumptions the tracker is trying to anticipate the quarry's actions, not only to find the next sign but also to produce an overall track picture.

Confirmation is the verification of the tracker's inter-deduction and assumptions. It could be the sighting of conclusive sign, such as

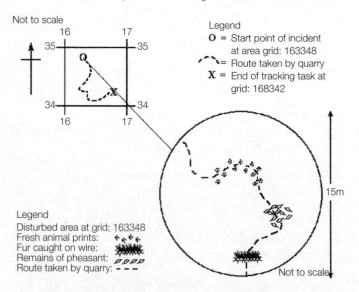

Sketch map of an incident at grid: 163348

Not to scale

Legend
O = Start point of incident at area grid: 163348
= Route taken by quarry
X = End of tracking task at grid: 168342

15m

Not to scale

Legend
Disturbed area at grid: 163348
Fresh animal prints:
Fur caught on wire:
Remains of pheasant:
Route taken by quarry: – – –

Fig. 42. Sketch map of an incident

Serial	Fact	Inter-Deduction
1	At grid 163348 the following were found:	
a	Four sets of fresh prints in the mud. Two sets smaller than the other two sets.	At least two animals, possibly dogs or foxes.
b	Considerable amount of disturbance to an area approximately 5m^2 around what appears to be the remains of a pheasant – feathers and uncongealed blood.	Quarries may have made a fresh kill—blood not yet clotted. Suggesting a very fresh track only five minutes old. Possibly with visual contact.
c	Fur caught up on barbed wire 10 m south of incident area where the sign entered a wood.	A close examination of hair left behind revealed that it was definitely that of a fox.
2	At grid 167342 the following were located:	
a	A strong odor was smelled blowing into the area from the south.	The strength of the scent lingering in the immediate area would suggest that the quarry, in this case a fox, was in close proximity.
b	Numerous fox runs found in the area with well padded-down paths superimposed by many scratch and paw marks.	Sign indicating an area that is used by more than two foxes, possibly a fox earth.
c	Approximately 50 m due north numerous fox earths were found. Outside the earth an array of articles were found: animal bones, fur, feathers, dried blood, foot-prints, bedding, and a large area (approximately 30–40 m) of flattening and the odor of a fox.	From areas of flattening and the great array of sign lying about, the earths were used by more than two foxes.

a boot print known to be worn by enemy troops, discarded material known to belong to enemy troops, or the actual sighting of the enemy.

The recording stage can begin with a sketch map of an incident, a rural case study, as shown in Fig. 42. Its accompanying tabulation (on page 181) highlights the subtleties and proves how much can be elicited from the facts when they are correctly analyzed.

From the above it is assumed that at least two foxes, possibly a vixen and cub due to the two different sizes of prints (consider the time of year vixens give birth), were out on a foraging mission and made a kill at grid 163348. They were probably disturbed by you, the tracker, which explains the very fresh sign at the incident area, and, considering the mother's instinct to protect her cub, headed for home.

To enable you, the tracker, to use any information gained, it is important that you compile a report during and after a tracking task so that you can build up a log about the animals that are in your area. This log should be supported with any sketches, photographs, and specimens that it is responsible to take from the countryside.

This chapter should be read in conjunction with Chapter 21, which gives more examples of how the deductive process helps the tracker.

As we saw with the two stories at the beginning of this chapter, there is nothing new in the world, and certainly the only aspect that is new in tracking is your personal development. This can be enhanced with practice, the study of tracking scenarios, and the exchange of ideas with like-minded people.

SUMMARY

THE THOUGHT PROCESS
Deduction is the final phase of the mental process that the tracker employs. To recap, the full process is:

Observe
Remember
Select and analyze
Deduce and comprehend

ASPECTS OF DEDUCTION

Deductions from a single print
A single print can give:

- The size of a footprint gives an indication of height
- The depth of the impression, all other things being equal, is in direct relation to the weight of the man and his equipment
- The angle of the print with respect to the line of march is indicative of the posture of the person—an athletically built person tends to walk with feet parallel
- Any scuff marks around the edges would suggest an idiosyncratic gait

Deductions from a series of prints
A series of prints from the same quarry lets the tracker judge:

- The speed
- The gait
- The load being carried—the heavier the load, the shorter the pace

Estimating numbers in a group

Analysis of groups

The analysis of peripherals

DEDUCTION AND THE MILITARY TRACKER

A military tracker is trying to assess:

- Direction of movement
- Age of the track
- Numbers in the group
- The speed
- Loads
- Tactics
- Weapons
- Sex

THE MILITARY PROCESS

When the military apply the deductive process to the work of their trackers, they use the following system:

- Facts—something physically present
- Interpretation ⎫
- Deduction ⎬ the tracker's reasoning: inter-deduction
- Assumption ⎭
- Reaction—this is to the conclusions from above
- Confirmation of the reasoning and the reaction
- Reporting of the sightings
- Recording—this is the final stage of the process when the written report is submitted

INTER-DEDUCTION

Interpretation and deduction, "inter-deduction," the essence of the tracker's mental processes. The tracker starts by listing all known facts. He then asks himself:

- How did it occur?
- Why is it like it is?
- When did it happen?
- Who caused the sign?

16

THE LOST TRACK DRILL

Trackers are human, however magical the skills may seem to the uninitiated. Because they are human, they are fallible. At some stage, however experienced a tracker, he will lose the track. At this point he falls back on the procedures laid down in this chapter. They will help him to re-establish the pursuit again.

When acquiring skills, a tracker must always be conscious of two important facts. First, losing a track can be a simple matter of taking only one or two steps in the wrong direction. And second, human nature will compel us to go on when there is no track and to fool ourselves into seeing a track where none exists.

Last definite sign

As explained in Chapter 12, the Track Pursuit Drill has been developed to assist the visual tracker in following a track made by the quarry. The corollary of this is that it prevents him losing the track—thus, the emphasis upon the importance of noting and remembering the last definite sign, and whether it was conclusive or substantiating. The tracker must always be able to locate this last sign and may often have to orientate himself by some definite mark in its vicinity—such as a tree stump, a large stone, a prominent bush or a fence post—to use as a reference point to re-establish his last contact with the quarry.

The last definite sign is the crux of the Lost Track Drill. Therefore it is worth mentioning a simple technique to help you keep sight of it. I find that if I am tracking in a relatively flat, featureless area it is useful to mark the last definite sign by a short thin stick that I carry in my day pack. You may, depending on the situation, tie a brightly colored piece of cloth to the end.

The Lost Track Drill is broken down into the following stages:

- Initial search
- Initial probe
- Initial cast
- Extended cast
- Streamline search
- Likely areas searches

The initial search
1. From your last definite sign, assess the general direction your quarry was last traveling in.
2. Describe a half circle in approximately one meter in radius. Scan it from left to right and right to left. Look in the distance, the middle distance, and the foreground. Do this from the standing, kneeling, and prone positions. Use a magnifying glass if necessary at this stage to identify sign that you might otherwise miss with the naked eye.
3. If you locate sign at any stage while carrying out the initial search, confirm that it is your quarry's by following it up a few meters. If you are happy that you are following the right track, carry on with the track pursuit drill.
4. If no track is located by use of the initial search you will now have to resort to the initial probe.

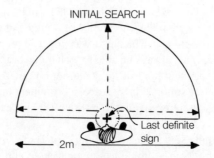

Fig. 43. The initial search

Notes:

- The initial search may take up to thirty minutes
- Your movements should be limited to those necessary to observe the area fully

The initial probe

1. From your last definite sign, probe forward to the left, front, and right, in each case moving only 4 to 5 meters maximum.
2. Every time you draw a blank retrace your steps to your last definite sign and probe again in a different direction.
3. The techniques carried out in the initial search above should come into effect on each probe.
4. If you locate sign at any stage while carrying out the initial probe, confirm that it is your quarry's by following it up a few meters. If you are happy that you are following the right sign, carry on with the track pursuit drill.
5. If no track has been located after completion of the initial probe, you carry on to the next stage, the initial cast.

Notes:

- The initial probe may take up to one hour
- A visual tracker must always remember his individual signs and should never move more than 3 to 4 meters beyond a definite sign of the quarry without another definite sign in front of him
- If no sign is located you must return to the last definite sign and start again

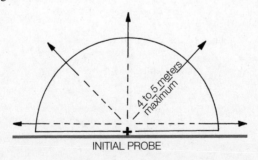

INITIAL PROBE

Fig. 44. The initial probe

The initial cast

1. From your last definite sign (Fig. 45) move back along the track in the direction you have come approximately 15 to 20 meters.
2. Begin walking in a circle 15 to 20 meters in diameter, using the last definite sign as the center of the circle.
3. Whether you move off to the right or left is optional. You will find that you will be influenced by the general direction of the quarry you are following, the ground, and in what direction you think you would be more likely to pick up the quarry's track again.
4. Your aim here is to cut the quarry's track. If you come across the quarry's track you must confirm that it is the same track that you have originally been following by checking the age of the new track. You then check visually backwards to ensure that the track connects with your last definite sign. Finally, inspect forward a few paces to ensure that it is not a dead end.
5. After confirming that you have located your quarry's sign, complete the circle. The reason for completing the circle is in case another animal of the same species has passed through the circle, in which case you would have to determine which is the quarry's sign, taking into consideration all the features of sign such as age, size of print, length of stride, and depth of print.

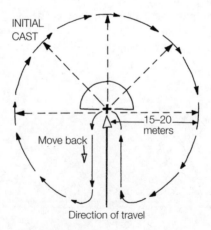

Fig. 45. The initial cast

6. If you still have not located the quarry's sign on your return to your last definite sign, you now have to carry out the extended cast.

Notes:

• The time taken to carry out the initial cast may be up to one hour, depending on your tracking ability, the ground, and tracking conditions—that is, the weather, time of day, age of tracks, and changes in the environment.

The extended cast
The drill for the extended cast is the same as for the initial cast but this time you go back 50 to 100 meters using the last definite sign as the center (see Fig. 46).

Notes:

• Although the above stages have been time-consuming, up to four hours in certain cases, you will now have to accept that you must remain in the area and move on to the final stages of the Lost Track Drill: the searches
• Before starting the next procedure you will need a rest. Don't forget tracking is a very tiring process because of the concentration

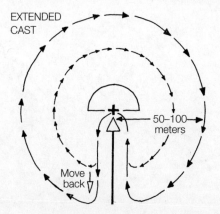

Fig. 46. The extended cast

that it demands from the tracker, along with the physical strain. Therefore stop, have a brew, put your feet up for an hour and relax.

Thus far, all the methods of trying to locate the quarry's track have started at the last definite sign. The searches do not. You are now using your powers of deduction and reason to select areas you suspect the quarry will have visited in the hope that you will pick up the trail anew.

The stream-line search
1. This is the most widely used type of search, but it is only one specific type of search. It is used for two reasons:
    *   Animals need water
    *   The ground around water courses tends to be a good medium for the preservation of sign
2. Assess the general direction in which your quarry was last traveling (see Fig. 47). If using a map, do a map study with the intention of locating any water on your axis of travel and forward from your present location.

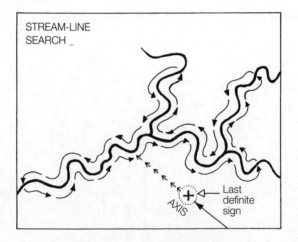

Fig. 47. Stream-line search

3. Whether the amount of water and its distance from your position makes it a viable water source for the quarry depends on the species. For large animals—humans, deer, badgers, and foxes— you will be studying your map for water supplies up to a distance of 5 kilometers. For smaller species you may be searching closer and considering much smaller supplies of water. And for all quarry don't overlook water sources that are not mapped, such as ditches and cattle troughs.

4. If you locate a water source from your map you think is worth searching, locate your position on the ground, set your compass, and navigate to the intended location of the search.

5. If you are searching a water course the following system is the most efficient:

   (a) On reaching the bank of the waterway use your map to confirm you are in the right place—remember that not all waterways are marked on the map.

   (b) Decide which direction you are going to follow the river and for how far. You must avoid retracing your steps and making unnecessary sign. Make a plan in your head and stick to it.

   (c) Check out the obvious first. Did the quarry go straight across the stream?

   (d) Before entering the stream, check the ground to ensure that no sign indicates the quarry came out at your entry point.

   (e) Do a limited search—20 to 30 meters of both banks, and in both directions to ascertain if there is an exit point.

6. The tracker has then to bring into play his knowledge of the sign associated with water courses:

   (a) Remember to check the water for discoloration. If the quarry went upstream, there is a possibility that debris, sand, leaves, and sticks will have been disturbed and floated downstream.

   (b) Overhanging branches will have a high water content and therefore they will be soft, making it easy for the bark to be scraped off and marked—look out for these indications.

   (c) If it is a clear water stream and the bottom is visible, it is still possible to track. Move along slowly, looking for impressions of prints, disturbed stones (practice and familiarization will enable trackers to recognize the natural position of stones lying on a stream bed), and a reduction in the numbers of sticks and other vegetation wedged or caught by the stones and boulders of the stream bed.

(d) Disturbed overhanging vegetation and the lack of spiders' webs across narrow streams will indicate the passage of some animal—this is not conclusive sign.

(e) All river banks are of soft soil and will certainly mark or crumble under the weight of a quarry exiting, often leaving foot impressions, skid, or slide marks.

(f) Any quarry exiting from a stream will certainly leave two telltale signs behind: water drops drained off in the immediate area of exit (the age of the track and the weather will significantly affect these) and, depending on the bottom of the stream, transferred material—sand, mud, or gravel.

(g) The tracker checking up or down stream should look out for overhanging branches because if they are near the water they present an obstacle and anything passing under or over them will undoubtedly leave some sign.

7. On coming across small tributaries (Fig. 47) you should go along the bank 50 to 100 meters, then cross, and go back down the other side until you hit the main river again.

Likely areas searches

In this strategy we are trying to get into the skin of the quarry and predict what he will do next and where. This is where building up the track picture in your mind's eye is so important.

The following factors should be considered:

• The possible task and intentions of the quarry
• The age of the track and the time of day when the quarry was at the place where the track has been lost—remember it will eventually get dark and you may have to abandon the track
• Consider the weather conditions that will have affected the sign— this depends on the age of the sign and therefore the tracker must have been monitoring weather conditions

The types of areas that give the best results are:

- Areas of likely campsites or, in the case of animals, likely living areas such as dens and tunnels
- Steep gradients
- Track junctions
- The sides of tracks, rivers, and roads
- Any other areas you feel your particular quarry may have gone

Finally

The aim of the Lost Track Drill is to help you, the tracker, to relocate the track. You must remember where your last definite sign is, and you must carry out the drills rigorously to ensure that you have not been bluffing yourself. If the sign is not located during the initial probe, then it is very likely that the quarry's last definite sign may be further back along the track. This is why the initial cast drill best assists you in re-locating the quarry's sign.

When following your quarry, at all times avoid stepping on your quarry's prints. In the case of small animals walk parallel to them; with humans and larger animals you can walk between their prints. The last thing you want when you lose the track and you have to go back to your last definite sign is to find your own footprints or those of a companion on top of your last definite sign.

Continually ask yourself the question, "What would I do if I were in his position?" But to be able to do this you must have developed the track picture so that you are aware of his general intentions and condition. This applies as much for an animal as for a man because the animal tracker has an acute appreciation of his quarry's habits that enables him to predict its movements.

We can lose a track through lack of concentration just as much as through the lack of sign and this mental aspect is worth considering:

Tracking is tiring
Don't bluff
Think like the quarry

SUMMARY

THE STAGES
The Lost Track Drill is broken down into the following:

- Initial search
- Initial probe
- Initial cast
- Extended cast
- Stream-line search
- Likely areas searches

If carrying out the first four drills has not located the lost track, the tracker should stop, relax, and have a brew. An hour of rest will help to focus your powers of reason and deduction on the searches.

PART THREE

ADVANCED SKILLS

17

TRAINING TRACKERS

You will already be aware that many sections of this book are specifically geared towards helping an individual who has a training role or responsibility. Where material is germane to a particular subject, such as stalking or observation, I have left it with that chapter. What you will find here are aids to tracker training in general and to the advancement of tracking skills.

The layout of this book can be used as a general guide to the order in which the subjects are taught.

With some groups and audiences it may be necessary to stimulate interest in a practical and spectacular way by trying to follow the tracks of something alive; but even then the preliminary stages of mental training, the training of the senses, stalking, and so on should be taken up as soon as possible. If habits of observation are not formed, the potential tracker's keenness on tracking will soon fizzle out as he becomes frustrated with continually losing the track.

The student has to be shown that the subject is a great deal deeper and more complex than he might at first think. But if he is led through the skills progressively by an enthusiastic instructor and the lessons are put across in an interesting way, it will be an encouraging challenge and not a daunting task.

For example, if you ask the potential tracker to follow the track of a motorcar on a soft dirt road, he will be able to follow it for half a mile with very little difficulty, but if you ask him to follow the track of a man across hard stony ground, he will lose it in under 25 meters. The training has to lie somewhere between these two extremes.

I am aware of the danger of accepting literature as a good substitute for actual practice. As with most things worth doing, tracking isn't easy and requires continual practice. Trackers think like trackers and see sign where the uninitiated don't: any environment is rich in sign to the senses of a tracker—the environment in which we live should not deter us from practicing the lessons. Having said this, there are tracking situations more suitable for the novice than others—snow, mud, and wet sand are ideal tracking mediums. And often the best time to practice is first thing in the morning when there is an abundance of fresh sign.

This chapter is directed to any person who finds himself with the responsibility of running training for trackers. There are the traditional groups such as:

- The military NCO of a reconnaissance or a special forces unit
- The rural police force, especially crime scene specialists
- The teacher or group leader with a background in covering outdoor pursuits, such as Scout leaders

But other bodies will also find it beneficial to study tracking in a structured fashion and therefore utilize the skills of a tracking instructor:

- Conservationists
- Bird watchers
- Protectors of endangered species
- Gamekeepers
- Farmers with a threat of rustlers
- Mountain rescue volunteers

Tracking exercises and lessons
First I will list the types of exercises and make a few observations. After that I will give a set of detailed instructions for each one.

The following are the main types of tracking exercises and instructional periods that I have used in the past to train military trackers:

- Observation stand

- Observation lane
- Age stand
- Pace tracking exercise
- Pace tracking lane
- Incident awareness stand
- Incident awareness lane
- Tracking competition
- Final exercise

The list above is in the order in which these activities should take place to gain the maximum benefit. The introduction to the age stand and the importance of being able to judge the age of sign have to be brought to the student's notice before he attempts the pace tracking lane.

In order to make the exercises and lessons a success, the instructor has to plan meticulously. The following details are given as an aid to that end. Firstly, there are some general considerations to be covered with regard to any exercise or lesson. The following list gives the administrative essentials to ensure that any exercise runs smoothly:

- Obtain permission to use any land
- Carry out a full rehearsal of the exercise
- Determine what mobile telephones receive a signal in the area; these may be needed in an emergency
- Compose a full list of equipment required of the instructor and of the students
- Issue a warning order giving the assembly time and place and what equipment the students need to have with them
- State the aim of the exercise
- Be aware of the students' details—numbers, age, experience
- Consider timings—travel time to the exercise area, duration of exercise
- Organize transport, meals, wet weather clothing, maps, equipment, alternative program in case of the exercise having to be postponed (transport breakdowns, misty weather during an observation exercise)
- Prepare a detailed set of instructions for any assistants and for the students

Observation stand

This exercise is similar to the one used by the Royal Marines, which I referred to in Chapter 7 under the section "Some Exercises for Youth Leaders." Here I will describe the method of laying out the stand and conducting the exercise.

First make a list of the items you intend to use in the observation stand. Then, having selected the piece of ground, mark out the left and right of arc and the foreground, middle distance, and far distance using broad tape similar to that used to demarcate hazards around building sites (Fig. 48).

Make a sketch of the observation stand area. Position yourself where the students will be. Then direct your assistant to lay out the items, starting from the far distance and working back towards where you are. Accurately record on your sketch where the items are.

Indicate from which position in the viewing area they can be seen and whether the observer has to be standing, kneeling, or lying. You

1	Rucksack	12	Football
2	Jacket	13	Tent
3	Fishing rod	14	Notebook – magazine
4	Cap or hat	15	Jumper
5	School bag	16	Radio
6	Push bike	17	Watch
7	Bike pump	18	Packet of chips
8	Person	19	Handbag
9	Person with dog	20	Pencil or pen
10	Belt	21	Loose change
11	Shoe	22	Conclusive sign

Fig. 48. Observation stand layout

also note why each item can be seen—shape, shine, shadow, spacing, silhouette, and movement. Other points to note are:

- All items should be listed and laid out in a sequence so that you do not lose any
- Instructor's sketch map will not be numbered until he gets on the ground and lays the equipment out because he may change his mind about placement of the items
- The kit list is only a guide. Put out what you think will most benefit the students

When everything is ready for the students, call them forward and brief them fully about the limits of the area they are expected to observe and their limits of movement, that is, within the viewing area only. Give the students a copy of the bare sketch map, or ask them to produce their own, depending on the time available and the training carried out up to this point. Inform the group that they will have to move about within the viewing area and adopt various positions to see all the items. Tell them what is required of them: they must place each item on the sketch map, describe it, and give a distance to it. Remind them to put their names on their papers, that referring or talking is not allowed, that they have five minutes to tune in, then set them a time limit, and inform them that they will be given a ten and five minute warning to indicate the approaching end of their allotted time.

After the test collect the papers and, in conjunction with your partner, indicate to the students, starting from the distance, where and what the items are. Remember this part of the exercise is an important part of the learning process, so don't rush it. The usual method is that the assistant stands behind the item and he then points to it. If there are students who still cannot see it, they are encouraged to change stance, to move and to carry out the figure eight search with their eyes around the object. After a few minutes, the assistant slowly lifts the item. It is convenient if the first item is a rucksack or a bag so that the rest can be stowed in it as they are collected.

As with any training, gradually build up the students' confidence by keeping the standard within their grasp.

A careful analysis of the papers is then required to determine the areas for each student that need attention. For example, some will see objects because of their shape, whereas others are attracted to the shine from surfaces but are inattentive to shadow and spacing. Other students have trouble with distant objects or items hanging from branches.

Observation lane

This exercise is a development of the preceding one but in this case a lane is delineated, either by tape as previously or by the bounds of an obvious track, which the students are not allowed to stray from. The length of an observation lane is usually about 50 to 100 meters. The items are outside the boundaries of the track (Fig. 49).

The students can set off as a group or the exercise can be conducted individually. Either way there should be no conferring and, if the students are going through as individuals, those who have finished the exercise should be isolated from the others.

Again, the debrief is very important. The same procedure as before should be used, where an assistant indicates the items and the students are given a second chance to try their observational skills.

1	Notebook	11	Person
2	Nature trail marker	12	Tent
3	Pair of shoes	13	Compass
4	Watch	14	Radio – on
5	Lighter	15	Nature trail marker
6	Person digging	16	Nature trail marker
7	Hat	17	Map
8	Jumper	18	Flashlight
9	Sleeping bag	19	Camera
10	Fire	20	Rucksack

Fig. 49. Observation lane sketch map for instructors

To add variety, the lane can have live aspects such as smoke from a fire, men occupying a camp, and people talking.

Age stand

A full description of this training technique is given in Chapter 14.

Pace tracking exercise

As was stated in the definitions in Chapter 2 this is "pace for pace" tracking carried out during the tuning in period or when the track becomes difficult to pursue.

Remember, as an instructor, to select the tracking medium suitable to the standard of your student—mud, snow, and sand for the beginner, dew-laden grass in the early morning at a later stage, leading to hard-packed dry earth and rock for the accomplished student.

It will be mainly ground sign that you will be following when pace tracking. You have to start from a known quarry's sign, whether it is conclusive or substantiating sign. Then make a comprehensive study of that particular sign to gain as much information as you can—direction, size of print, width, depth, left or right foot, fore or hind in the case of an animal, sex, and age. Once you have taken all these into consideration, your next task will be to find the next sign.

Let's run through an easy example (see Fig. 50):

In this case there is a conclusive sign made by a human's right shoe (a), box 1. From your position (b) look forward from the end of your toes and the width of your body to a maximum distance of one meter.

Look to the obvious area where the left shoe should be (c).

Once you have established the next print, in this case the left shoe, place your right foot parallel to but not on the quarry's right footprint (see box 2).

Next bring your left foot forward but *do not* put it down on the ground, sweep it from left to right over the ground between the quarry's right foot (a) and the quarry's left foot (c).

Now place your left foot down between (a) and (c).

Bring your right foot forward, placing it between the quarry's left and right foot, then kneel down (see box 3).

The reason you carry out this sweep is fourfold:

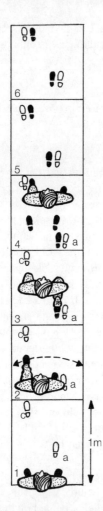

Fig. 50. Pace tracking

First, to establish the length of the quarry's pace so that you adapt your pace to suit the pace of your quarry. This enables you to anticipate where the quarry's next sign will be.

Second, so that you don't foul the quarry's sign by placing your foot on top of it.

Third, from the kneeling position you can get a closer look at the quarry's next sign, using a magnifying glass if required.

And finally, to make sure that the quarry has not put an indicator pace in between (c) and (a), which would reveal a change of direction.

Once you are confident that you have established where the quarry's left foot was, place your left foot beside it (see box 4).

When you have built up confidence in pace tracking you will find that you will be able to follow a quarry at a normal walking pace (see boxes 5 and 6) only carrying out the sweep when necessary.

When pace tracking always be aware of the quarry changing direction—look for the indicator pace. Do not be tempted to jump sign as you will only lose the track and end up fouling the sign. Pace tracking means exactly that, following the track pace for pace, and the tracker keeping in step pace for pace. A further point for consideration in pace tracking is the speed of the quarry. In the case of humans you should have no problem finding out if they are walking, jogging, or running when you do the sweep.

The same principles apply to pace tracking animals, but in this case measure the walk or hop of a bird with a stick and use this to locate the next print. With animals there is an added problem, since a human has a reason for going from A to B and will generally go in a straight line. Animals, however, are much more unpredictable. With four-legged creatures the ideal situation would be establishing all four prints in, say, mud, snow, or sand. Usually you will be following only two or three prints and the direction may be less predictable.

The organization of a pace tracking exercise is mainly about avoiding one group inadvertently causing foul sign for another. So to that end the instructor divides the group into two, say the red and the blue teams. Pair off each member of the red with a blue team member. Indicate a start line, for instance the edge of a bridle path, line the red team members up along the path at ten-meter intervals and have their counterparts on the blue team stand behind them back to back.

The group laying the track make a conclusive sign and plant a marker by it as the start point for their partner in the other group. They then walk off in the given direction (the instructor ensures that the tracks are parallel) for a given distance, say 50 to 100 meters, and sit down out of sight of the tracking group who are then shown their respective first conclusive sign and are told to pace track from there.

After each track, follow it up with a lessons learned debriefing session. The groups then change roles. The instructor should encourage the students to be slow and methodical at this stage. It is not a race. They will learn from each piece of sign and each pace if they proceed steadily.

The practice can be varied as the students improve by having the quarry group putting in indicator paces using deceptions, varying the speed, walking with a stick, or joining a group.

A pair of student trackers can carry out this exercise on their own as long as they set themselves a cut-off time if they do lose contact with each other. They can re-establish contact by whistle blasts or heading for the emergency rally point (see "Safety" below).

Pace tracking lane

The pace tracking lane is the next development in the tracker's training. The instructor chooses a piece of virgin ground, probably in a woodland area but not necessarily. He tapes off the left and right boundaries, leaving an untouched corridor a meter wide and not necessarily straight. The quarry (probably the instructor himself or his assistant) then walks the length of the corridor between the tapes. He then seals off the ends with tape.

The students then move down the boundaries of the corridor and record in their notebooks any observations relating to the passage of the quarry and the sign it has left. Or, if possible, the student walks down the side with the instructor and points with a stick to any sign and describes it and the deductions made from it. He tells the instructor whether the sign is conclusive or substantiating. He should be able to tell the direction of travel.

These corridors can be varied to introduce groups and men carrying equipment that brushes the vegetation.

Incident awareness stand

The stimulation of interest is often best achieved, especially with sophisticated youngsters and adults, by making the training relevant to realistic situations that they are likely to encounter or to which they can relate. Incident scenarios are an invaluable tool.

The trainer of trackers can use the scenes of incidents to great effect. Not only do they add realistic variety to the training but they engage the trainees' senses, deductive powers, and their imagination as they try to get into the character of the quarry.

Some of the scenarios that I have used in the past to stimulate the grey matter of a group are:

- A road traffic accident where somebody is missing
- A mountaineering search
- A poaching incident
- A fisherman missing from the river bank
- A kidnapping
- The reconstruction of a crime from the sign left on the ground, or in a room, is a good exercise for our deductive faculties, but the setter of the stage should have a very clear idea of the story he means to convey by the sign
- And, of course, any number of military and counter-terrorist scenarios, such as the site of an ambush or an attack, after which the tracker team is detailed to locate the fleeing enemy

Incident awareness lane exercise

The incident awareness lane is a development of the previous exercise that puts even more pressure upon the deductive powers of the students. The following is the administrative detail required to set one of these up (see Fig. 51).

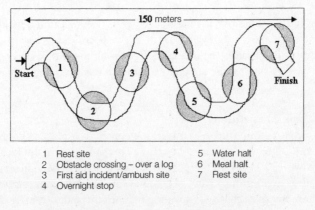

1	Rest site	5	Water halt
2	Obstacle crossing – over a log	6	Meal halt
3	First aid incident/ambush site	7	Rest site
4	Overnight stop		

Fig. 51. Layout of an incident awareness lane

The lane should be about 150 meters long; over its length the student should be able to identify about six sites. Each site should have sign that indicates an activity. The sites are to each side of the lane so that the students can observe them without fouling the sign for the next group. The following is a list of sites with the appropriate sign to be left by the instructor:

- Rest site—cigarettes, rucksack scuff marks on trees against which they have been leaned, areas where four people have sat, complete with heel prints where they have been resting, urination site
- Meal halt—food remains, some of the same points as for the rest site
- Water replenishment site—footprints meandering around the area, sign where water bottles have been placed down, transfer of water onto other areas
- Overnight stop—four sleeping areas, knife cuts in the vegetation, latrine area, buried waste area, fire site
- Ambush site—vegetation bent over to produce arcs of fire, vegetation used to produce camouflage, flattened areas where they have lain
- First aid incident—after an obstacle such as a steep slope or a large tree across the track that had to be negotiated, there should be sign where a man has slipped and fallen and then limped away, sat down, and then been bandaged by a medic, some discardables from the medic pack

It should be noted that if judging the age of the sign in the incident awareness lane exercise is one of the aspects being tested, the instructor must set up the incident scenes with this in mind to ensure that the sign and its age are compatible with what is being depicted.

Tracking competition

It is often a fitting finale to a tracking course to run a competition. The most effective way to organize the competition is in the form of what we call in the military a round robin, where the students go round in small groups from event to event. The layout is important because the subjects are arranged in order of difficulty (see Fig. 52). The elements I tend to include are:

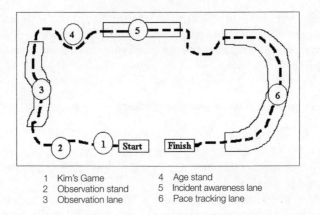

1	Kim's Game	4	Age stand
2	Observation stand	5	Incident awareness lane
3	Observation lane	6	Pace tracking lane

Fig. 52. Layout for a tracking competition (round robin)

- Kim's Game—see Chapter 6
- Observation stand—see page 200
- Observation lane—see page 202
- Age stand—judging the age of sign—see Chapter 14
- Incident awareness lane, deducing what happened at the site—see page 207
- Pace tracking lane—see page 206

Final exercise

The culmination to all this tracker training would be a tracking exercise, which is simply a group or an individual setting off as the quarry along a route set by the instructor. The quarry must follow the given route so that the instructor has control over the exercise. The tracker group then attempts to follow from the given start point, which will probably be an incident scenario.

I have taken part in an exercise such as this in the Malayan jungle. It proceeded for five days and culminated in the tracking team locating an enemy camp and then mounting an attack on the same. The first exercises should only be six or eight hours long and can be less ambitious, but to make them work the students' standard of tracking has to be of a fairly high level and the exercise needs to be well co-ordinated by the instructional team, who need good communications among themselves, the quarry, and the tracking team. To guarantee control, especially with an inexperienced group or over difficult terrain, one of the instructors can travel with the tracking team as an observer.

Some practicalities of training trackers

Safety—the emergency rally point (ERP)
To help you as an instructor keep control of the group during outdoor exercises and training, it is a good idea to instigate a procedure known as the ERP.

The chief instructor designates the ERP at the start of an outdoor activity. Only he can change it—and if he changes it during an activity, he is personally responsible for making everyone in the group aware of the location of the new ERP. It must be a point on the ground with which the group is familiar, such as the point where the transport dropped the group off, a gate in a field, a tent, or a house. The ERP is not selected from the map without confirming its physical presence.

The function of the ERP is that in an emergency or if groups become split, this is where they make for. If you have the manpower, one of the instructor team or an administrative person is detailed to man the ERP for the duration of the activity or until everyone is accounted for.

Group size
There is a limit to the number of people one instructor can train at various stages of the tracking syllabus. With many of the classroom lessons the group is only really limited by the classroom, but when we commence the practical exercises there are severe limitations. For instance, when following a trail (a track made up of sign laid for the purposes of training trackers) the maximum is three students. If there are any more, the crowding causes confusion and can obliterate the sign.

Stress/pressure
I have found that the people at the back of a group of trainees see more sign than the person actually doing the tracking. The explanation for this I firmly believe is that those at the back are not under any pressure and, as a result, are more relaxed. This

phenomenon of the learning process needs to be taken into account and employed beneficially by the instructor.

Stimulating interest for the younger student
Three simple means of giving practice and stimulating interest might be suggested. First, in town or country a small outdoor tracking ground could be carefully smoothed and different pieces of food left on it overnight. The next day the tracks that are almost certain to appear on the ground may be carefully examined. The food selected should be such as to tempt the birds and animals that are likely to frequent the locality.

Second, in the country in the winter there are many fields that are marked by the tracks of the stock and wildlife in them. Each individual can be given a different set of prints and told to trace the animal. This exercise should only be undertaken provided the group do not disturb the stock itself in any way and only with the permission of the livestock owner.

Third, students should be made aware that tracking does not necessarily mean following marks upon the ground. Birds can be tracked by their calls, their plumage, their flight pattern. Birds of prey can also be located by the bones and feathers of small birds and animals scattered below the trees where they nest.

Training techniques

I would like to emphasize the fact that even traditional trackers undergo training—trackers are not born, they are trained. Sometimes their training takes years and is very arduous. There is a great deal to be said for absorbing a subject over a long period, since it will then become a part of the person and the skills won't disappear after a short layoff.

Training has to be progressive, moving logically from subject to subject with breaks and revision periods designed into the program for consolidation. Then the subjects have to be amalgamated to produce a practical skill. These skills have to be tested under realistic but controlled conditions in order to validate the instruction. By laying out tracker training in this fashion we progress and meld the skills without drab repetition. The secret of success in tracker training is to secure and sustain interest by providing variety.

The following are some of the techniques I have used in the past with civilians.

Trail as opposed to track

I am using the word "trail" to designate a track that is made artificially, as opposed to the track that is made by the feet of an animal, human or otherwise. This is not the standard definition of the word, but I wish to distinguish between the tracking of an unwitting quarry and a designed tracking exercise.

In utilizing trails we work progressively from stage to stage and try to provide variety. The most elementary form of a trail is that made by scattering paper on the ground so that those behind can follow, that is to say a paperchase. A further definite stage is reached, however, by the laying of a wool trail. Odds and ends of wool or cloth are cut up into pieces 5 or 6 centimeters long and used in place of paper. There are several benefits to cloth or yarn: by using different colors separate trails can be laid for each individual running along more or less parallel lines and converging on a common point. The cloth can be placed on bushes as well as on the ground and be tied to branches or twigs overhead, thus training in all-around observation. When we come to tracking proper we will not always find all the sign on the ground, so practice in looking up as well as down is a good thing. Obviously, this sort of exercise is particularly appropriate for the younger student.

Progressive methods in this kind of trail can be utilized by scattering the material thickly at first, gradually reducing the number of pieces put down and increasing the interval between each. An important point to remember is that anything strange, say an early flower, can be brought to the notice of those following by laying a piece of cloth alongside it.

The next stage, as far as our progressive steps are concerned, is the laying of what is known as a nature trail. That is where the trail layer leaves indications. Either these indications can be to supplement the sign, such as turning over a leaf, placing an oak leaf on a holly bush, breaking a twig, or, by some pre-arranged convention between the trail layer and the following groups, they can indicate direction, for instance by tying small bunches of grass together, breaking a twig and laying it in a certain direction, or arranging piles of stones. Fig. 53 shows some examples of trail markers.

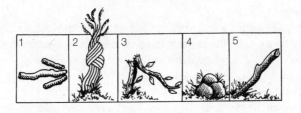

Fig. 53. Trail markers

The last stage is the introduction of sign proper and not contrived clues, such as those above. At first the signs should be made at frequent intervals and be large in size; then distances between each sign should be increased and their size decreased. As the skill level increases, deceptions can be incorporated and the tracking medium altered from easy mud and wet sand through grass and leaf-strewn woodland to rocky terrain.

In this last stage especially, anyone who is laying a trail to be followed would be wise to call in another instructor to see if he can follow it before setting the potential tracker on the job. When you lay a trail yourself, it seems quite easy to follow, but when you try to follow a trail laid by someone else it is not quite as easy. There is an obvious safety aspect for the adult laying such trails for young student trackers: the trail has got to be so designed that students don't get lost even if they lose the trail.

Age stands
Age stands are fully described in Chapter 14 and are a necessary part of any long-established tracker training unit because judgment of the age of sign is an indispensable skill in the tracker's armory.

Sandboxes
With the aid of sandboxes, the instructor can explain how the speed of the quarry, its weight, and any other characteristics affect the print.

So far I have touched upon the main stages that might be adopted in laying trails, but have not discussed variety. Here the instructor's imagination is the key factor in making any training interesting.

The young tracker
The following guidelines for young trackers should be noted by anyone with a responsibility for training young people:

- Leave a note of your route and the expected time of return
- Ensure you have some food with you—it is difficult for anyone to concentrate if they are hungry
- Dress sensibly, wear stout footwear and clothing that does not rustle when you move, and wear or carry a hat suitable to conditions
- Notice which way the wind is blowing and approach the area of suspected sign downwind
- When stalking move slowly, a few paces at a time; stop regularly and observe in all directions
- If accompanied, arrange a series of signals with your companions before you start—don't talk unless it is essential
- Make notes and sketches when it is appropriate on all that you see; it is not easy to remember later when you come to make your report
- Carry a good set of binoculars
- If you see the quarry, keep perfectly still. Don't try to get too close. Use your binoculars to see details.
- If the quarry moves away, don't try to follow too soon
- As a general rule, never touch or frighten away any young of the animal kingdom, if you are lucky enough to come across them. Admire from a distance and then move away very quietly.

- Keep an eye on the time; remember that someone will be worried if you are late
- Carry a whistle—if you get lost, blow it at regular intervals to attract attention
- Take all the items necessary for a successful and safe day's tracking—see below.

Equipment

The following suggested kit list will assist you to carry out a tracking task successfully, safely, and in relative comfort. The list will assist the beginner to be more efficient and to achieve better results when carrying out a tracking task. I use many of the items listed below and some that are not (reading glasses and a hearing aid!). The general rule for kit items is, "If it is of use, take it," but don't fall into the trap of dressing up like a Christmas tree. A good many trackers that I have had the privilege of being associated with have never heard of most of the items listed, never mind used them, and even if they had it wouldn't have made them any better trackers than they already were. There is no substitute for experience. Before wasting money on a lot of fancy kit, do some local area tracking to see if this is the hobby for you. Don't give up after a few hours: I have seen people struggling for days and then it just clicks. Remember, find an easy area to start with that has plenty of sign.

The kit list

Essentials:

- Day pack
- Suitable outdoor clothing
- Hat—woolly in winter; small brim in sunny or wet weather
- Map(s) protected in a plastic bag or map case
- Flashlight—medium size with a switch that can't be inadvertently put on
- Silva compass
- Long tweezers
- Notebook and pencil (rather than pen; keep these in a plastic bag)

- A set of lightweight waterproofs, jacket and trousers (if not already being worn)
- A short home-made flag, maximum length 0.75 meters
- Exact change for the telephone, or a phone card, or a mobile phone for use in emergencies (keep switched off during exercise)
- Binoculars—the ideal binoculars for watching wildlife areas is 7 × 50 or 8 × 40. Higher magnification binoculars are very difficult to hold still without a support, and you may want to use them in some pretty awkward positions. For a young person whose budget is tight, a pair of ex-military binoculars in good condition will suffice. These can be easily obtained from the many ex-military surplus stores.
- Magnifying glass
- Cold snacks, to last a day
- Thermos flask, with a hot drink
- Water bottle
- Tape measure
- Small personal medical kit (bandages, headache tablets, insect repellent etc.—ask the advice of your local pharmacist if in doubt)
- Small waterproof container of plaster of Paris and the kit required to make a plaster mold
- This book in a plastic bag
- Small penknife
- Whistle
- Watch

Optional items:
- Camera
- Tape recorder
- Hand-held GPS (check reception in area)
- Night viewing aids

Remember prior to departure:
- Inform someone of your intentions, including estimated time of return
- Lay out and check all the items you intend to take with you on your tracking task

SUMMARY

TRACKING EXERCISES AND LESSONS

The following are the main types of tracking exercises and instructional periods:

- Observation stand
- Observation lane
- Age stand
- Pace tracking exercise
- Pace tracking lane
- Incident awareness stand
- Incident awareness lane
- Tracking competition
- Final exercise

EQUIPMENT

Essentials

- Day pack
- Suitable outdoor clothing, including hat
- Map(s) protected in a plastic bag or map case
- Flashlight—medium size with a switch that can't be inadvertently put on
- Silva compass
- Long tweezers
- Notebook and pencil (rather than a pen; keep both in a plastic bag)
- A set of lightweight waterproofs, jacket and trousers (if not already being worn)
- A short home-made flag, maximum length 0.75 meters
- Exact change for the telephone, or a phone card, or a mobile phone for use in emergencies
- Binoculars—the ideal binoculars for watching wildlife areas is 7 × 50 or 8 × 40. Higher magnification binoculars are very difficult to hold still without a support, and you may want to use them in some pretty awkward positions. For a

young person whose budget is tight, a pair of ex-military binoculars in good condition will suffice. These can be easily obtained from the many ex-military surplus stores.

- Magnifying glass
- Cold snacks to last a day
- Thermos flask with a hot drink
- Water bottle
- Tape measure
- Small personal medical kit (containing bandages, headache tablets, insect repellent etc.—ask the advice of your local pharmacist if in doubt)
- Small waterproof container of plaster of Paris and the kit required to make a plaster mold
- This book in a plastic bag
- Small penknife
- Whistle
- Watch

Optional items
- Camera
- Tape recorder
- Hand-held GPS
- Night viewing aids

REMEMBER PRIOR TO DEPARTURE
- Inform someone of your intentions and return time
- Lay out and check all the items you intend to take with you on your tracking task

18

MILITARY TRACKING

Trackers in the military are used for two main purposes. The first is to gain information about the enemy and so provide useful intelligence to the commanders. The second is to locate the enemy and destroy him.

Tracking skills are also taught to many who will never become trackers, working on the principle that, if a soldier has a knowledge about how a tracker operates, it will help him evade a tracking team.

The intelligence gathering role
A visual tracker must realize that gaining information starts at the beginning of a pursuit and is confirmed time and time again throughout the task. Each individual piece of sign, whether it is direction, numbers or age, is telling the tracker something about the quarry. The information gained by the tracker may be of vital use later and affect decision-making. However, all information gathered during a pursuit task will give the tracker a better understanding of the quarry; with this knowledge he will be able to counter any moves the quarry may employ.

The tracker has to establish in which direction the quarry is heading and check the map for the best route. A calculated guess can help plot the quarry's route and, if the trail is lost, this will make it easier to find. The military tracker above all others has to get into the skin of his quarry—he has to think like the enemy, so he is able to anticipate what may be deadly moves.

All the time he has to be asking himself, "What would I do?" This will help him follow the track if it gets less obvious. There are only a few ways around an obstacle like rocks or fallen trees, and a trained eye will spot these places. The place that you would use to cross a river will probably be the one that the quarry used—that is, if it is unaware of your follow-up.

An enemy in a hurry will take the most direct route. It is possible to predict this and then, as the Rhodesian Selous Scouts did, place ambush teams forward. More recently, colleagues of mine advised an anti-poaching unit in Botswana to try this tactic against well-armed rhino poachers—with results fatal to the poachers.

The intelligence value of tracking is so important that the New Zealand SAS (probably the foremost military unit in tracking skills) dedicate a whole section of their tracking course to this subject, called Incident Awareness. The following is based upon my experiences serving with them.

Recognizing an incident site

The recognition of an incident site is a crucial feature because this is where information is gleaned and the track picture enhanced. Unfortunately, some sites are not obvious because of their size, their position, or the enemies' attempts to disguise them.

Aids to recognition of sites

Some techniques the military tracker employs to help him identify an incident site are:

- Anticipate incidents, for example be looking for the next camping site at about a suitable distance from the last one
- Note changes in direction due either to the enemy looping back, breaking off the track, or where pointers indicate a more abrupt change
- Be aware of localized increases in sign
- Watch for discardables such as food wrappers, indicating a meal stop
- Study areas where incidents are likely to happen, such as at water resupply points, where there are obstacles to be crossed, or where halts will be taken, such as at the top of steep climbs

Help in finding a lost track
A thorough search of possible incident sites is invaluable if the target sign has been lost.

Dangers of incident sites
If the enemy is alert to trackers, incident sites can be used to lure the tracking party into booby trapped localities or into a registered target for their support and indirect fire weapons.

The sequence of events
If the following procedure is used, nothing will be missed and time will not be wasted. The sequence is:

- When a potential incident site is identified move back and go into all-around defense
- Plan the search, which may include looping to determine the size, layout, entry, and exit points
- The tracker and his cover man conduct a systematic search and record all facts on a sketch. The sketch has to include as a minimum: north, entry and exit points, positions of all sign
- Depending upon the size of the incident area, the rest of the patrol can surround the perimeter or give cover from features outside the immediate area
- Briefly record the interpretations and brief the patrol commander or another tracking team if handing over
- If the incident warrants it, send a track report signal to the base
- Continue with the task

The type of information and the intelligence deductions drawn from it are covered in detail in Chapter 15.

Offensive action tasks
Special forces are usually trained in the arts of tracking. Their patrols are a lethal combination of the primordial skills of tracking and the most technically sophisticated techniques of directing a barrage of accurate, long-range fire power from ships, aircraft, or

artillery. The modern special forces patrol has become a very potent mix of the ancient and modern.

But even alone a special forces tracking team can inflict damage on an enemy out of all proportion to its size because of the element of surprise gained during the pursuit of an unwary or complacent enemy. The following case studies exemplify the use of trackers in an offensive mission.

In Malaysia in 1956 an Australian tracking patrol successfully followed and almost overtook a party of approximately fifteen CTs (communist terrorists) tracked for over 10 kilometers through jungle in 18 hours. The team of trackers consisted of two Australian trackers, one a dog handler; an Iban tracker (brought in from neighboring Borneo); and a local aborigine. Whenever the sign became warm, the Iban and the local aborigine tracker would tend to become frightened and suddenly lose the trail. When this occurred one or both of the Australians would take over the lead and continue the track. The team commander achieved outstanding results by exploiting the peculiar composition of his team.

In the same campaign in an area only 30 miles northwest of Kuala Lumpur the SAS were involved in a protracted search and destroy mission. The unit tracked down a group of CTs over a fourteen-week period. Sergeant Bob Turnbull was one of the extraordinary group of the SAS soldiers in the Malay campaign who became better at tracking than the Ibans. Others in this group were Sergeants Creighton and Hawkins. During one follow Turnbull tracked a four-man group for five days until he was able to close with them and kill them.

More recently, the South African Army employed Bushmen trackers in offensive follow-up operations into Namibia. These tracking units were so offensively organized that they had their own RPG 7 and mortar sections.

Evasion

The evasion skills of my tracker training in the SAS were often put to good use on the escape and evasion exercises that were a regular part of the training cycle. Being accustomed to what creates good sign makes it a fairly straightforward task to avoid leaving an obvious track of your passage through an area.

The importance of a knowledge of tracking to a soldier's survival, especially a soldier in an unconventional unit, is highlighted by the following. These are the standing orders for Rogers' Rangers, a unit that fought the French and Indians in the days when North America was still being contested. These orders, dated 1736, read as follows:

Standing Orders—Rogers' Rangers
Major Robert Rogers

Don't forget nothing.

Have your musket clean as a whistle, hatchet scoured, sixty rounds powder and ball, and be ready to march at a minute's warning.

When you're on the march, act the way you would if you was sneaking up on a deer—see the enemy first.

Tell the truth about what you see and what you do. There is an army depending on us for correct information. You can lie all you please when you tell other folks about the Rangers, but don't lie to a Ranger or officer.

Don't never take a chance you don't have to.

When we're on the march we march single file, far enough apart so one shot can't go through two men.

If we strike swamps, or soft ground, we spread out abreast, so it's hard to track us.

When we march, we keep moving till dark, so as to give the enemy the least possible chance at us.

When we camp, half the party stays awake, the other half sleeps.

If we take prisoners, we keep 'em separate till we have had time to examine them, so they can't cook up a story between 'em.

Don't ever march home the same way. Take a different route so you won't be ambushed.

No matter whether we travel in big parties or little ones, each party has to keep a scout twenty yards ahead, twenty yards on each flank, and twenty yards in the rear, so the main body can't be surprised and wiped out.

Every night you'll be told where to meet if surrounded by a superior force.

Don't sit down to eat without posting sentries.

Don't sleep beyond dawn. Dawn's when the French and Indians attack.

Don't cross a river by a regular ford.

If somebody's trailing you, make a circle, come back onto your own tracks, and ambush the folks that aim to ambush you.

Don't stand up when the enemy's coming against you. Kneel down, lie down, hide behind a tree.

Let the enemy come till he's almost close enough to touch. Then let him have it and jump out and finish him up with your hatchet.

The above may make graphic reading today but the awareness of the tracker's skills are implicit in many of the rules and were reiterated in more modern prose by the SAS so that they could evade and survive in the jungles of Malaya and Borneo. Their rules for "Lead Scouts and Jungle Soldiers" run to thirty points and mention sign and the tracker's skills many times, as you can see below.

1. Do not "signpost" your routes. Laid down tactics will determine whether all camp rubbish is to be buried or carried out.
2. Keep yourself fit, your weapon clean, and your equipment ready at all times.
3. Always move with stealth and never at such a speed that your presence in the area is telegraphed ahead of your visible distance.
4. Your life and the lives of others often depend on the intelligence and "info" that you gain and pass on. State clearly whether your information is fact, deduction, assumption, or an intelligent guess. Never lie or knowingly pass on false information.
5. Physical fitness is a personal responsibility, but even a fit and alert Scout can get tired. Never "bash on" when you are so tired that you find your concentration and alertness slipping.
6. Never look at the ground while moving forwards.
7. When faced with thick undergrowth, if possible go around. If you have to go through, weave your way under or over. Never cut or allow your pack or body to get caught up in the branches or vines and so cause sounds and movement at the tops of young trees.
8. Remember that the sound made by the rattle from poorly packed equipment, unnecessary talking above a whisper, a cough, or a broken stick will travel outwards in all directions. Don't alert and warn an enemy in the area of your presence and approach,

thus giving him time to come into the aim before you could possibly spot his movement.

9. When acting as a Lead Scout for a patrol, ensure that your cover man is always a tactical distance away from you.

10. Never forget your own "sign"-leaving tendency; ground sign, top sign, and the phantom twig snapper. If necessary detail tail-end Charlie to brush over and camouflage your tracks. Always consider the possibility of using deception tactics.

11. Always vary your route and timings, out and back from all patrols, unless you want to be ambushed.

12. Patrol with, visit with, eat with, sit with, and sleep with your weapon at all times. Never let it out of your sight or farther than arm's length away from you.

13. "Belt order" will contain your survival equipment, together with other laid-down items. Wear your belt order at all times and have it at arm's length while asleep.

14. Always remember that as the Lead Scout, it is your responsibility to ensure that you do not lead your patrol into the killing zone of an enemy ambush. Make use of the "listening halts." Develop all your senses to a high pitch and if you ever become suspicious of the area ahead, stop the patrol and have a "listening halt" or go forward and check it out with your cover man. Look through, not at, the vegetation and undergrowth to the second or third layer.

15. Observe and become familiar with the natural sights and smells of the insect world, the animal kingdom, the bird life, and all forms of vegetation in your area of operations. Be alert to any sign that indicates man's presence in the area.

16. Once on patrol "switch on" and stay "switched on" for the complete duration of the patrol. Move with stealth and with every man spaced out at the correct tactical distance; cross all obstacles tactically and ensure that all halts—the smoke halt, the meal halt, the water halt, the listening halt, the radio comms halt, the navigational check halt, and the overnight bivouac halt—are carried out in a tactical manner.

17. Ensure that you are familiar with and well practiced in all RV (rendezvous) drills and procedures.

18. Approximately 100 yards before stopping for a meal halt, leave a drop-off man to check rear. This could be the second Scout. Before commencing the meal halt, check up to 100 yards out-

wards and forwards of area to ensure you are not beside an enemy location. This would be the Lead Scout's job. Front, rear, and all-around security must always be maintained both while on the move and during all halts.

19. Well-disciplined and immediate reactions on contact with or on coming under fire from the enemy can often result in a routed foe.

20. Always be aware of the patrol's mission, be familiar and well practiced in all contact drills. On occasion it may be necessary to avoid contact and let the enemy go by, then report his presence and activities rather than getting involved in a "fire fight."

21. On all suspicious sights, sounds, and smells, react as the wild animal does and remain perfectly still. If an enemy appears and moves across your front, there is a very good chance that he will not see you. If the enemy appears to be walking towards you, slowly and silently go down on one knee, at the same time bring your weapon into the shoulder aimed at the approaching sound, or carry out Immediate Action drills.

22. Always make positive identification before shooting.

23. If possible, always let the first members of an enemy patrol pass you by, then shoot the third or fourth man. Here again, laid down drills will dictate which member of your patrol will spring the ambush. Remember that in the heat of battle, particularly with today's automatic weapons, the tendency is to fire high, often missing the target altogether. *Aim low and shoot to kill.*

24. When operating with an SAS patrol, after the evening meal move on until just before dark, then carry out the "Basha up" drill (the overnight stop). Always ensure that you are packed and ready to move before first light. Make a final check of the area on first light, then move off to the breakfast halt.

25. When camping, selection of the site will be in such a place that a surprise night attack would be impossible. Use hammocks for camps on near vertical slopes or crawl into the center of thick, noise-making vegetation. No lights, no noise, no cooking; all unused equipment to be placed in containers.

26. Again, when operating as an information-gathering patrol, avoid all contact with the enemy. The deeper you get into his secure areas the more relaxed he becomes and so the easier for you to observe and gain intelligence of his movements and activities.

Do not leave tracks or signs to tell him that you are in his area. Do not use tracks or trails—loop them.

27. You will be required to make decisions that will influence the lives of other people. Learn quickly to make the correct decision and do not be afraid to express your views. Do not let yourself be talked out of your beliefs.

28. Learn all you can of the enemy in your area: his habits, tactics, customs, and practices. Always keep an open mind to new learning—and never become so overconfident that you think you know it all, as often different areas and enemy personnel will present completely different sets of tactics and drills.

29. Make use of all up-to-date intelligence information and briefings. In particular the "Going Maps" i.e. tracks, maps, both animal and human, wild fruit trees and vegetable growing areas, the good fishing and game trapping areas, old enemy campsites, ambush positions, track sitings, and known courier routes.

30. It has happened that an enemy has ambushed and killed twice in the same location using the same tactics. Don't let this happen to you. Read and take note of all "Contact Reports" and "Lessons Learned" reports.

The maxim for the modern soldier is:

> *Once on patrol*
> *Switch on*
> *Stay switched on.*
> *Remember*
> *There is always someone ready*
> *To switch you off*
> *PERMANENTLY!*

The next chapter is closely associated with the military world, but because it is such a specialist subject I have set aside a separate chapter for a description of the use of dogs in tracking.

SUMMARY

INCIDENT AWARENESS

Aids to recognition of sites
- Anticipate incidents
- Changes in direction
- Localized increases in sign
- Discardables
- Study areas where incidents are likely to happen

Help in finding a lost track
A thorough search of possible incident sites is invaluable if the target sign has been lost.

Dangers of incident sites
If the enemy is alert to trackers, incident sites can be used to lure the tracking party into booby traps or into a registered target for their support and indirect fire weapons.

The sequence of events at incident sites
- When a potential incident site is identified move back and go into all-around defense
- Plan the search, which may include looping to determine the size, layout, entry, and exit points
- The tracker and his cover man conduct a systematic search and record all facts on a sketch—the sketch has to include as a minimum: north, entry and exit points, position of all sign
- Depending on the size of the incident area, the rest of the patrol can surround the perimeter or give cover from features outside the immediate area
- Briefly record the interpretations and brief the patrol commander or another tracking team if handing over
- If the incident warrants it, send a track report signal to the base
- Continue with the task

19

DOGS AND TRACKING

This subject has two diametrically opposed facets in the military context. One is the employment of tracker dogs by a tracking team; the other is the study of the techniques of evading a tracker dog and its team.

The employment of tracker dog teams dates back to ancient times but there are still occasions when they are of great benefit to police and also to the military. For instance, in the early 1960s the British Army employed tracker dogs in conjunction with visual trackers to great effect in follow-up operations against the rebels in Brunei.

I will first describe how a scent tracker, a dog, can be a great asset to the visual tracker team before going on to describe the evasion techniques employed by special forces to combat tracker teams.

Scent tracking—an illustration
This is a policeman's account of a pursuit, which exemplifies how visual trackers and scent trackers can become a formidable pursuit combination.

After going over fairly easy ground for 10 or 12 miles we got into a dry, stony district, where the runaway, knowing he would be tracked, had jumped from rock to rock—a basic deception tactic. The visual tracker was still able to follow the track, which consisted of scratch marks on the rocks and small amounts of transferred material.

When we came to a camp of a work party the track was fouled and the visual tracker handed over to the dog handler. The dog ran around the camp and indicated that the fugitive had left in a particular direction.

The visual tracker confirmed that the ground sign was a crude deception—the runaway had changed his boots in the camp and had at this point been walking backwards—another deception tactic that indicates the quarry was still aware that he had a pursuit team following him. Very soon it was noticed that the quarry had got tired of wearing strange boots and had started to wear his own again.

After many miles we came to a river; the footprints led straight on into the water. We put the dog across but he didn't find any scent on the far side. He swam back again and found scent of the quarry heading downstream near the river bank. We followed it along the river bank for 3 miles where the quarry had turned on to a path along which a herd of cattle had recently passed.

The man had obviously nipped in ahead of the herd hoping that they would obliterate his sign, which in fact they did but the dog had no such problem and when the man's route parted company with that of the cattle the dog barely paused—the visual tracker then confirmed the prints as being those of our target and we carried on.

The visual tracker then reported that the sign was very fresh where earth kicked up was damper than the surrounding ground and the edges of the track were sharp, and not rounded over from the sun or wind. We proceeded cautiously and were able to successfully terminate the pursuit.

It is this same combination of man and dog that is so effectively used by the mountain search and rescue teams.

The dog
Despite long domestication, the dog retains most of the characteristics found in its wild relatives. Primitive man was quick to spot the dog's advantageous traits and to use them to help in hunting and guarding, although there is a recent theory suggesting that about 100,000 years ago the wolf, the forerunner of the domesticated dog,

actually adopted man as a means of easy food by scavenging around his leftovers. Either way, modern mankind has adapted the dog's traits to aid in the maintenance of law and order, to support search and rescue, and to assist the visually and aurally impaired.

When properly trained and managed, dogs can be used to pursue a man efficiently for up to eight hours, depending on terrain and climate, although dogs used in relays can go on much longer than this. Big dogs when fresh can run at speeds between 30 and 40 miles an hour over a distance of about 100 meters, but slow quickly after that. They can maintain a steady 8 to 10 miles per hour for several hours but, if employed in long pursuits, they are usually limited by the speed of the handler. Thus the average speed is about 4 miles per hour.

The dog is naturally inquisitive. In many cases its reactions have to be interpreted by a human and herein lies a weakness. The handler may misinterpret or ignore a dog's reaction.

From the shape and structure of the dog's eye came a theory that the dog is short-sighted and sees only in black and white. We know it has difficulty in discerning static objects at a distance of more than 50 meters. However, it has great powers of spotting movement at considerable distances. There is no evidence that a dog's night vision is any better than a human's.

The dog has much more sensitive hearing than a human. It has a greater power of locating the source of a sound and can hear noises of a much higher frequency than those detected by man.

The scent faculty

The dog's sense of smell is vastly superior to a human's—estimated at seven to nine hundred times more acute. It can detect minute traces of substances or their vapor in the air, on the ground, or in contact with objects. Even minor disturbances of the surface of the ground or floor can be sensed by virtue of the alteration of the scent picture around those disturbances.

It is not unreasonable to think in terms of a scent picture for a dog. A dog thinks in smells, another world from a human's. Whatever happens, a dog seems to appreciate all the odorous characteristics in an environment. We can analyze the scent picture in two basic ways: air scent and ground scent, or we can be more specific and say that it is composed of:

- Objects themselves—animate or inanimate
- Chemicals associated with the objects—deodorants and toiletries on a person, oil on a gun, polish on shoes
- Human smells associated with inanimate objects thrown away or hidden—discardables
- Disturbances of the environment around an object or caused by its passage, such as freshly dug earth, disturbed dust, broken vegetation, smells around hides, or vegetation crushed and disturbed by footfalls

The factors affecting the scent picture

Being of a particulate and volatile nature, scent is subject to chemical decay. The first factor adversely affecting the scent picture is therefore the passage of time. The longer the interval between the track being laid and the follow-up, the weaker the smell. Other factors, however, accelerate or retard the decay of the scent:

- Wind may dissipate scent
- Heavy rain or running water may wash it away
- Strong sunlight will speed evaporation of the scent
- Frozen ground tends to hold scent and release it gradually when it thaws
- A soft warming wind or gentle sunlight will enhance the scent picture by drawing out smells from the environment
- Factors may combine to provide conditions for a good scent picture, for example at night when the warm ground gives off its scent into a cool atmosphere, which tends to retain any scent

Tracker dogs

Dogs are employed to find the line of the quarry's progress on foot. They work mostly from ground scent, but after the passage of time they may follow the evaporating scent given off in the air. Therefore the visual tracker, working in conjunction with a scent tracker, should not be misled by the tracker dog's seemingly erratic progress and the fact that its head is lifted as it moves.

No memory key such as sniffing clothing belonging to the quarry is needed. A handler will experimentally cast a dog around an area until he observes his dog following a particular line. The dog has been trained to follow any distinct track.

Scent trails

Tracker dogs are taught to follow a certain scent trail. These are strongest in soft going or when the quarry has moved through long grass or vegetation. The scent trail is considerably easier to follow when moving into the wind. The scent trails remain for quite some time, evaporating soonest from hard surfaces within six to eight hours.

Masking scent

There are no guaranteed substances available to stop a tracker dog from following a scent. Successful evasion of dogs depends on the intelligent use of dog evasion techniques and any improvisations that can be utilized to put the tracker dog and his handler off the pursuit.

Some chemicals may destroy scent, but if applied they will have characteristic telltale odors of their own. What definitely will not happen is a smell being masked by the application of another. Anything added, such as anise, just becomes another part of the scent picture to a dog and is a giveaway of human presence and intent to deceive.

Also, if a human covers himself in animal excrement, he just smells, to a dog, like a human covered in animal excrement—the key sign is the human smell, which is unchanged.

Scent checks

There are no guaranteed scent checks to throw a tracker dog off a human scent. Three categories of substances are used or have been developed to confuse a dog:

- Attractants: This is meant to resemble the scent of a bitch. The obvious reasoning behind this is that the dog would prefer to follow this rather than the human scent. The down side to the use of this type of substance is that if any should inadvertently get onto the soldier's clothing it will only make the pursuit easier. Also this scent is powerful. The handler will be able to smell it and realize what has happened—by casting around the handler will be able to continue the track. Then, too, the tracker dog may be a bitch!

- Repellants: These are primarily designed to put dogs off bitches in heat. They are disagreeable smells, but they will not deter a highly trained dog that is in good working form.
- Decoys: These are designed to be more powerful than the human smell. The idea is for the quarry to drag this for a little distance before discarding it. The hope is that the dog will lose the quarry's scent in the decoy smell and that if a well-chosen discard point has been made, the scent trail will be broken and lost.

Performance levels

Dogs are trained to different standards and are temperamentally very different. The normal teaching methods for dogs is the reward system, where they are kept hungry and rewarded with food when they find their quarry.

Some dog breeds are particularly suited to this type of work, such as the typical hound breeds and gun dogs, but some are less enthusiastic than others. I have worked with dogs that lost interest after only half an hour.

Tracker dog teams

Military tracker dog teams normally consist of two or more dogs, plus a visual tracker, snipers, and good communications, usually ground to air. Depending on the context of the operation, a tracker team can be placed onto a scent trail very quickly by helicopter and replaced by fresh teams working in relays.

A variation of the employment of dogs in a tracking-related scenario is their use in searches for survivors of earthquakes, avalanches, and during mountain rescue operations. These dogs can be trained to work on or off the lead and either to sit in the area of the casualty when it is located or to return to the handler and sit in front of him as an indication that the dog has located a body.

Tracker dog evasion

This is first and foremost a military skill that a special forces' patrol (and in this case I mean a long-range raiding or reconnaissance patrol working deep in enemy territory) needs to study if the intelligence indicates the enemy will be deploying tracker dog teams in their search and destroy missions.

Evasion techniques
The aim of the evading special forces soldier is to:

• Delay the pursuit
• Break the scent trail

He is taught that the recommended tactics for delaying are:

• Crossing obstacles—it takes twice as long for the dog and handler
  to cross
• Moving with the wind, not into it—the scent will be blowing
  away from the pursuit and will be much harder to follow
• Avoid changing direction at obvious places. For example, instead
  of following a route over a mountain pass, turn off before the pass
  and contour around the hillside, or turn off and change direction
  before a track junction rather than at the junction
• Laying false tracks and backtrack
• Using streams and hard surfaces such as rocky ground, roads, railway lines, fences, and dry stone walls—the scent will disappear
  more quickly from these, particularly in sunlight
• Mingling his scent with recent human scent, such as moving
  down a path or road that has recently been used by locals for a few
  hundred meters if tactics permit—animal smells or droppings can
  also assist but are not as effective as human scents

For breaking the scent trail the special forces soldier is taught:

• Gain time in order to allow the scent to become faint due to
  evaporation
• Use streams to good effect by laying false trails immediately
  upwind of the entry point, and then by moving downstream and
  downwind; then if possible exit onto rocks or any other hard
  surfaces
• If the situation permits march the last mile or so along hard surfaces or in water
• He should stop and hide as near first light as possible, thus per-
  mitting the day heat to weaken and eventually disperse his scent
• The only known, totally effective scent-breaking method used by
  evading troops was to ride on an animal or bicycle

SUMMARY

SCENT TRACKING
There are air scents and ground scents that come from:

- Objects themselves—animate or inanimate
- Chemicals associated with the objects—deodorants and toiletries on a person, oil on a gun, polish on shoes
- Human smells associated with inanimate objects thrown away or hidden—discardables
- Disturbances of the environment around an object or caused by its passage, such as freshly dug earth, disturbed dust, broken vegetation, smells around hides, or vegetation crushed and disturbed by footfalls

FACTORS AFFECTING THE SCENT PICTURE
- Wind may dissipate scent
- Heavy rain or running water may wash it away
- Strong sunlight speeds evaporation of the scent
- Frozen ground tends to hold scent and release it gradually when it thaws
- A soft warming wind or gentle sunlight will enhance the scent picture by drawing out smells from the environment
- Factors may combine to provide conditions for a good scent picture

SCENT CHECKS
There are no guaranteed scent checks to throw a tracker dog off a human scent, but three categories of substances are used to confuse a dog:

- Attractants
- Repellants
- Decoys

TRACKER DOG EVASION TECHNIQUES
The aim is to:

- Delay the pursuit
- Break the scent trail

Tactics for delaying are:

- Crossing obstacles
- Moving with the wind
- Avoid changing direction at obvious places
- Laying false tracks and back track
- Use of streams and hard surfaces such as rocky ground
- Mingling your scent with other recent human scent

Tactics for breaking the scent trail are:

- Gain time
- Use streams
- Use hard surfaces
- Stop and hide at first light
- The only known, totally effective scent-breaking method used by evading troops was to ride on an animal or bicycle

20

MAP-READING

Equipment
This chapter assumes that the reader is using a Silva, or Silva-type compass. From a tracker's point of view I have found that the best types of map to use for tracking are the different series of the Ordnance Survey. The smallest scale that is of any real use is 1:50000. Ordnance Survey maps with larger scales contain proportionally more detail. Depending on the area and speed with which you are moving, you can decide which map is the most appropriate, taking into account the difficulties of handling many large scale maps if you are moving rapidly over an area. Other countries produce similar quality maps if you are working abroad.

I have been asked why map-reading and compass bearings are important when one can use modern technology (SatNav, etc.). My answer is another question: What happens when your technology fails? Your skills will be essential to survival.

The uses of map-reading to a tracker team
I deliberately left out map-reading as a quality of a tracker in Chapter 5 because many of the world's best tracking groups have probably never seen a map, let alone know how to read one. But, having said that it is not a necessity, I still maintain that it is a great adjunct to a tracker's skill set for the following reasons:

• Selection of the quarry's likely route
• Location of your own position

- Prediction of the quarry's actions
- Collating the information and intelligence from other trackers or other pursuits
- Planning pre-emptive operations based on tracking information and intelligence

Map-reading subjects and skills

The following subjects and skills have been selected as being of particular relevance to a tracker. Map-reading and navigation are a huge subject. Therefore, the following critical selection provides the student of tracking with subjects he needs to understand and skills he must master to track over unfamiliar terrain.

- Conventional symbols and other information contained in the map's margins
- Features of the compass
- Setting the map
- Measuring distances
- Using grid references
- Understanding the different north points
- Converting bearings from grid to magnetic and vice versa
- Taking bearings from the map and assessing your direction of travel
- Plotting position by resection
- Estimating distance covered—speed

Conventional symbols and other margin information

The most important skill in map-reading is to be able to "read" the map. A good map-reader can look at the map and immediately start to form a mental picture of the ground. This takes time and practice but is a skill that can be learned by all with time and patience. The secret to this technique is the interpretation of the signs and symbols used on the map, especially the contour lines that help to visualize the relief of the ground.

Maps are used everywhere in daily life. There are many different types of map. You will have used a road map from a garage, or a map of the subway, or a street plan of your home town. Each map type is designed for a particular purpose but they all are two-dimensional representations of the real world. They convey information to the reader via the symbols they use. The key to these symbols is always on the map's margins, along with other essential information such as the scale and the date of publication. See Fig. 56 on page 244 for examples of legends that show the symbols and their meaning.

Features of the compass

The Silva compass itself (Fig. 54) is usually mounted at one end of a transparent plastic plate, measuring approximately 12 cm by 6 cm, which will have a direction of travel arrow—usually luminous. Incorporated within this base plate you may find a magnifying lens. The short side away from the compass is beveled. Along the sides of the base plate are various measures, and the short end away from the compass is usually designed as one of a set of romers (see Using Grid References below).

The compass housing rotates and on this rotating bezel are the fixed calibrated compass points. The orienteering or Silva-type compass is calibrated either in degrees or, for the military, in mils—this system need not concern the civilian tracker. The bottom of the

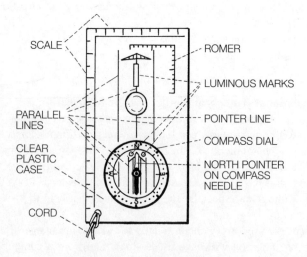

Fig. 54. The Silva compass

compass plate is marked with a series of lines running parallel to the north-south calibration and marked with a north arrow. The compass needle, the north half of which is red with a luminous tip, swings freely within this housing.

Setting the map

By setting, or orientating, the map we mean holding it in such a way that the details on the map correspond to the features on the ground.

There are two ways to set a map: the inspection method and the compass method.

The inspection method

This is the easiest way but you must have some idea of where you are on the ground. If you are standing on a straight section of road with a road junction either side of you and sign posts, line up the road on your map with the road you are standing on, making sure the map is pointing in the right direction with reference to the locations indicated on the sign posts. If you are not on a road, another linear feature will serve the same purpose. Or you may have to find prominent features on the ground that you can identify on your map, such as a church, bridge, crossroads, river, or stream junction. By identifying features on the ground and on your map you will be able to move your map so that it corresponds to the lie of the land. This is orientating or setting your map by features recognized both on the ground and on the map.

The compass method

This is done by holding the map so that the north of the grid lines of the map are pointing to the north. To effect this, one has to take into account the magnetic variation. Using a Silva-type compass, set the magnetic variation on the direction of travel line (see Taking Bearings below and the Different North Points). Then place the compass on the map so that the direction of travel arrow coincides with the north direction of the grid lines. Then rotate the map with the compass laid on top of it until the compass needle coincides with the north pointer of the parallel lines (see Fig. 55). The map is then set.

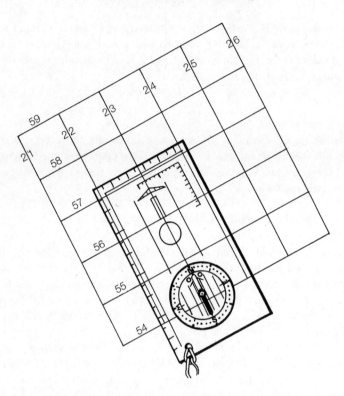

Fig. 55. Setting a map by the compass method

Measuring distances

It is important that you should be able to estimate and measure distances from your map. If you are moving across country, you don't want to miss your objective because you have miscalculated the distance and time it takes to get there.

Scale is the relationship between the size of your map and the area of ground it depicts. Scale is determined by the number of times the map is smaller than the area of ground it depicts. The scale shows you the direct relationship in terms of distance between map and ground. By looking at the scale on the map you can tell how many centimeters on the ground are represented by one centimeter on the map. The standard Ordnance Survey map has a scale of 1:50000. If you walk 50,000 centimeters (500 meters) you will have covered one centimeter on the 1:50000 scale map.

Check the scale of your map and ensure that you know what size the grid squares are (see Using Grid References below). On most maps you will find that the grid squares are one kilometer square, each side being 1000 meters in length. Therefore the distance from corner to corner is for approximate calculations 1.5 kilometers.

Most maps will have a scale bar marked along one edge of the map. The easiest method of measuring a straight line distance is to take a strip of paper and mark the two points between which you want the distance on the paper, and then read off the distance on the scale bar. To measure the distance along a road or river that winds about, simply consider the road to be a number of straight sections. Lay a piece of paper along the first leg and pencil in the start and finish of this leg, then starting at the finish point of the first leg, pencil in the start for the second leg, and so on until the total distance is marked out along the edge of the piece of paper. Measure this on the scale bar to find the distance on the ground.

Using grid references

A grid is a series of equally spaced, parallel, numbered lines superimposed on the map detail, both vertically and horizontally, to produce a pattern of squares. By the use of this pattern of squares it is possible to give a unique numerical description of a position. This is known as the grid reference. To be absolutely accurate it is an alphanumeric description because a full grid reference is prefixed by two letters that the Ordnance Survey has allocated to it to distinguish the number from where it will repeat itself elsewhere in the country.

To be able to give and apply grid references it is necessary to understand eastings and northings. The eastings are the vertical lines of the grid system, running north to south on maps and numbered from left to right (east). Northings are the horizontal lines of the grid system running west to east and numbered from the bottom to the top (north).

A four-figure grid refers to one complete grid square. It is defined by the lines that cross at the bottom left-hand corner of the grid square—the southwest corner. In Fig. 56 the four-figure grid of the square with the X is grid reference 2257. A four-figure grid

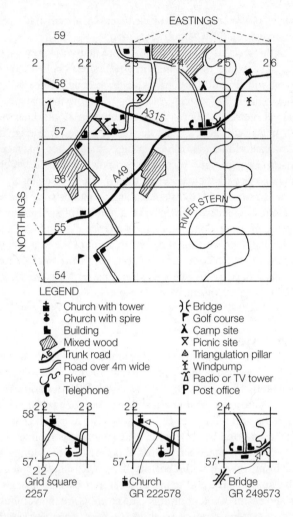

Fig. 56. Sketch illustrating the use of grid references

reference is made up from the two digit eastings, followed by the two digit northings. Easting 22 and northing 57 together give the grid reference 2257, which defines the grid square with the cross in it. Use this system when you want to refer to an area contained within a grid square on your map or when there is only one object or feature of the same type within the grid square, for example, the church with a tower in grid square 2257 and the bridge in grid square 2457.

It is essential to remember that when giving or reading a grid reference we always put the eastings first, followed by the northings. There are many ways to remember this such as "E" comes before "N," or that you go across the map for the eastings and up the map for the northings; therefore, "You go through the door before you go up the stairs."

Look again at grid square 2257 with the X in it; you will see that there are two churches, one with a tower and one with a spire. To identify either of these churches you would have to give a further description or, alternatively, you can identify your church by giving a six-figure grid reference.

This refers to one point on the map and it is accurate to within one hundred meters. The grid reference of the church with the tower in grid square 2257 would be 222578 and the bridge in grid square 2457 would be 249573. The two extra numbers in the six-figure grid reference are the third and sixth figures. These extra numbers represent tenths of the grid square. The grid square is divided into tenths, both across and up the square. You then judge how many tenths across and how many tenths up that the feature is. In grid square 2257 look at the location of the church with the tower in the northwest corner. The easting is 22 plus 2 tenths, giving 222, the northing is 57 plus 8 tenths, making 578. This gives a full six-figure grid reference of 222578.

A device called a romer, which has a right angle marked in tenths for both the vertical and horizontal axis, enables you to give a six figure grid reference at a glance (see Fig. 57). Simply place the corner of the romer on the feature and read off the third and sixth figure for easting and northings. Silva-type compasses have a built-in romer that cuts out the estimation in giving or plotting a six-figure grid reference. Two features of romers need noting. The first is that they are calibrated for specific scales and therefore you have to use the correct one. Secondly, if the point falls between two marks, always take the lower number, not the nearest number. This is because the grid reference as pointed out with a four-figure grid reference refers to the southwest corner of the particular square you are describing.

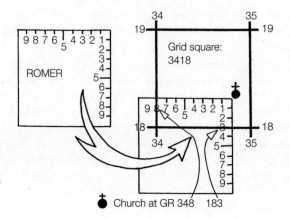

Fig. 57. The use of a romer

Remember, with a six-figure grid reference, first give all three figures across, the eastings, before you give the northings.

The different north points

There are three norths indicated on Ordnance Survey maps. They are:

- True North
- Magnetic North
- Grid North

True North is the direction of the North Pole and is shown by the lines of longitude on a map or chart.

Magnetic North is the direction in which a freely suspended compass needle points and because of the physical characteristics of the earth it varies annually and by different amounts in different regions. All this information will be written in the margins of the large scale maps that you use as a tracker.

Grid North is the direction of the grid lines on the map. This is different from True North because the grid lines on a flat map cannot geometrically fit identically to the lines of latitude and longitude of the curved surface of the earth.

Converting bearings

The bearing you take off a map is a grid bearing, whereas the one shown by your compass is a magnetic bearing. Therefore you need a system to be able to convert from one to the other.

The method is to check the information on the map about the magnetic variation (whether it is east or west of grid north), its annual rate of change for the area, and the date of publication of the map. From these facts you can work out the magnetic variation today.

A way to remember which way the conversion goes from magnetic to grid bearings is:

> From Mag to Grid Get Rid
> From Grid to Mag Add

Note: This rhyme only applies if Magnetic North is to the east of Grid North; otherwise the rule is reversed. But for the most part, in Britain the rhyme applies.

Taking bearings from the map and assessing your direction of travel

Using an orienteering-type compass, line up the edge of the compass base plate on the objects between which you want the bearing. Ensure that the direction of travel arrow is pointing in the appropriate direction—that is normally from where you are to where you want to go (Fig. 58). Rotate the compass housing until the parallel lines in the base of the housing are parallel with and, in the same direction as, the north-south grid lines of the map.

This is the grid bearing between the two points. Before you can use the compass to assess your direction of travel you have to adjust this for the magnetic variation (see above).

When you have rotated the compass housing so that the reading against the direction of travel arrow takes into account the magnetic variation, usually by adding several degrees in Britain, you now have the magnetic bearing set on your compass.

Your intended direction of travel is found by holding the compass horizontally (so that the compass needle is free to swing) and by moving it around until the north of the compass needle is superim-

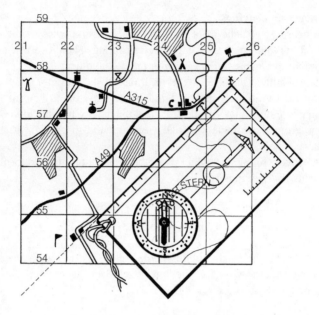

Fig. 58. Taking a bearing from a map

posed over the north pointer of the parallel lines in the base of the compass housing.

Plotting position by resection

If you are unsure of your position, you can plot it accurately on the map by using resection. Basically all you have to do is locate two objects or features on the ground that you can identify on the map, take bearings visually to them from where you are, convert these magnetic bearings to grid bearings, plot the two bearings on the map. Where the lines cross is your position.

To find a bearing from you to a feature simply point the direction of travel arrow at the object and then, holding the compass horizontally, rotate the compass housing until the north pointer on the housing base is under the compass needle. Remember this is a magnetic bearing and needs to be converted before putting on the map.

Estimating distance covered—speed

As well as being able to use the above-mentioned skills, you should take time to consider how far you are able to move in different types of country and weather conditions. You can estimate this by knowing what your average pace is for the various conditions. For example, walking on a flat road you may cover 4 miles per hour. Therefore if you have been walking for 45 minutes you will have covered 3 miles. Another way is to count your paces—pacing. If you know how many paces you take to cover 100 meters, then it is quite easy to work out the distance you have covered. The best way to do this is to measure your pace over a known 100-meter distance counting every time your right foot touches the ground. Do this walking, then again running, and note the difference. You will find a difference going up or down hill and in different terrain and weather conditions. As a basic guide I average about 64 paces per 100 meters walking and 40 to 45 when running. In the time it takes to walk 200 meters on the flat you could climb a 25-meter slope, cover 150 meters through primary forest, or travel 50 meters through thick undergrowth. With experience you will be able to make a good informed estimate of the distance you have traveled.

As I mentioned earlier, map-reading can never be considered a prerequisite for tracking, but if you intend to track anywhere other than your own area it is an important skill. Not only does it make the relaying of information easier, but it adds interest and can be essential for safety in remoter areas.

SUMMARY

EQUIPMENT
- Silva or Silva-type compass
- Ordnance Survey map (1:50000) or map of similar quality

USES OF MAP-READING TO A TRACKER TEAM
- Selection of the quarry's likely route
- Location of your own position
- Prediction of quarry's actions
- Collating information and intelligence from other trackers or other pursuits
- Planning pre-emptive operations based on tracking information and intelligence

MAP-READING SUBJECTS AND SKILLS
- Conventional symbols and other information in margins
- Features of the compass
- Setting the map: by inspection method; by compass method
- Measuring distances
- Using grid references
- Understanding the different north points: True North, Magnetic North, Grid North
- Taking bearings from the map and assessing your direction of travel
- Plotting position by resection
- Estimating distance covered and speed of travel

21

HUMAN PRINTS

A breakdown description of a bare footprint will enable a tracker to describe fully what he has seen without omitting any detail—he will be able to extract from the print the maximum amount of information. We then move on logically to a full description of how a tracker studies a print made by a quarry wearing footwear. The next stage is to analyze the walking action to see how a track—that is, a series of prints—is produced. The chapter concludes with what can be deduced from these detailed observations by noting what causes peculiarities in a print or a track.

Bare footprints
To find some reference point the footprint is divided as in Fig. 59. There is a fixed axis and a line at right angles to this. The axis of the foot is a line that passes through the heel to the center of the big toe. From this axis the other reference line is that which just touches the lowest edge of the little toe. As a further help a third line has been drawn from the tip of the big toe to the tip of the little toe.
    The analysis follows the scheme below:

- The toes—count them; there are not always five
- The pad under the toe—this is the only part of the toe that normally comes into contact with the ground when walking
- The length of the toes—long or short
- The relative length of the toes—in some cases the second toe is longer than the big toe

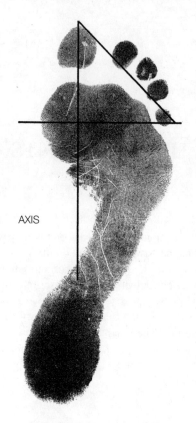

AXIS

Fig. 59. Human footprint

- The position of the toes with reference to the diagonal line—in some cases the third toe is furthest from the diagonal line, in other cases the fourth
- Spacing—in some cases there is a space between the second and third toes, in others there is a larger space between the third and fourth
- The configuration of the forward edge of the impression of the sole and the toe prints
- The shape of the outer edges of the print
- The form of the instep—pronounced or weak
- The size and shape of the heel

- The size and shape of the ball of the foot
- The pattern of the area connecting the heel and ball pads
- Any peculiarities—creases, cracks, and scars

When we consider these features of the human footprint and the differences that can exist, it is easy to comprehend the possibility of a trained tracker being able to tell one person from another by footprints.

The tracker confronted with a foot and a footprint made by the foot has to realize that they will not necessarily be one and the same in form because of weight distribution, gait of the quarry, and ground irregularities. Also if the quarry is attempting to confuse a tracker he may change his gait, which can alter the appearance of his footprints. For instance, a shuffle, or placing the foot at a different angle, or a slight twist as the foot meets the ground will make all the difference to the impression made.

Footwear prints

The footwear print is a result of the footwear itself (that is, how it left the factory or the cobbler's last), how it has been worn since then (duration of wear and characteristics of the wearer), and how it was placed on the tracking medium by the quarry.

In setting out to study a footwear mark, the following points should be noted:

- Length of footwear mark from heel to toe
- Breadth of sole at its broadest point
- Length of the heel from the front edge behind the instep to the back of the heel
- Breadth of the heel
- Height of heel, if on soft soil
- Number, shape, and position of nails, if any
- Any distinctive marks made by the sole or heel
- Any logos or writing
- Wear marks
- The shape of the various parts of the print: the toe, heel, and sole
- Any indication as to the composition of the footwear: rubber, leather, rope, canvas, or plastic

- If there is a succession of footmarks, length of stride from the toe of one footmark to the back of the heel of the next successive footmark
- Any indications of sex or age from such features as size or footwear style

When trying to match a print to a particular piece of footwear, be careful not to make the obvious mistake of fitting the specimen footwear over the original sign—fouling or obliterating it.

As with all important pieces of sign, it is well worth recording details by sketching or photographing them. Always leave a scale marker alongside the print for future reference.

Prints and the walking action

To gain full insight into what we are looking at when we study a human footprint, it is necessary to have an understanding of the walking action. A slow-motion picture shows you the movements made in walking. This type of demonstration is useful to illustrate the walking action and how it influences the sign. The muscular motions that propel a man forward have their counterpart in the track he leaves on the ground.

The following is a description of the walking action (see Fig. 60). From the standing position a man leans forward. This throws his center of gravity in the direction in which he intends to go. As he does this he commences to bend the knee of the leg he intends to move forward first. We will assume that he intends to step off with the left leg. He bends the left knee and at practically the same time, in order to relieve the ankle, he raises the left heel from the ground. As the leg moves forward the whole of the sole of the foot leaves the ground, the toe being the last to lose contact. At the same time he leans slightly over to the right throwing his weight gradually on to the right leg and foot until they bear the full weight of his body. The right foot is flat on the ground and the weight of the body distributed equally along the length of the sole from heel to toe until it bears the full weight of his body. The left leg is advanced, and simultaneously the center of gravity is thrown further forward; when there is a danger of the balance being lost, the left leg straightens out and the left heel touches the ground.

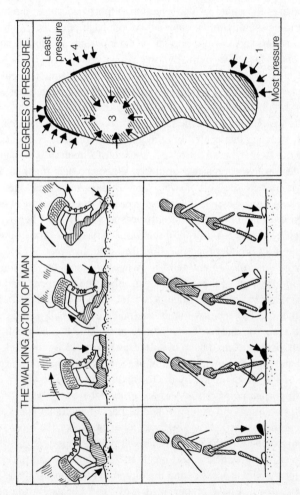

THE WALKING ACTION OF MAN

DEGREES of PRESSURE.

Least pressure

Most pressure

Fig. 60. The walking action of man

In the meantime the right leg is bent at the knee and the right heel is forced to leave the ground, with the result that the weight of the body is borne on the back of the left heel and the front of the right toe, the center of gravity of the body being swung forward and to the left by the push of the right toe. The direction of this force causes the man to strike the ground with the outer side of the back of the heel, which goes downward and forward into the ground, pushing the soil, if soft, in front of it. This soil is gradually forced down and forward as the left foot comes to the ground from heel to toe. Before the right toe leaves the ground it gives a final push towards the left foot, which has the effect of pushing the soil away in a contrary direction.

All the weight is then borne on the left foot and the right swings forward, causing the center of gravity again to change direction towards the right. The effect of this change of direction is to cause the left foot to exert pressure similarly. When the heel touched the ground it pushed the soil forward and slightly outwards, then it pressed it straight down as the pressure passed directly above it and now it presses it to the rear and outwards as the left heel begins to lift for its second step. This roll of the foot is what makes the impression of the foot broader than the foot itself actually is.

Studying this movement tells us where to look for the most marked impressions of the foot on the ground. The two most marked are those made by the outer side of the back of the heel and the inner side of the toe. The next two are those made by the ball of the foot behind the big toe and by the outer side of the foot behind the little toe. Then there is a small heap of soil thrown forward by the back of the heel and pressed down by the flat of the heel and finally a certain amount of soil thrown back by the toe and not pressed down.

Two important points arise. On hard ground there may be no other mark left on the ground except where the heel first struck the ground and where the toe last left it. The faster a person walks, the more soil will be dispatched by the toe and that soil will be loose.

In the ordinary walk the heel meets the ground first and the toes point slightly outward, following the direction of the thrust made by the opposite foot. I have emphasized "ordinary" because if the person is thinking about how he walks, he can alter this profile.

We now have the ordinary marks left by an average man at an ordinary walk. The relationship of the left footmark to the right will vary according to the man. The distance between each footmark will be slightly over thirty inches. If a string were stretched along the center of the line of walk, it would pass over both heels, but the left toes would fall to the left of it, and the right toes to the right.

Speed

If the walk is slower, more balance will be required: on one's feet, as on a bicycle, the heels will lie more off the center line to the left and right respectively. The slower the walk, the more there will be a tendency to place the feet wider apart, and the toes at a greater angle (Fig. 61/1).

When a man trots (Fig. 61/2), he merely speeds up his walk and the track he leaves is speeded up accordingly. The same characteristics in regard to the parts of the print most marked and the soil pressed forward or back will be present but to a marked degree. The distance between each step will be lengthened and, since he has more balance because he is going faster, there will be a tendency for the marks to be in a straighter line. It is to be noticed that the impression of the toes will be deeper and that of the heels correspondingly lighter, but in soft soil the marks of the heels will be easily apparent.

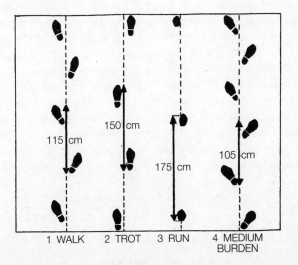

Fig. 61. Tracks of the same quarry under different conditions

Gradient

In walking up a slope the heel strikes less and less deeply as the hill gets steeper because when the foot is brought to the ground the leg is bent at the knee. There is also a tendency to walk with the toes pointing straighter forward. In walking down a slope at an ordinary pace the feet are kept practically straight but more flat to the ground so that the toe and the back of the heel strike less deeply than when walking on the level. In hurrying down a slope, however, the heels are stuck sharply into the ground to act as brakes and the paces are considerably longer.

Training or panic flight

A significant difference can be seen in the track of a man trained to run fast versus that of an untrained runner. A trained runner sprinting will bring the ball of his foot only to the ground and thrust off with his toes. He leaves no marks of his heels. His paces are much longer than at a trot and the marks left by his toes are in a straight line with very marked backwards-facing push marks (Fig. 61/3).

An untrained man running fast will probably show a different kind of track altogether. It is quite possible that he will bring his heel down to the ground first in the same way as in walking only with increased force. His feet tend to point out again, as in walking, and the line of his track will not be so straight. The untrained man running fast is manifesting a phenomenon known as "panic flight," to which even a trained runner is prone in times of danger.

I have personal experience of "panic flight." One summer's day as a young boy I was accompanying my father on a fishing expedition. On our way to the river we had to cross a few meadows. We were climbing out of a dip and coming over a low crest when we were surprised by a bull. We just managed to exit the field ahead of the snorting animal.

The walk, the trot, and the sprint are the human animal's three main gaits, but for the purposes of classification of human tracks I propose to add four more:

- Those made by a man walking backwards
- Those made by a man carrying a load

- Those made by a man who is exhausted
- Those made by men suffering from some physical infirmity

Walking backwards

The movements and the sign left by a man walking ordinarily have been fully described. It stands to reason that if he is going to reverse the direction of these movements, the effects of them on the ground will also be reversed. This is, of course, precisely what happens, thus:

- Instead of pushing off from his toe at each step he pushes off from his heel
- Instead of his heel first striking the ground at the completion of each step, his toe does
- The mark he makes on the ground then shows a push back from the heel
- There is no push back from the toe
- The steps are shorter
- The line of walk is uncertain
- The toes may turn in
- There may be a shuffle of the soil in a backward direction from toe to heel

Carrying a load

If a man is carrying a burden he has to propel himself forward and, in addition, he has to force the extra weight forward (see Fig. 61/4). These characteristics show in the track:

- The steps are shorter
- The feet are planted wider apart laterally
- The line of march is uncertain as the extra weight affects the balance
- The indentations are deeper than they would ordinarily be, especially at the toe

There is the obvious dilemma as to whether the quarry is heavy or whether the quarry is light and carrying a pack. The uncertainty of the line is the strongest clue to differentiate; there may be corroborating evidence such as pack marks at resting places or against trees.

Exhausted

If a man is exhausted, he loses some control over his legs. Anyone who has run a grueling race realizes this fact to the full. Those who haven't probably have seen such a race and noticed how runners stagger off the track. This isn't histrionics for the camera. The track gives a true picture of the extent of the exhaustion. The marks left on the ground show that:

• The feet have strayed from a central well-balanced line
• The feet are inclined to cross over each other
• The line of advance is very uncertain
• The outer edges of each impression are deeply indented
• There is no cleanness or definite pattern in the track as a whole—it shambles about

A similar track would be left by either a wounded man, where there may be other evidence such as blood stains or medical discardables, or a drunken man, in which case there may be discardables such as bottles or there may be vomit or many urination sites.

Other deductions from prints

This material should be cross-referenced with Chapter 15 to give a full description of the intelligence to be gleaned from prints by the trained tracker. It cannot be over-emphasized how important it is for the tracker to sketch the first good print he finds of his quarry. The sketch will be an invaluable record later on in the pursuit to which he will be able to refer. The following gives a detailed analysis:

• An estimate of height can be deduced from the length of the stride and from the length of the footmark
• Weight can be deduced from the depth of the impression; it has already been noted that this can be affected by the load the quarry is carrying
• The combination of the height and weight will give an indication as to build but further characteristics are seen in the case of

obese persons, who are inclined to plant their feet farther apart to afford them more balance and are also inclined to turn their toes outwards

- The socioeconomic group by the type and upkeep of the footwear

Physical condition of the quarry
This has a considerable effect on a track:

- Knock-kneedness shows up with the heels apart, the right heel falls a little to the right and the left heel a little to the left of the central line of the track. The inner side of the back of his heel, and not the outer side, will strike the ground first and leave a correspondingly marked impression
- A wound, injury, or malformation of the leg will frequently entail a difference in the length of stride
- Lameness is indicated by two footmarks close together followed by a space and another two prints—usually the short pace is made by the sound leg as this is bearing the weight a disproportionate amount of the time thus allowing the lame leg to be thrown forward further
- A damaged heel's impression will be light, as will a sore toe
- If the leg is stiff, the steps may be of equal length, but there may be signs of the foot brushing into place on the ground, usually from an outward and backward direction
- A blind person leaves a short pace, the line of march is apt to be uncertain, the feet are planted wider apart, there may be marks of a stick or a dog
- Age influences the walk to a considerable degree in that older people are apt to become infirm, their powers of balance are lessened, entailing spread out feet, line of march not as straight, shorter steps, and sometimes a shuffling action

SUMMARY

The analysis of a human footprint follows this scheme:

- Count the toes
- Study the pad under the toe
- Length of the toes
- Relative length of the toes
- Position of the toes with reference to the diagonal line
- Spacing of the toes
- The configuration of the forward edge of the impression of the sole and the toe prints
- Shape of the outer edges of the print
- Form of the instep—pronounced or weak
- Size and shape of the heel
- Size and shape of the ball of the foot
- The pattern of the area connecting the heel and ball pads
- Any peculiarities—creases, cracks, and scars

The analysis of a footwear mark:

- Length of mark
- Breadth
- Length of the heel
- Breadth of the heel
- Height of heel
- Number, shape, and position of nails
- Any distinctive marks
- Any logos or writing
- Wear marks
- The shape of the various parts of the print
- Any indication as to the composition of the footwear
- If there is a succession of footmarks, length of stride from the toe of one footmark to the back of the heel of the next successive footmark
- Indications of sex or age

FACTORS AFFECTING THE PRINT
- Speed
- Gradient
- Level of fitness
- Level of tiredness
- Load carrying
- Deception tactics

22

ANIMAL PRINTS

For anyone interested in wildlife, this chapter gives the background information essential to a fuller development of the associated tracking skills. From a brief study of anatomical differences we progress to a description of the methods of locomotion and how this affects the subject's sign. The sign of some of the more common mammals found in temperate areas are then described before the chapter concludes with an account of the main variations in the sign of the major bird groupings.

The reader who lives in or intends to visit a tropical or subtropical area is encouraged to read an area-focused text such as *Signs of the Wild* by Clive Walker for Southern Africa.

Fig. 62 gives a few examples of some of the spoor likely to be encountered on a safari.

Anatomical classifications

The formation of the foot has changed over time so that today we have three marked divisions under which the feet of animals can be classified.

Animals that walk on the flat of the foot are termed sole-walkers or plantigrades. The sole-walkers, as a class, are the most widespread. We ourselves are sole-walkers and have as our companions such diverse animals as bears, porcupines, hedgehogs, monkeys, gorillas, badgers, otters, hares, and rabbits.

There are those that walk on their toes, toe-walkers, or digitigrades. This class includes all the members of both the canine and the feline genus.

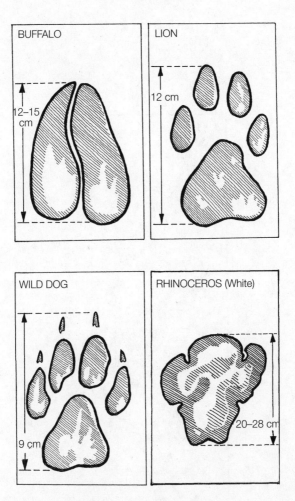

Fig. 62. Four African mammals

The third group are those that walk on the points of their toes, like ballet dancers. In the process of time their toes, or four of them at least, have grown together until they have become hooves. This class is known as the nail-walkers or ungulates and can be subdivided into two: animals with a solid hoof, and animals with a cloven hoof. Examples of this class are: horses, mules, zebras, cows, deer, sheep, and goats.

Fig. 63. Squirrel on the move

For tracking purposes we are then interested in another classification of animals dependent upon the structure of their limbs.

The first class comprises those animals whose legs are of about equal length. In this large class are included horses, cattle, pigs, deer, canines, and felines.

The second class contains animals whose hind legs are much longer than their front legs, such as hares, rabbits, squirrels, and kangaroos (Fig. 63).

To the third class belong those animals whose legs are short in proportion to their bodies, such as otters, weasels, stoats, ferrets, mink, and martens.

The fourth class includes those animals whose legs are very short in proportion to their bodies, and whose bodies are also very large such as badgers, hedgehogs, and porcupines.

It is not easy to classify every animal accurately in only one of the above classes according to the way it moves, but the groupings are a useful aid to the wildlife tracker. Some animals will show characteristics of gait appearing to belong to two classes, sometimes walking and sometimes hopping, for instance the squirrel.

Method of locomotion and how it affects sign

The normal walk is the basis of all tracking comparison, whether with human beings or other animals. Just as we considered the gait of humans in the previous chapter, so we have to study the various methods of locomotion to be in a better position to analyze the sign left by the nonhuman quarry.

First category—equal length limbs

As with the walk of man, watching a video or a slow-motion film will highlight the order and way in which an animal lifts and places his legs. When a horse walks it plants its feet diagonally (see Fig. 64). If the near (right) forefoot touches the ground first, the off (left) hind foot is placed next, then the off-fore foot, and lastly the near-hind foot. Thus it moves all four feet one after another, so that four footfalls may be heard, but it does not move the two on the same side one after the other.

The pig tracks shown in Fig. 67/5 show the distinctive side by side position of the prints. All animals in this class move in this way

The Walk

Fig. 64. The walking action of a horse

except the camel. The camel does not move diagonally but lifts its feet in the following rotation: near-fore, near-hind, off-fore, off-hind. This progression sets up a swaying movement from side to side that proves inconvenient and sometimes disastrous for the novice rider.

The track left by the horse at a walk differs according to the individual. Where the hind registers in relationship to the fore is a significant recognition feature, that is, whether it is behind, superimposed on, or in front of the mark made by the fore hoof. In a very heavy horse, such as a carthorse, the hind hoof will show behind the fore hoof, whereas in a light riding horse the hind hoof will be in front of the fore hoof. The relative positions of these marks also depends on the speed.

The trot (Fig. 65) is merely a hastened walk, and the gait is just the same but quicker. The feet touch the ground in the same rotation, but because two feet touch the ground almost at the same time only the noise of two footfalls will be heard. The track itself appears more in a straight line because the animal has more balance in consequence of the speed, and plants its feet more under the center of its body. The mark of the hind foot will almost invariably show in front of the mark of the fore foot, and the distance between paces will obviously be greater.

The gallop is a series of leaps, as Fig. 66 shows. The hind legs serve mainly to propel the animal forward and the forelegs to balance or brace the body. For this reason the hind legs are planted more or less side by side, while the forelegs are planted apart from, and one behind the other. The resultant track is like a magnified rabbit's track—owing to the speed at which the animal is moving, the hind hoofs hit the ground well in front of the fore hoofs.

Unequal length limbs
Animals whose hind legs are longer than their forelegs progress by a kind of leapfrog movement—see rabbit tracks in Fig. 67/4. The hind feet come round the forelegs and are thrown ahead of the forefeet. In this class of animals the hind feet are longer than the forefeet and can be easily distinguished.

Short legs/long body
The jump made by members of this group is a curious loping snake-like movement—see mink and marten tracks in Fig. 67/1 and 67/2.

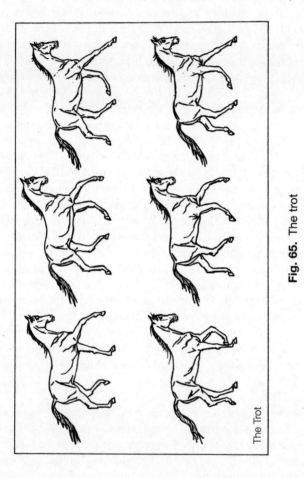

The Trot

Fig. 65. The trot

The Gallop

Fig. 66. The gallop

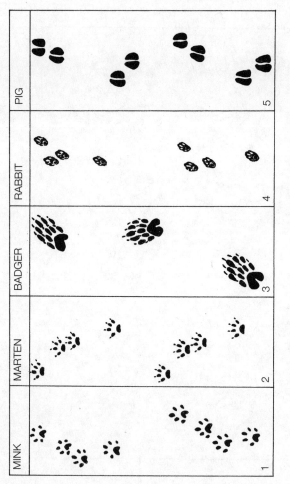

Fig. 67. Tracks of four different animal categories

The movement is rather like that of a porpoise in the water—a series of curves. The two forefeet leave the ground and come down together side by side, the animal's body doubles up like a drawn bow, and the hind feet follow, landing almost directly on the same spot, while the forefeet go off on the next bound, so that the trail shows apparently one pair of tracks side by side at regular intervals. Occasionally some animals in this class will make short bounds with all four feet at the same time. At a faster pace the hind feet may seemingly outstrip the forefeet to land in front of them.

Short legs/large body
The animals of the fourth class (see badger tracks in Fig. 67/3) usually walk turning their hind feet in to a marked degree and spreading all four feet out wide apart laterally. As a general rule the hind foot registers over the mark of the forefoot and across it, heels out, toes in. Occasionally, when alarmed, they will leap but, because of their bulk, the distance between successive tracks is short.

These classifications, foot and gait, have been adopted in order, by a process of elimination, to narrow down the possibilities of the identity of any one track that is noticed. They help to throw light on the characteristics and habits of the quarry.

Distinguishing marks
Animals, like human beings, leave sign specific to the individual. As with a human quarry, it is a matter of observant, concentrated, systematic study of the print that allows the tracker to distinguish his quarry from that of another member of the same species.

Even with a solid-hoofed animal it is possible to distinguish the print of one from another—likewise if the horse is shod, there are differences in the shoe.

Also, when we study the track as a whole, there are differences in the length of stride and the position in which the feet are placed in relation to one another.

In the case of cloven-hoofed animals, the splitting of the hoof and the shape of the two halves of the hoof are also points that will help the tracker to identify the spoor of his quarry. The split in the hoof in most cloven-hoofed animals varies according to age and sex, apart from any accidents that the animal in question has experienced. The male usually has a squarer toe. The two halves of the foot are not uniform in shape and size; the difference between the two is an important clue in identifying individuals.

Domesticated animals
Cattle, sheep, and pigs leave their prints in two parallel lines, one on each side of the central line of the track. The impressions of all four feet are clearly seen. In cattle there is a general tendency for the hoof to open out more at the toe than the heel in fully grown animals. The sheep has a smallish, pointed hoof, while the pig, on soft ground, shows the marks of the dew claws behind the marks of the hooves. Goats usually place their hind feet well in front of the fore and have a more irregular cleft.

Fig. 68 shows some of the more common animal prints and tracks with a worldwide distribution and a few of the larger species. These examples will help the student to start to differentiate between species and then between individuals within that species.

Deer
In most kinds of deer the tracks register, that is the marks of the forefeet are covered by the marks of the hind. A deer track will show

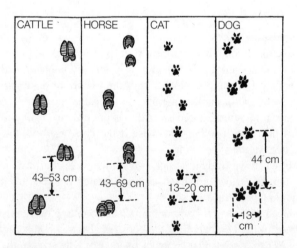

Fig. 68. Prints of animals with a worldwide distribution

the condition of the animal to a great extent. The doe nearly always registers and when heavy with young the feet will be spread wider apart laterally. The buck varies according to the season. When full of strength in the early spring, its hind feet will overstep the marks made by the forefeet. As the rutting season progresses they will drop back and register, and when the buck is worn out and out of condition, the hind feet lag behind the forefeet.

Fox
A fox leaves a pad-mark rather like that of a small dog, but there are several points of dissimilarity. The impression is narrower by comparison with its length. The hind pad is smaller compared with the size of the toes. And a careful examination of a clear print will show traces of hair between the toes and the pad leaving a furry margin, as opposed to the more clear-cut impression of the dog's paw.

The fox's track seems to be more akin to that of the cat than the dog. The dog splashes along and seems to take special delight in putting its feet in muddy places, while the fox walks deliberately and avoids wet and dirty places, behaving in this respect like a cat. Usually, the fox registers its hind paw over the impression made by the forepaw, again as the cat does.

Cats and dogs
The toe-walkers comprise the two great tribes of canines and felines. A comparison of the track of the dog with that of the cat brings out an extraordinary number of differences. These are entirely due to the characteristics of the two different types of animal out of their mode of life.

The dog leaves a zigzag track, like a horse, with the marks of all four feet showing in two parallel lines. The marks of the nails can be seen. The cat leaves a comparatively straight track that shows only one line of marks more or less on a central line.

As its wild cousins the leopard and the tiger do to this day, the cat lived in the jungle and stalked its prey by stealth. Speed was not so much a consideration as quietness. It stalked carefully along, planting its hind feet in exactly the same spot where its forefeet had been, so that only the marks of the hind paws were left on the ground. This was important, because if the hind paw snapped a twig the noise might alarm its prey. As a stalker the cat is a past master and can balance in any position.

Note: There is one interesting point in connection with the toe-walkers that might be mentioned, and that is that the back of the forefoot is concave and the back of the hind foot convex, just as the back of the palms of our hand is concave and the back of our heel is convex.

Rabbits and hares

The best way to distinguish between the various types of animal whose hind legs are longer than their forelegs is by the size of the actual track and the distance between the successive marks. For instance, it might be easy to distinguish the print of a kangaroo from that of a hare but not so easy to distinguish the print of a hare from a rabbit. But with the whole track there should be no such problem, especially if the tracker takes into account all the evidence including the locality.

In these leapfrog tracks, an important point to be certain of is the direction in which the animal is traveling. At first it is difficult to grasp that a four-footed animal's hind legs can come in front of the forelegs.

Rats

The third class—animals with short legs and long bodies—again show peculiar characteristics between the various types, although most of them are also sole-walkers. These characteristics depend more upon the length of the bound than upon the size of the individual marks. Many will show the marks of the tail as a drag between the two parallel lines of the track. Rats seem to leave their tails behind them more than mice do, but the different varieties of each leave a slightly different track. A water vole and a common brown rat may be difficult to distinguish from each other by the track they leave, but in this case the environment should be taken into account.

Otters

The tail marks the otter, coupled with his size, and the fact that he walks the occasional few steps.

Badgers

Among the short-legged/large-bodied category of animals, the badger will register the hind foot across the fore.

Birds

Because of the great similarity between the tracks of many birds, it is important for the naturalist using tracking skills to realize that locality is the most important point to be considered.

The main differences are between birds that perch in trees, birds that walk on the ground, and birds that live on the water. The tree-percher (sparrow, chaffinch, thrush) generally hops along the ground with both feet together and in line with each other. The ground-walkers (pheasant, grouse) walk along somewhat like we do, first one foot then the other. The water birds (duck, goose, swan) all waddle along with their toes turned in.

Perchers

Among the tree-perchers (see Fig. 69/1), it is possible to identify one track from another only by the size and now and then by the tail and wing marks. For instance, the chaffinch leaves a small mark, with sometimes the flick of the tail showing on the ground, whereas the sparrow's track shows larger marks, and the thrush even larger ones with greater distances between them.

Walkers

The ground-walkers (Fig. 69/2) are mostly game birds. It will be found that the toes of game birds are set much wider apart than those of, say, crows and blackbirds. The angle of the outside toes of game birds are set at, or greater than, a right angle, whereas the angle formed by the outside toes of other birds is less than 90 degrees. Again, it will be noticed that the toes of the game bird are of even thickness almost to the tips, while the toes of others taper. Pheasants and partridges especially have peculiarly smooth toes that leave a clean-cut impression, while such birds as pigeons have coarser scales that leave a far rougher mark. The pheasant's track, however, is larger than that of the partridge, and its middle toe stands almost in a straight line with its tail. The cock pheasant trails his tail behind him. The sandpiper makes neat tracks, which might be mistaken for the tracks of other birds if it were not for the little round holes here

Fig. 69. Tracks left by different categories of birds

and there that show where it has probed for food. The woodcock's tracks are similar but larger, and again beak marks are found.

Water birds
The tracks of water birds are usually so much alike that again only the difference in size makes it possible to distinguish between the

species. Their webbed feet clearly distinguish them from the ground-walkers and tree-perchers (Fig. 69/3).

Waders

The feet of the waders may show slight webbing but more usually it will be found that the toes are long and stand well out from each other so as to give a greater surface on which the birds can walk in the mud (Fig. 69/4).

Conclusion

The trained keeper in pursuit of game birds usually pays more attention to signs other than the tracks he may be able to see on the ground. Feathers will be found in places where birds have taken sand-baths; small paths leading here and there in the grass will show where birds have eaten. The place where a bird has been feeding, as well as the food itself, will give a clue to its identity.

Undoubtedly, snow is the ideal medium for bird tracks. Snow not only shows the marks made by the feet of birds but the marks of their wings and tails as well. For instance, when a magpie alights on snow it will leave a clear impression of its tail-feathers as well as of its outspread wing-feathers (see Fig. 70).

Fig. 70. Sign left by birds taking off from snow-covered ground

SUMMARY

ANATOMICAL CLASSIFICATION

Feet
Plantigrades—walk on the flat of the foot (sole-walkers)
Digitigrades—toe-walkers
Ungulates—nail-walkers

- Solid hoof
- Cloven hoof

Relative limb length
Equal length
Hind legs are much longer than front legs
Legs are short in proportion to bodies
Legs are very short in proportion to large bodies

BIRDS
Tree-perchers
Ground-walkers
Water birds
Waders

23

VEHICLE SIGN

As defined in Chapter 2, a sign is "any physical indication left on the environment by the passage of any animal or inanimate object." No account of tracking can be complete without considering the study of the sign left by vehicles.

The traffic police and insurance assessors have built up vast forensic data relating to speed, direction, and road-worthiness that they can extract from vehicle marks left at the scene of a traffic accident. I do not intend trespassing on this specialist area because this book's purpose is tracking, which, by definition, is following the line of the sign.

Tire tracks

Just as a tracker studying the print of an animal or a human has a checklist of features, he has one when recording the details of a vehicle print. The following are details in which the tracker is interested:

- Depth of tread (see Fig. 71)
- Depth of impression
- Distinguishing features of the tread—wear pattern
- Pattern of the tire
- Width of the tire tread—weight of the vehicle and its load, the pressure of the tire
- Variations of the different wheels

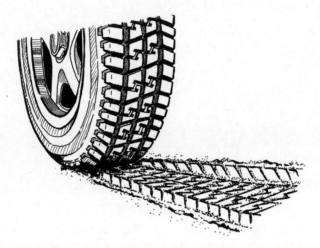

Fig. 71. Typical tread pattern left by a car tire

- Width of track will indicate the type of vehicle
- Direction of travel:

  - indicated by the tread pattern
  - stones are pushed forward slightly and then kicked back
  - passing over a bump, the tires will broaden out momentarily as they impact on landing
  - small areas of dust, mud, and water will be thrown out and slightly backwards
  - puddles of water, if driven through fast, will push the water forward
  - reversing—uncertain line

Just as in other tracking scenarios, the tracker is trying to gain as much information from the sign as possible. To this end the emotional state of the driver can be estimated to a degree by the presence of skid marks where the vehicle has been drawn to a halt or where it has sped off.

Vehicle loads
Often the load of a vehicle, especially a goods vehicle, can leave a

great deal of useful information for the tracker that will link a vehicle to two sites and a particular route.

Deposits can be left on the road/ground in the form of drips from a bulk liquid carrier or in overhanging vegetation from other types of load.

Bicycles

Two-wheeled vehicles have an inherent advantage for the tracker in that when they move more slowly the rider has greater difficulty maintaining his balance. The physical state of the rider and/or the direction of travel of a bicycle can be judged by the track, in that the straighter it is, the faster it is moving, so a tired rider (or one who is riding uphill) will leave a front wheel track that swings left and right of the axis.

Tracking combined vehicle/foot journeys

As was mentioned in Chapter 19, there is only one guaranteed method of thwarting a scent tracker and that is by riding on an animal or a bike. But the tracker who is aware of the significance of vehicle prints and has studied them will be able to link in with the scent tracker and frustrate this ploy by linking the vehicle prints at one entry/exit point with those at another.

The two entry/exit sites may not only be linked by vehicle and footprint impression but by transfer of material from one site to another where it is totally foreign.

Animal-drawn vehicles

The fact that you as a tracker have identified the quarry as an animal-drawn vehicle is in itself very useful distinguishing information. You then have the advantage of being able to draw conclusions from two sources—the prints of the animal and those of the vehicle.

Skiers, men on snowshoes, and snowmobiles

Tracks made in snow will become fixed if the temperature drops and may remain for a long time. The military are well aware of this hazard of operating in snow. They try to use dead ground or tree cover to hide themselves from aerial surveillance, but neither dead ground nor top cover from the tree canopy is a problem to a tracker following on the ground.

However, knowing what the military do to try to overcome the serious disadvantage of moving through snow helps the tracker to realize what he must be thinking about. The military attempt to deceive the enemy by laying more tracks to create an illusion of greater numbers or by hiding their tracks among any existing ones.

Therefore, the tracker must from the start of the track identify the particular features of the skis or snowshoes that belong to the target. He should note the width, the length, the depth of indentation, any deformities of the blade, and any features of the ski poles and how they are used by the skier. But the tracker will have to be alert for the obvious deception of changing skis, which in itself will create tell-tale sign at the point of changeover.

The direction of the skier and even the snowmobile will be the most obvious on gradients, as with the cyclist, and therefore when there is a gradient and there are several sets of tracks, those going in the wrong direction can be immediately eliminated. On the level, the marks of the ski poles will give the direction as they kick back on the push-off. On a bumpy surface, the direction of a snowmobile is easy to ascertain since the track will have slight gaps in it or shallower depressions as the vehicle takes off and leaves the surface momentarily after the crest of the rise.

SUMMARY

DETAILS OF TiRE TRACKS
- Depth of tread
- Depth of impression
- Distinguishing features of the tread—wear pattern
- Pattern of the tire
- Width of the tire tread—weight of the vehicle and its load, the pressure of the tire
- Variations of the different wheels
- Width of track will indicate the type of vehicle
- Direction of travel:

  - indicated by the tread pattern
  - stones are pushed forward slightly and then kicked back
  - passing over a bump the tires will broaden out momentarily as they impact on landing
  - small areas of dust, mud, and water will be thrown out and slightly backwards
  - puddles of water if driven through fast will push the water forward
  - reversing creates uncertain line

OTHER VEHICLE SIGN
- Loads can leave deposits on the ground or disturb vegetation
- Bicycle tracks can reveal direction of travel and physical state of its rider
- Combined vehicle/foot journeys can be linked at entry/exit points
- Animal-drawn vehicles offer two sources of sign: prints of the animal and of the vehicle
- Tracks in snow require extra vigilance—against enemy deception tactics as well as identifying target features

24

PRESERVING PRINTS

For the tracking instructor or the naturalist who is studying a species, it is often a requirement to be able to preserve a specimen of a print. In this chapter I will outline the usual method.

Other methods can also be used to preserve the information from a print. See Chapter 25 and the section on digital photography.

Plaster of Paris is widely available from art shops as well as the usual suppliers, such as pharmacists and builders' merchants. The best plaster is that used by dentists—fine Italian plaster. In any case, care must be taken that the plaster is absolutely fresh and that it is kept in an airtight container; exposure to the air will render it stale so that it will not set readily when mixed with water.

The technique

When a track has been found, carefully remove any loose material, whether vegetation or debris, that may be lying across it but take great care not to mark the print itself. Forceps or a photographer's blower brush are useful at this stage (Fig. 72/1).

If the track is shallow or on sloping ground it will be necessary first of all to build a wall or embankment around the mark with twigs or mud or even strips of cardboard so as to keep the plaster on the track while it is in a liquid form.

Pour some water into a container and sift the plaster into it, breaking up any lumps as much as possible (Fig. 72/2). Stir constantly and keep adding plaster or water until the mixture is the consistency of thick cream and can just be poured out of the container. The

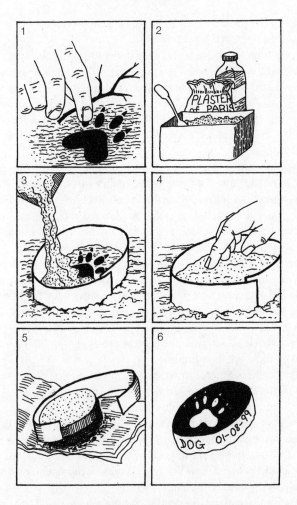

Fig. 72. Making a plaster cast of a print

quantity of the mixture required will vary with the size of the print, but it is better to make too much than too little. Tap the container on the ground or with a knife to get rid of air bubbles.

Pour the mixture gently into the crevices of the print (Fig. 72/3) and to the sides of the print, taking care to avoid air bubbles. Be sure that the cast is thick enough by adding successive layers of the mixture; otherwise it will break in transit.

Drying time for the cast will vary according to atmospheric conditions and the dampness of the ground itself. A pinch of salt added to the mixture usually has the effect of making the cast dry more quickly and of rendering its composition stronger. Monitor drying by gentle finger pressure (Fig. 72/4). It usually takes between fifteen and thirty minutes to set, depending on how much water was mixed with the plaster.

When the cast is nearly dry, scratch on the back of it the place, date, your name, and the name of the quarry or some identification. At the same time make a record in your notebook of all details in connection with the print: type of ground, weather conditions, age of track, quarry's identity, its age, sex, and any other relevant information.

When the cast is dry, cut out the soil around the plaster and remove completely (Fig. 72/5). Pull back the supporting card, wash off all mud and earth, and pack carefully in newspaper for transit. If it is necessary to move the cast before it has set completely, leave any debris attached to it and remove it later. It can be hardened by baking it slowly. Take care, however, not to apply too high a heat as the cast will be apt to crumble.

Be particularly careful to wash out the mixing container as soon as the mixture has been poured out onto the print; otherwise what is left will harden and be difficult to remove.

Before the plaster cast is quite set, a loop of string or wire can be inserted into it at the back so that the cast can subsequently be hung up. If casts are to be kept in good condition for any length of time they should be stored in a flat box. Bubble wrap underneath them can help to prevent movement.

What you have at the moment is a cast of a foot (Fig. 72/6), which is very useful for making sign on the age stands (Chapter 14).

To produce a replica of the sign gently press the cast into plasticine. This gives a clean impression of the sign.

To make a plaster cast representation of the original sign as a more permanent record than the plasticine, build a plasticine embankment around the base of your original cast. Next paint the face of the cast with a soap solution. Mix up some more plaster and pour it into the embankment. When the plaster has set, you can gently prise the two casts apart, after removing the embankment. If this proves too difficult you may have to break the original cast in order to preserve the new positive cast.

The first cast you made, the negative, can be used as a tool with your age stand. By pressing the cast into your age stand or tracking lanes you can make an impression of the original sign. This can be observed to note the aging process, allowing you to record the sign's deterioration over time. When you do this, make sure that the weather conditions are favorable, that is, not too wet.

PART FOUR

THE FUTURE

25

DEVELOPMENTS IN TRACKING

You have reached the end of the book but not the end of the story. This is the start of your tracking career. Whether you are involved with tracking in your profession or as an art in itself, this book will have given you a good basis upon which to build.

I would like to indicate areas that in my opinion will become important in the medium term to people involved in tracking. I can see three main areas for future development: professional, technical, and personal.

Professional

When I ran military tracking courses, my main aim was to turn highly trained special forces students into potential lead scouts—trackers capable of following enemy forces by the sign they leave with the short- or long-term aim of killing or capturing them. If I were to teach tracking today, I would have to adjust the tracking course program to suit various organizations, purposes or individuals.

Bearing that in mind, I have never known anyone to fail a tracking course. The course has been designed with two objectives: First, one needs to identify the tracker with real potential for further training, with the aim of making that individual into an excellent lead scout tracker, capable of working alone or in a tracking team in a hostile environment. Second, one is building awareness in individuals without tracking potential—once you become aware of the capabilities of a tracker, you learn to leave as little sign as possible for the enemy to follow your sign and kill you. Taking that on board, you end up with two types of tracker: one who can track, and one who knows the capabilities of a tracker.

Before teaching students, I would make sure that all the tracking *instructors* could "track." Be very aware of the self-proclaimed experts. (This is true in all walks of life.) Remember, this is a serious subject, especially if you are training law-and-order personnel and big-game hunters. It could mean the difference between life and death. Don't take instructors at face value; any sound organization should check out its employees' references and test their experience. You cannot justify running a tracking course on theory only.

To check tracking ability, set up a tracking test. Using this book, lay a track approximately 100 meters long without the potential tracking instructor to be tested seeing you do so. Put as much sign into the track as you think is relevant without going overboard. Then get the potential tracking instructor to follow the track with you so that you can appraise his tracking standards.

An instructor also has to have the ability to *teach* the subject on the ground. (We call this "hands on" in the military.) Once you have appraised the standards of the potential tracking instructors, and you know how well they can track, use them to your best advantage. If they cannot track but know the capabilities of a tracker, also keep them on. As you'll know from reading this book, there are other subjects to be taught for them to take. Also, you can slot them in with other tracking students so that they can improve their tracking abilities.

This brings me to an important point: I spent most of my military career in the SAS, where we treated one another like family. We all had something different to offer. I took to tracking like a duck takes to water, but that doesn't make me any better than any other members of the family with different skills. What's suitable for one person is not for another. What my tracking expertise does give me is an advantage over a nontrained tracker in a hostile tracking environment—making the difference between life and death.

Technical

As with any other skill traceable to ancient times, there is often resistance among tracking practitioners to the latest technological breakthroughs. There are, however, a few areas that I consider to be of great help to the modern sophisticated tracker.

Thermal imaging
The use of thermal imaging (TI) technology is well established in the military, the fire service, and with search and rescue organizations for seeing in obscured environments such as smoke, moonless nights, or earthquake rubble. This application can be used by the tracker team, but TI can also be used to detect heat sources.

Applying the equipment to this effect will give the tracker two advantages:

- The tracker will be able to detect the presence of the quarry otherwise hidden from view
- The tracker will be able to give a better estimate as to the age of sign

Night vision goggles and infrared flashlights
The use of night vision goggles will enable the tracker to carry on tracking well beyond the normal hours permitted by nature, especially if they are augmented with infrared light sources. It must be appreciated that this equipment is not without its drawbacks. For instance, the peripheral vision of the wearer is severely restricted, and with most designs the depth of field is very difficult to judge.

Information technology
Intelligence and information gathering play a huge part in the tracker's role. Because of this emphasis it would be remiss of the modern tracker not to take advantage of all the efficient methods that are available today to transfer, collate, and record these data—in addition to your notebook and memory!

Digital photography
This subject is in its infancy with respect to its application to tracking but, with the advent of digital cameras and digital video recorders, there is an area ripe for development. Computers can be used to store, collate, and compare, as well as to enhance the imagery with 3D effects and to modify the color and tonal properties of a picture. The digital images can also be swiftly shared with colleagues anywhere.

DNA tracking
A day doesn't seem to pass without a report in the newspapers about the latest application of DNA studies in the solving of crimes, some dating back many years. To this end the modern tracker must be aware of the importance of preserving, gathering, recording, or marking the location of any material left by the quarry.

Global Positioning System (GPS)
South African game parks are now utilizing the latest GPS technology to keep records of their wildlife. With the aid of hand-held computers using a graphics display, trackers with poor or non-existent literacy skills can record the location of prints and animals. In this way, the parks can use the vast amount of information that the trackers see but have been previously unable to record, to build up a picture of the movement patterns of the animals. It is a classic harnessing of modern technology and ancient skills to produce valuable results.

Personal
I hope that this study will enhance your knowledge and appreciation of your hobby or your profession. I'm sure that the outdoor pursuits teacher, the conservationist, and the wildlife enthusiast will gain as much from this book as the military tracker because, as with all experts and dedicated people, they do not stop learning and developing in new directions. Even if they have never considered tracking as being in their remit, they will see the benefits that can spin off from it into their sphere.

What is important is the recognition of personal development. To that end I have included a few blank pages at the back of the book for you to record any comments, observations, or experiences that relate to tracking. One can see one's development as a continual progression; the more the earlier practices are applied, the more progress will be made.

The following will encourage and stimulate your personal development:

• Courses and structured training
• Discussion and feedback via the Internet
• Practice and the critical analysis of the lessons learned

26

TRACKING AIDE-MÉMOIRE

DEFINITIONS

TRACKING
Tracking can be defined as the art of being able to locate, identify, and pursue sign, and from intelligent interpretations and deductions gain reasonably accurate information about the quarry concerned.

SIGN
This is any physical indication left on or in the environment by the passage of any animal or inanimate object.

GROUND SIGN
These are ground level marks or disturbances.

TOP SIGN
This is defined as any sign above the ankle.

CONCLUSIVE SIGN
This is sign directly linked to the quarry.

SUBSTANTIATING SIGN
This is sign probably made by the quarry.

KEY SIGN
This is the most prominent sign.

SIGN PATTERN
This is the sign that serves to indicate the habits or the peculiarities of a quarry.

TIME BRACKET
All sign in the initial stages is placed into a time bracket—that is, the time lapse between the earliest possible time the sign could have been made and the time it was located.

STRAIGHT EDGE
This is the line found on leaves or blades of grass caused by the application of pressure.

SPOOR
This Afrikaans word derives from the Dutch word for footprint and is reserved for that sign left by an animal (including man), as opposed to the sign left by a vehicle or inanimate object.

THE TRACK
This is the line of sign.

VISUAL TRACKING
This is the art of being able to track a human being, animal, or vehicle by the marks it has left.

SCENT TRACKING
Scent tracking is normally performed by dogs.

TRACKING PICTURE
This is the overall picture gained by the tracker over any given length of track.

TRACKING MEDIUM
This is the generic term used for the material in which the sign was left by the quarry.

EXIT AND ENTRY POINTS
These are points or passageways through which a quarry may pass from one environment to another.

POINTERS
These are the signs that serve to indicate the direction of movement.

FOUL TRACK
Is defined as a track that has entered an area where numerous other tracks exist.

DECEPTION
When a quarry attempts to lose the tracker by leaving misleading sign.

INDICATOR PACE
This is the footprint immediately before or after an intended change of direction.

CASTING
This is the method of locating or relocating sign that has been lost.

TUNING IN
This is the initial reading of the sign that enables the tracker to think and act like the quarry.

PACE TRACKING
This is "pace for pace" tracking carried out during the "tuning in" period or when the track becomes difficult to pursue.

TRACK ISOLATION
This is where the tracker, having anticipated the intended route, is able to abandon the track and leapfrog ahead.

TRAITS
These are the characteristic features or qualities distinguishing a particular quarry.

PHYSIQUE
This relates to the general appearance of the quarry.

DIET
This relates to the food and drink that the quarry regularly consumes.

HABITAT
This is where the quarry lives. It can be rural, suburban, city, or remote territory.

SIGN

CHARACTERISTICS OF SIGN

Regularity
This is an effect caused by straight lines, arches, or other geometrical shapes being pressed into the ground leaving marks not normally found in nature.

Flattening
This is the general leveling or depression caused by pressure on an area compared to the immediate surroundings.

Transfer
This is the deposit carried forward over an area after the quarry has moved from one environment to another.

Color change
This is the difference in color or texture of sign from the area that surrounds it.

Discardables
This is anything that is left behind by the quarry.

Disturbances
This is any other change to or rearrangement of the natural state of an area caused by the passage of the quarry.

CLASSIFICATION OF SIGN

Substantiating sign
These signs may or may not have been caused by the quarry.

Conclusive sign
This sign has definitely been made by the quarry you are tracking.

Temporary sign
Some types of sign are termed temporary because they are particularly affected by weathering agents.

Permanent sign
Permanent sign is very resistant to weathering.

FACTORS AFFECTING SIGN
Four main factors affect sign:

- Spoor and sign left by other animals and vehicles
- Features of the terrain
- Climatic conditions
- Time

Third-party spoor and sign
Spoor and sign belong to one of three groups:

- You the tracker and your team
- The quarry, which can be one or more persons or vehicles
- A third party

The terrain
The major types of terrain that offer very distinctive attributes for the tracker:

- Grass and cultivated areas
- Rocky ground
- Sandy desert
- Primary forests
- Secondary forests and dense undergrowth
- Inland waterways and marshy areas
- The seashore
- Snow-covered regions
- Urban and built-up areas

The climate
The three climatic factors that affect the track are:

- Direct sunlight
- Strong wind
- Heavy precipitation

All these factors will adversely affect the sign of a track. The degree this effect will have is varied and depends upon:

- The strength of the element
- Whether they were working in combination or separately
- The duration the element impinged on the sign
- The type of terrain

Time
Time is the fourth of the factors that affect sign. To be able to assess the time bracket between when a spoor mark was made and when it is found is one of the crucial tracking skills.

Interdependence
The tracker must be aware that the four factors that affect sign do not influence the track independently. They work in unison on the sign and spoor to weather it and to change its nature. Sometimes one of the factors becomes dominant and at other times it is the interplay of the factors that produces the transformations.

THE ATTRIBUTES OF A TRACKER

To be a competent tracker you must possess or develop the following qualities:

- Patience
- An inquisitive mind
- Honesty
- Perseverance
- Acute observation
- All five senses must be well attuned
- Above average endurance
- Above average standard of field craft

- Mental and physical determination
- A good knowledge of the local fauna and flora
- Curiosity

SELF-KNOWLEDGE
A good tracker is aware of his limitations both in terms of fatigue and tracking ability. In short, he is honest with himself and others.

PSYCHOLOGY OF THE QUARRY
Attempt to picture in your mind the party making the track. Try to get into his skin and into his mind.

THE FIVE SENSES
Sight, hearing, smell, taste, and touch have to be used to note everything and then remember it.

MEMORY

Memory is the process of storing and retrieving information, or retention and recall.

STORAGE TECHNIQUES
- Association
- Groupings or clusters
- Visualization

RETRIEVAL TECHNIQUES
- The Greek system of a familiar room
- Knot in the tie or some item that is out of place
- Mnemonics

Recall is state dependent.

Memory is either short- or long-term.

Forgetting is when information becomes inaccessible, either because it is no longer in storage or it cannot be retrieved.

FACTORS INVOLVED IN FORGETTING
- Time
- Interference
- Distortions
- Memories can be entirely false
- Memories are not fixed but change over time and can also be affected by other memory inputs

ENHANCING THE MEMORY
- Fantasy
- Visualization
- Association
- Exaggeration

OBSERVATION

SCANNING AND SEARCHING
Divide the area into:

- Foreground
- Middle distance
- Distance

WHERE TO LOOK
The following are places where sign will be most obvious:

- Near any source of water
- On muddy and sandy patches
- In high grass or thick undergrowth
- On steep hillsides
- On the edges of clearings
- Where obstacles have to be crossed

WHAT TO LOOK FOR

As you are scanning and searching, you should remember each of the factors that make an object visible:

- Shape
- Shadow
- Silhouette
- Surface/Shine
- Spacing
- Movement

BEFORE AND AFTER STUDIES

The format:

- Natural state
- Disturbed state
- Confirmatory actions

FORMAT FOR DESCRIBING AN INDIVIDUAL

Sex

Age—in a 5-year bracket. Use dress, surroundings, activity, as well as physical appearance to assess age.

Height—in a 5-centimeter bracket. Use reference points. A door is 2 meters. Compare with a known person to estimate.

Build—slim, medium, large

Posture—bent, straight, lopsided

Hair—color, parting, length, style, clean, dirty

Face—complexion, shape, features, facial hair, scars

Eyes—spacing, color, large, staring, glasses

Gait—speed, stride, limp, swagger, military

Dress—so as to avoid omissions work from the head to the feet

Carrying—describe any articles that the person is holding or carrying

Distinguishing feature—if the person has any unusual characteristics note them

Other remarks . . .

Reminds me of . . . If it is possible, name a person to whom the individual has a likeness

STALKING

DEFINITION
It is the art of approaching an object under cover, or by stealth. It is more generally described as the ability to move rapidly, or fairly rapidly, from place to place, without being seen, heard, or otherwise detected while at the same time seeing and observing.

THE GOLDEN RULE
Take risks early.

PRACTICE OF CAMOUFLAGE AND CONCEALMENT
Remembering why things are seen.

KNOWLEDGE OF THE QUARRY
A principle of stalking is that you must understand and know as much as possible about your quarry. It is a mistake to underestimate your quarry. The following is a list of use-

ful questions about the quarry the stalker should try to answer:

- How does it feed?
- Where does it feed?
- What precautions does it take to guard against surprise?
- How quick is it to take alarm?
- What sort of place does it frequent?
- What kind of cover does it go to?
- How does it get there?

THE WIND

Carries scent and sound. Sometimes it has an adverse effect and sounds carry towards the quarry, whereas at other times the noise generated by the wind can cover the sound of your movements.

SCENT

The tracker has to be aware of the scent that he may be giving out that will alert his quarry whether it be human or animal.

Eliminate any possible chance of the quarry detecting you by smell. It may be necessary to avoid any of the following for two or three days before going on a tracking task:

- Toothpaste
- After-shave lotion, perfume, deodorants
- Soap
- Hair gel
- Talcum powder
- Shaving soap
- Shampoo
- Medications such as liniments
- Spices and garlic

In addition, the visual tracker, especially the military tracker, must use his sense of smell to warn him of any danger. The following would alert a soldier on a tracking mission:

- Cooking smells
- Human sanitation
- Domesticated animal smells
- Campfires
- Slaughtered animals
- Freshly dug earth
- Cigarette smoke, ash, or butts

STALKING TECHNIQUES
If one word should be remembered by a stalker, it is "stealthily."

METHODS OF MOVEMENT

The cautious approach
This consists of walking calmly and quietly.

The upright crouch
The ball of the foot should touch the ground first, followed by the heel.

The feline crawl
When the distance between you and your quarry is lessening and when cover is getting scarce, it will be necessary to employ the feline crawl. You crawl along on hands and knees. The hands feel for suitable places on which to rest and the corresponding knee comes up to the same position.

The flat or belly crawl
This procedure is used for the final stage of the stalk. It is necessary to go down full length on the ground, flat on the abdomen, with the head down. You work yourself forward, bit by bit, a few inches at a time, using the hands and the sides of the feet.

Freezing
Used if you are liable to be spotted. This technique is most effective with a non-human quarry. It does have a place in the repertoire of skills to be used when stalking a human,

although then the background, distance, and light conditions are more critical.

ROUTE PLANNING AND THE STALK

Wind direction and strength
As we know, the wind carries not only smell but also sound; therefore, you should stalk with the wind in your face.

Vegetation
As the vegetation cover alters, the stalker has to select new material to top-up his personal camouflage.

Movement
Each leg of the stalk will probably require a different method of movement. For instance if you are behind a hedge and not visible from the quarry a crouching posture will be ideal, whereas if you are working your way through a wheatfield overlooked by the quarry it will be necessary to adopt the feline crawl. Divide the route into bounds.

Landmarks
During the stalk you will require reference points for orientation purposes.

Cover
Check that the obvious features—such as ditches, walls, hedges, buildings, and river beds—will actually cover you to your destination and that the cover is complete.

Dead ground
This is a military term used to describe an area that, although overlooked by an observer, is a blind spot to him because of the folds in the ground.

Obstacles
The route planning has to take into account any obstacles before the stalker sets off.

Roads and waterways
Try to plan to cross roads and waterways at bends or corners.

Plowed land
Use the furrows as cover.

Long grass or cereal crops
Keep changing direction so that there isn't a uniform, predictable movement of the foliage causing color change.

Observation points
There should be pre-planned points at which you will halt and observe the quarry.

Noise
The stalker has to take advantage of existing noises such as streams, the wind, rain, vehicles, the sea, or aircraft to cover any sounds that he may make.

Animals
Any wildlife that you disturb will alert the quarry. The curiosity of domesticated animals will, apart from the more obvious barking of dogs, be noticed by the observant enemy.

Hillsides
If you are stalking on a mountain or hillside, try to put yourself into a position above the quarry but avoid skylining.

Stalking animals
Grazing animals tend to raise their heads at frequent but irregular intervals, so do not be tempted to make a sudden dash or any quick movement as you can be caught out and they will be put to flight.

Alternative routes
After choosing the main route, consider other paths in case you have to abort or modify the stalk.

Rehearse hand signals

Control the tracking group
The tracker has to be aware that he must control the group he is with.

NIGHT MOVEMENT
- We see less than in daylight
- We develop night vision
- We see shapes, not detail
- We see skylines and silhouettes—and so does the quarry
- We may see movement
- If caught in the light of a vehicle, freeze, quickly close one eye to protect your night vision
- Be aware that vehicle lights turn night into day
- Use night vision aids if available
- Hearing and smell become more important—turn your ears towards any sound
- Stop and listen, keep close to the ground
- Freeze if you hear a noise
- Keep quiet
- Don't have loose equipment (check before starting out)
- Be aware of skylining and shadows
- Move carefully using the ghost walk, the cat walk, or the kitten crawl
- Clear your route
- Don't step on dry vegetation
- Use any available cover
- Breathing into the air on cold nights will create a cloud above the stalker—breathe into your jacket or the grass or disperse your breath with a scarf

THE TRACK PURSUIT DRILL (TPD)

INTRODUCTION
The following assists the student in interpreting the sign:

- The sign must be studied very carefully
- Distinguish the sign from among the many others

- As soon as possible, the condition of the quarry being followed must be assessed—that is, whether it is lazy, tired, alert, confident, or any other indication as to its state
- Idiosyncracies and traits must be noted
- Any slight change in the sign, no matter how small, must be investigated thoroughly
- Anticipate the quarry's moves, direction of travel, and any likely deceptions
- Build up a complete picture from all the available sign
- Continuously monitor the ground and country in relation to the direction of travel

THE TPD SEQUENCE

The TPD is a distillation of lessons learned in the art of tracking. It has been devised and formulated by the military to provide a framework from which the tracker can work. It is particularly useful for the student because he has the guidance of a sequence. There are seven steps that are in effect a cycle: When the end of the cycle is reached, the sequence is started again. This drill continues until the culmination of the track.

Step 1: assessment of the general direction

The tracker looks ahead along the perceived track to the maximum visibility and back to where he is standing for the general direction of the track.

Step 2: eliminate all openings and finalize the general direction

If there are two or more openings, compare the ages and eliminate old tracks, assuming the track that you are following is the most recent one.

Step 3: look for the farthest sign and connect it back to your position

This is to ensure that there is not a split track and that no other form of deception has been practiced. This ensures that you, the visual tracker, are still following the same track.

Step 4: look through the vegetation for the quarry

This step is an ongoing process and that is the reason it is placed midway through the sequence. It is very important and must be carried out at every opportunity. The visual tracker must always be aware of the possibility that the quarry is close.

Step 5: check the area to the left and right for deception tactics

By carrying out this drill you ensure that your quarry has not gone off your line of travel and that there isn't any access to the sides. There are many ways in which the quarry can confuse the tracker (Chapter 13). This step is to combat being led astray.

Step 6: plan and memorize your next footsteps

Here the tracker is working out the best route to the farthest visible sign made by the quarry. Remember we are minimizing all unnecessary movement, which could give our position away.

Step 7: move forward with stealth

The most vulnerable time for the visual tracker is when he is moving. Any sudden movement might catch the quarry's eye. This will result in the quarry being put to flight, or in the case of a military tracker, in being ambushed. When the tracker arrives at the farthest sign of the quarry, he again visually checks all the area to the front for the quarry's presence before restarting the cycle.

SIGNS THAT A TRACK HAS BEEN OVERSHOT

- Individual tracking signs, conclusive or substantiating, are absent
- The ground is fresh
- Cobwebs that would normally be broken by the quarry are intact
- Dew is still present on the vegetation and ground

- Vegetation as a whole will be in a natural state showing no signs of disturbance

DECEPTION TACTICS

The following is a list of deception methods:

- Walking backwards
- Conversion of sign
- Brushing the track
- Stone hopping
- Tiptoe walking
- Fade out
- Splitting up if the quarry is in a group
- Crossing or walking in a stream or river bed
- Looping back

REASONS FOR USING DECEPTION TACTICS
- To gain time
- To lose the tracking team
- To kill the tracker

JUDGING AGE

THE IMPORTANCE OF THE TIME BRACKET
The sign needs to be placed into a time bracket for the following reasons:

- To distinguish between old and fresh sign
- To determine the approximate time lapse since the quarry passed through the area
- To establish the correct track picture

316   The SAS Guide to Tracking

- To use foul tracks to your advantage and not be misled by them
- To gather information for use by intelligence analysts

THE FOUR FACTORS AFFECTING SIGN
- Time
- Features of the terrain
- Climatic conditions
- Spoor and sign left by third parties

THE TERRAIN AS A MEDIUM
The terrain is the medium upon which the quarry writes as he passes. What he writes is the sign. Is the medium of a nature that will retain the sign or not, and if so, for how long?

WEATHERING
Consider if the sign has been exposed to the elements or sheltered.

METHODS FOR JUDGING THE AGE OF SIGN
- Comparison of color
- Breaking and comparing sticks and twigs
- Comparison of impression
- Time brackets created by precipitation
- Wind
- Superimposed game tracks
- Wildlife
- Prints in mud
- Exposed earth
- Dry leaves
- Sticks
- Growing vegetation
- Man-made objects
- Fires
- Worm casts

- Ants and termites
- Animal droppings
- Smell
- Age stands

DEDUCTION

THE THOUGHT PROCESS
Deduction is the final phase of the mental process that the tracker employs. To recap, the full process is:

Observe
Remember
Select and analyze
Deduce and comprehend

ASPECTS OF DEDUCTION

Deductions from a single print
A single print can give:

- The size of a footprint gives an indication of height
- The depth of the impression, all other things being equal, is in direct relation to the weight of the man and his equipment
- The angle of the print with respect to the line of march is indicative of the posture of the person—an athletically built person tends to walk with feet parallel
- Any scuff marks around the edges would suggest an idiosyncratic gait

Deductions from a series of prints
A series of prints from the same quarry lets the tracker judge:

- The speed
- The gait
- The load being carried—the heavier the load, the shorter the pace

Estimating numbers in a group

Analysis of groups

The analysis of peripherals

DEDUCTION AND THE MILITARY TRACKER
A military tracker is trying to assess:

- Direction of movement
- Age of the track
- Numbers in the group
- The speed
- Loads
- Tactics
- Weapons
- Sex

THE MILITARY PROCESS
When the military apply the deductive process to the work of their trackers, they use the following system:

- Facts—something physically present
- Interpretation ⎫
- Deduction   ⎬ the tracker's reasoning—inter-deduction
- Assumption   ⎭
- Reaction—this is to the conclusions from above
- Confirmation of the reasoning and the reaction
- Reporting of the sightings
- Recording—this is the final stage of the process when the written report is submitted

INTER-DEDUCTION
Interpretation and deduction, "inter-deduction," the essence of the tracker's mental processes. The tracker starts by listing all known facts. He then asks himself:

- How did it occur?
- Why is it like it is?
- When did it happen?
- Who caused the sign?

THE LOST TRACK DRILL

THE STAGES
The Lost Track Drill is broken down into the following:

- Initial search
- Initial probe
- Initial cast
- Extended cast
- Stream-line search
- Likely areas searches

TRAINING TRACKERS

TRACKING EXERCISES AND LESSONS
The following are the main types of tracking exercises and instructional periods:

- Observation stand
- Observation lane
- Age stand
- Pace tracking exercise
- Pace tracking lane
- Incident awareness stand
- Incident awareness lane
- Tracking competition
- Final exercise

EQUIPMENT

Essentials
- Day pack
- Suitable outdoor clothing, including hat
- Map(s) protected in a plastic bag or map case
- Flashlight—medium size with a switch that can't be inadvertently put on
- Silva compass
- Long tweezers
- Notebook and pencil (rather than a pen; keep both in a plastic bag)
- A set of lightweight waterproofs—jacket and trousers (if not already being worn)
- A short home-made flag, maximum length 0.75 meters
- Exact change for the telephone, or a phone card, or a mobile phone for use in emergencies
- Binoculars—the ideal binoculars for watching wildlife areas is 7 × 50 or 8 × 40. Higher magnification binoculars are very difficult to hold still without a support, and you may want to use them in some pretty awkward positions. For a young person whose budget is tight, a pair of ex-military binoculars in good condition will suffice. These can be easily obtained from the many ex-military surplus stores.
- Magnifying glass
- Cold snacks to last a day
- Thermos flask with a hot drink
- Water bottle
- Tape measure
- Small personal medical kit (containing bandages, headache tablets, insect repellent etc.; ask the advice of your local pharmacist if in doubt)
- Small waterproof container of plaster of Paris and the kit required to make a plaster mold
- This book in a plastic bag
- Small penknife
- Whistle
- Watch

Optional items
- Camera
- Tape recorder
- Hand-held GPS
- Night viewing aids

REMEMBER PRIOR TO DEPARTURE
- Inform someone of your intentions and planned return time
- Lay out and check all the items you intend to take with you on your tracking task

MILITARY TRACKING

INCIDENT AWARENESS

Aids to recognition of sites
- Anticipate incidents
- Changes in direction
- Localized increases in sign
- Discardables
- Study areas where incidents are likely to happen

Help in finding a lost track
A thorough search of possible incident sites is invaluable if the target sign has been lost.

Dangers of incident sites
If the enemy is alert to trackers, incident sites can be used to lure the tracking party into booby traps or into a registered target for their support and indirect fire weapons.

The sequence of events at incident sites
- When a potential incident site is identified move back and go into all-around defense

- Plan the search, which may include looping to determine the size, layout, entry, and exit points
- The tracker and his cover man conduct a systematic search and record all facts on a sketch—the sketch has to include as a minimum: north, entry and exit points, position of all sign
- Depending on the size of the incident area, the rest of the patrol can surround the perimeter or give cover from features outside the immediate area
- Briefly record the interpretations and brief the patrol commander or another tracking team if handing over
- If the incident warrants it, send a track report signal to the base
- Continue with the task

SCENT TRACKING

There are air scents and ground scents that come from:

- Objects themselves—animate or inanimate
- Chemicals associated with the objects—deodorants and toiletries on a person, oil on a gun, polish on shoes
- Human smells associated with inanimate objects thrown away or hidden—discardables
- Disturbances of the environment around an object or caused by its passage, such as freshly dug earth, disturbed dust, broken vegetation, smells around hides, vegetation crushed and disturbed by footfalls

FACTORS AFFECTING THE SCENT PICTURE
- Wind may dissipate scent
- Heavy rain or running water may wash it away
- Strong sunlight speeds evaporation of the scent
- Frozen ground tends to hold scent and release it gradually when it thaws

- A soft warming wind or gentle sunlight will enhance the scent picture by drawing out smells from the environment
- Factors may combine to provide conditions for a good scent picture

SCENT CHECKS

There are no guaranteed scent checks to throw a tracker dog off a human scent, but three categories of substances are used to confuse a dog:

- Attractants
- Repellants
- Decoys

TRACKER DOG EVASION TECHNIQUES

The aim is to:

- Delay the pursuit
- Break the scent trail

Tactics for delaying are:

- Crossing obstacles
- Moving with the wind
- Avoid changing direction at obvious places
- Laying false tracks and back track
- Use of streams and hard surfaces such as rocky ground
- Mingling your scent with other recent human scent

Tactics for breaking the scent trail are:

- Gain time
- Use streams
- Use hard surfaces
- Stop and hide at first light
- The only known, totally effective scent-breaking method used by evading troops was to ride on an animal or bicycle

MAP-READING

EQUIPMENT
- Silva or Silva-type compass
- Ordnance Survey map (1:50000) or map of similar quality

USES OF MAP-READING TO A TRACKER TEAM
- Selection of the quarry's likely route
- Location of your own position
- Prediction of quarry's actions
- Collating information and intelligence from other trackers or other pursuits
- Planning pre-emptive operations based on tracking information and intelligence

MAP-READING SUBJECTS AND SKILLS
- Conventional symbols and other information in margins
- Features of the compass
- Setting the map: by inspection method; by compass method
- Measuring distances
- Using grid references
- Understanding the different north points: True North, Magnetic North, Grid North
- Taking bearings from the map and assessing your direction of travel
- Plotting position by resection
- Estimating distance covered and speed of travel

ANALYSIS OF PRINTS AND MARKS

HUMAN FOOTPRINT
- Count the toes
- Study the pad under the toe

- Length of the toes
- Relative length of the toes
- Position of the toes with reference to the diagonal line
- Spacing of the toes
- The configuration of the forward edge of the impression of the sole and the toe prints
- Shape of the outer edges of the print
- Form of the instep—pronounced or weak
- Size and shape of the heel
- Size and shape of the ball of the foot
- The pattern of the area connecting the heel and ball pads
- Any peculiarities—creases, cracks, and scars

FOOTWEAR MARK
- Length of mark
- Breadth
- Length of the heel
- Breadth of the heel
- Height of heel
- Number, shape, and position of nails
- Any distinctive marks
- Any logos or writing
- Wear marks
- The shape of the various parts of the print
- Any indication as to the composition of the footwear
- If there is a succession of footmarks, length of stride from the toe of one footmark to the back of the heel of the next successive footmark
- Indications of sex or age

FACTORS AFFECTING THE PRINT
- Speed
- Gradient
- Level of fitness
- Level of tiredness
- Load carrying
- Deception tactics

ANATOMICAL CLASSIFICATION FOR ANIMAL PRINTS

Foot
Plantigrades—walk on the flat of the foot (sole-walkers)
Digitigrades—toe-walkers
Ungulates—nail-walkers

- Solid hoof
- Cloven hoof

Relative limb length
Equal length
Hind legs are much longer than front legs
Legs are short in proportion to bodies
Legs are very short in proportion to large bodies

Birds
Tree-perchers
Ground-walkers
Water birds
Waders

DETAILS OF TIRE TRACKS
- Depth of tread
- Depth of impression
- Distinguishing features of the tread—wear pattern
- Pattern of the tire
- Width of the tire tread—weight of the vehicle and its load, the pressure of the tire
- Variations of the different wheels
- Width of track will indicate the type of vehicle
- Direction of travel:

  - indicated by the tread pattern
  - stones are pushed forward slightly and then kicked back
  - passing over a bump the tires will broaden out momentarily as they impact on landing

- small areas of dust, mud, and water will be thrown out and slightly backwards
- puddles of water if driven through fast will push the water forward
- reversing creates uncertain line

SUGGESTED READINGS

A Question of Memory by D. Berglas and G. L. Playfair
Signs of the Wild by Clive Walker
"The Most Dangerous Game," short story by Richard Connell
The Jungle Is Neutral by F. Spencer Chapman
The Yom Kippur War by Abraham Rabinovich
The Journals of Lewis and Clark by Meriwether Lewis and William
    Clark
The Annotated and Illustrated Journals of Major Robert Rogers by
    Timothy J. Todish
Training in Tracking by Gilcraft
Footwear Impression Evidence by William J. Bodziak
The Scout by Stephen Plaut
Kim by Rudyard Kipling
The 39 Steps by John Buchan
Follow the Rabbit-Proof Fence by Doris Pilkington-Garimara
The Tracker, film directed by Rolf de Heers

INDEX